HARVEST OF JOURNEYS

"I am always finding myself a stranger in other people's worlds," Hammond Innes once said. He has lived and worked with a survey team in the Rockies, with whalers on a catcher, with railway construction gangs in the bleak heart of Labrador. He has ridden with Arabs to the mud skyscraper cities of the Hadhramaut, to Buraimi Oasis and the explosive Yemen border. He has penetrated the Zone of Insecurity in the Sahara and the Eskimo North of Hudson's Bay. These are not easy things to do in places where outsiders are unknown and unwanted.

Glimpses of these outposts of civilization have become one of the most striking features of Hammond Innes's books. But many of his private adventures could not be included in his novels, and he has gathered some of them together in *Harvest of Journeys*.

HAMMOND INNES

Harvest of Journeys

FONTANA / Collins

First published 1960
First issued in Fontana Books 1965
Seventh Impression December 1973

© Hammond Innes, 1960

Printed in Great Britain
Collins Clear-Type Press London and Glasgow

Front cover photograph reproduced
by kind permission of J. Allan Cash

Contents

CONTENTS

VI. THE ELEMENTS

VII. THE SEA

Illustrations

INTRODUCTION

This book is a record of my travels during the last ten years, a collection of pieces, most of which were written in that first flush of excited discovery that follows a journey into a new land.

Most of the journeys described were undertaken with the primary object of getting material for my novels. To this end I was fortunate in being able to travel farther and farther off the beaten track. But a work of fiction imposes its own discipline, often necessitating a long lapse of time whilst the story grows of its own accord out of the background. Such discipline would have proved frustrating had I had no other outlet.

In 1953 the editors of that fine American magazine, *Holiday*, asked me to contribute a piece about Norway. This request was due to the fact that I had already written two books backgrounded on my experiences in that country, for the policy of this magazine has always been to employ European novelists wherever possible to write about the European scene. The resulting piece—*Viking Land*—was the beginning of my association with *Holiday*, an extraordinarily happy association that has lasted now for six years. Arabia followed—the pirate coast of the Trucial Oman, the skyscraper cities or the Hadhramaut—and then the Low Countries, the Biscay coast, Yugoslavia, subjects of my own choosing. Looking back now on this period of my life, I realise how much I, and others like me, owe to Ted Patrick and Harry Sions of *Holiday*, for not only encouraging the novelist to travel, but for providing the vehicle by which he could pass on his experiences to others.

The dozen or so journeys recorded here were not all written for *Holiday*—barely half, in fact. But, like the *Holiday* pieces, they were all of them written because I wanted to write them. This particularly applies to the section at the end, entitled *The Sea*.

I enjoy travelling. Nevertheless, it is as much a part of my working life as the actual writing, my time almost equally divided between the two. But with the sea it is different. I have written about it. Indeed, it seems to infiltrate into my books of its own accord. But it is still not associated in my mind with work. To hoist sail and see the coast of England fade away astern, then all the world seems suddenly within one's grasp. I cannot explain its effect on me—the freedom, the sense of peace, the exhilaration.

In the pages that follow I ask you to sit back and come with me into the lands through which it has been my good fortune to travel. And if I have managed to convey something of the excitement that was mine at each fresh discovery, then I shall to some extent have repaid the debt I owe to all those countless friends of the moment who gave me of their kindness, hospitality and help, and who did it because they were proud of the land that was theirs or of the job they were doing.

HAMMOND INNES

I. ARABIA AND THE PERSIAN GULF

I. THE PIRATE COAST

The Persian Gulf is like a shallow pot of salt water simmering everlastingly in the sun's fire. To the north the rim of the pot is fashioned out of the serried ranks of the Persian mountains; to the south are the burning sands of Arabia. A sixty-mile dam across the straits of Hormuz, where the Persian Gulf meets the Gulf of Oman, might convert the bed of this shallow sea into a new Garden of Eden irrigated by the waters of the Tigris and Euphrates. But that is just a pipe dream; nobody is interested in making the desert—let alone the sea—flower when beneath Arabia's sands lies the " black gold " that the mechanised world hungers for.

The magic word Oil draws men to this humid hell like moths to a candle flame. They go there for money. Few ever go there just to see it. I was one of the few.

An invitation from a cousin of my wife's, posted to command of a frigate of the Persian Gulf squadron, sparked the flame of interest that had been smouldering ever since I had soldiered in the Middle East. Arabia! But I needed more than the Navy if I were to get to grips with the country itself; I needed desert transport. And so I turned to the R.A.F. for help.

Twice I had written novels with an Air Force background—the battle of Britain, the Berlin airlift. Nevertheless, it was in a mood of some uncertainty that I visited an office in the Air Ministry. And there, miraculously, the doors of Arabia swung open for me; not Saudi Arabia, which with increasing fanaticism had become allergic to infidels, but all the coastal states from Bahrain east along the Gulf, the seven sheikhdoms of the Trucial Oman; the Buraimi Oasis, too; and if I could get myself to Masira

Island, then the fabulous Wadi Hadhramaut, the Yemeni border.

We talked for hours about places, people, transport, the clothes I should need, departure dates and visas, and I came out in a heady daze with a whole world of romance, colour and excitement in my pocket, everything arranged —only one thing left in doubt; how I was to get myself from the Persian Gulf to Masira Island far to the south in the Arabian Sea. For the moment it was enough that I had achieved so much. But the problem of how to bridge this gap was to loom ever larger in the course of my travels.

A month later I flew out of a blizzard-swept airfield in Wiltshire, flew south and east into a world of brilliant sunshine, of incredible pastel shades. It was January and the climate of the Gulf was that of an English summer, the sun's pitiless heat tempered by the *shamal* blowing boisterously out of the north-west.

Bahrain was my jumping-off place. It is an island crossroads set conveniently halfway along the southern coastline of the Gulf. It has a history that goes back beyond the Bible story of Hagar and Ishmael, beyond the origins of Arabia. It is all sea history and there is even a theory that the inhabitants piloted their strange, dhow-sailed craft up the Euphrates, crossed to the Syrian coast and built the forerunners of the Mediterranean *feluccas*—that they were, in fact, the Phœnicians about whose origins there has always been considerable mystery.

There is no real evidence to support this theory. But if you drive inland from the port of Manama there is evidence in plenty of an ancient history; where the palmerie ceases abruptly and the ground slopes upward there is a broad, sandy plan covered with ancient burial mounds, heap on heap—an estimated fifty thousands of them; the world's largest tumuli burial ground. Professor Glub, a Danish archæologist who was digging among them at the time, told me they were about four thousand years old; his most important find was a little bronze dish—filled with water it had constituted man's first attempt at a mirror and the British Museum had confirmed it as the oldest in the world.

Probably that water mirror had once reflected a dusky neck encircled by pearls of the wonderful lustrous nacre that belongs only to the Gulf, for Bahrain has been famous for its pearls since earliest Bible history. Standing on the long viaduct that joins the main island port of Manama to little Muharraq, watching the cluster of dhows waiting to go through the swing bridge, listening to the sounds of hammering made by two Arab carpenters as they worked on the only dhow being built, I tried to visualise what it had been like a hundred years ago. Pearling was at its height then and twenty thousand men would sail out of Manama and Muharraq, attracted by stories of sudden, fabulous wealth, to the hard and dangerous work of diving; fifteen hundred *booms, sambuqs* and *jalibuts* crowding out to the banks, sharp prows etched black by the sunset, great curved sails mirrored limp in the polished-metal gleam of oily-calm water.

What a sight it must have been ! But now all that colourful life is gone, killed by the Japanese cultured pearl. I stood there regretting it and the sunset flamed red on the neat white buildings of Manama, red on the deserted mud berths along the waterfront. And past me streamed a procession of shiny new Buicks and Cadillacs driven by men with dark virile faces framed in the white *kayffiah* and white *agal* of the Bahraini. They were bound for the two Arab clubs on Muharraq.

A bare quarter of a century ago those same men would have been riding their camels or standing with bare toes curled round worn-wood tiller, piloting a *jalibut* out to the pearl banks. Oil has produced a strange and rapid change in the life of the Gulf Arab, and it was on Bahrain that it was first discovered.

An Australian—a Major Frank Holmes—came to the

islands, prospecting, after the First World War. He drilled
and found only water. Nobody was surprised, for they say
Bahrain floats on fresh water (certainly the pearlers never
took water out to the nearby banks, for a goatskin lowered
to the sea bed would be spring-filled with as sweet water
as ever came out of a sultan's well). Short of backing,
Holmes took the line of least resistance and went into business as a driller of artesian wells.

But he still had a bee in his bonnet about oil in Bahrain
and though most people regarded him as a crank, he
eventually persuaded an American company to back his
theory. And in 1932 the first well came in. Now, low-
lying Sitra island is an iron maze with its cat-cracker, tank
farm and oil pipes; out across the tide flats runs a metalled
highway on stilts, carrying tiers of pipes into the sunset to
feed oil products into the bottoms of a thousand tankers a
year; and piped along the bed of the sea comes more crude
oil from the mainland of Saudi Arabia to add to the output
of the huge refinery. The whole thing is a steel monument
to a man's belief in a theory, a theory that included all the
coast of the Gulf and that took him to Kuwait, before
anyone knew there was oil there, to negotiate a half
interest for America.

This comment was made to me by Sir Charles Belgrave:
"Fortunately it all developed quite slowly here in Bahrain
and we had time to adjust ourselves." There was a note
of relief in his voice. For half a lifetime this tall, stooped
Britisher acted as adviser to the rulers of Bahrain and it is
not difficult to imagine the problems he would have faced
if it had all happened suddenly. We were both of us thinking of Kuwait, the little sheikhdom at the head of the
Gulf which in three short years replaced the whole output
of Persia.

But a bare twenty years for men to change from the
camel to the Cadillac—even that is like something out of
the Arabian Nights. And nearly all the dhows gone from
Manama and Muharraq, the arrow-shaped fish catcheries

IRAN

PERSIAN GULF

Bahrain I.

Ras al Khaima

Khor al Fakhan

Sharjah

Doha

Dubai

Gulf of Oman

TRUCIAL OMAN

Buraimi Oasis

Muscat

OMAN

ARABIA

Masiri I.

Rub al Khali Desert
(The Empty Quarter)

Salala

Wadi Hadhramaut

Tarim

Shibam

Seyun

W. Du'an

ROT.

ARABIAN
SEA

Baihan

Qaidun

YEMEN

Sif

Rijan

Mukeiras

Am Ruseis

Mukalla

ADEN

Aden

Socotra I.

GULF OF ADEN

Scale of Miles

0   100   200   400

of palm fronds out in the shallow sea falling into disrepair and Professor Glub digging amongst the tumuli within sight of the Sitra refinery. And only just over a century ago —in 1820—the British entered the Gulf because the coasts were infested with pirates which interfered with the Indian trade !

The Pirate Coast! That is what the Victorian English dubbed the sea-board states east of Bahrain, and the name has stuck—unofficially. Officially they are known as the states of the Trucial Oman because under the various truces made with Britain the independence of each sheikh-dom is guaranteed. provided they keep the peace. Their names are Abu Dhabi, Dubai, Sharjah, Ajman, Umm al Qaiwain, Ras al Khaima, and Fujaira, each ruled by its own sheikh, each entirely independent under the guidance of the British Political Resident.

Anyone with a visa can go to Sharjah—there is a regular air service from Bahrain—and from there a piece of iron-mongery that calls itself a taxi will take you the twelve miles to Dubai along a track of black sand packed so hard and flat that it is more like a metalled highway. But to get anywhere else is not so easy, particularly as you need desert transport, and the only people who have Land Rovers are the sheikhs, the political agents, the Trucial Oman Levies[1], and the oil companies.

Rain and a gale—and the vagaries of the Foreign Office —delayed me for three days in Bahrain. And then suddenly I was free to leave and in the cool after a night of torrential rain I left for Sharjah in one of the old Ansons that the R.A.F. were still using to patrol the Trucial Oman border. The old Etonian pilot had orders to show me as much of the country as possible, and he took those orders literally.

We flew across the Gulf of Bahrain with our belly to the ripple-corrugated water, across the Qatar peninsula

[1] Since I travelled with these Bedouin Levies they have been re-named the Trucial Oman Scouts.

with its flat sands dotted with camel scrub and blotched
with the darker patches of sea water seepage, the plane
life-size in sun-shadow below us; on over the sea again to the
wilder sand country of the Abu Dhabi sheikhdom, across
the eye-searing white gypsum flats of the Sabkhat Matti to
the beginnings of the big dune country. It was like driving
in a double-decker bus, except that we were travelling in
country no vehicle could drive through, dune on endless
dune, crescent-shaped, the steep inner side etched deep in
shadow.

My impressions of that flight are somewhat kaleido-
scopic : a sheikh's palace twisting slowly at the end of a
wing-tip as we banked, neat and rectangular in contrast to
the chaotic huddle of mud and *barasti* palm-frond shacks
that were the town; oil camps, neat and ordered, with their
vehicle parks and huts in rows, and the inevitable litter of
empty fuel drums; a strange gusher of water spurting up
out of red, sun-blistered sand—sulphurous and useless; a
dhow seen as a glimpse of a curved white sail rushing past
with the face of the *nakhuda* staring up at us under a ragged
turban, grinning, too astonished to be scared; camels
shambling into a gallop, ungainly in their fright; fishermen's nets patterning the foreshore for miles as we approached Dubai : and Dubai itself, a dog-leg estuary
packed with dhows, the houses crowding along the waterfront, many-windowed and elaborate like Italian palazzi
with tall Persian wind-towers funnelling air into the rooms
and looking like half-grown campanili—the whole place a
little Venice in Arabia.

So much of Arabia packed into one flight ! And at
Sharjah I stepped out on to the sodden sand of the half
washed-out airfield, straight into a desert world : a watch
tower stood sentinel against the inland sky and below it a
camel caravan ambled bulkily, guarded by wild-faced
Bedou, sun glinting on the silver trappings of their rifles; and
on the far side of the airfield the fort stood out, starkly

white like bleached bone, and beyond it was Sharjah port, mud houses and palms crouched in the sand and the blue line of the sea behind it.

Neat, organised Bahrain with its copy-book East-meets-West atmosphere seemed suddenly a world away.

Sharjah and Dubai are like twins, but Sharjah has gone down in the world, its mud houses crumbling, tracery half-obliterated, wood shutters rotting unpainted. The bar across the estuary mouth is silting up and though Sheikh Saqr (Sugger) has cut the import duty to half what it is for Dubai, hardly a dhow comes into the port now.

In a wild night of storm, with a violent *shamal* blowing, a small dhow tried to come in over the bar for shelter and was wrecked. Next morning I saw the crew of three huddled under a wisp of canvas with all that remained of their boat stacked beside them, a little pile of timbers and rough-hewn planks. Seen across the wind-whipped estuary with the remains of a deserted village behind them, they looked utterly forlorn in the teeming rain. They were there in desperation, for that boat was all their possessions in this world and over the months of blazing summer heat they would slowly and painstakingly recreate it. It was their only hope of survival.

Dubai, on the other hand, bustles with activity. Big, gaily-painted dhows crowd the waterfront close against the wind-towered houses, and the illusion that this is an Arabian version of Venice is enhanced by crude craft jostling at the landing places, black-faced 'gondolieri' soliciting custom at the tops of their voices.

This is the richest of the ports of the Trucial Oman, though when I was there it was only just recovering from the depression caused by Persia's near-bankruptcy under the Mossadeq régime. Like Sharjah, Dubai was once a pirate lair, but when the British captured Ras al Khaima, the main pirate stronghold, the men of Dubai prudently took to smuggling, and now they have the bulk of the Persian trade. The *suks,* ankle-deep in unheard-of mud, were crowded with men from the smugglers' dhows, a motley of gay colours, skins ranging from Arab mahogany to the jet black of slave ancestry.

And behind these ports the watch towers stand against the desert, manned day and night by a guard who enters by a hole halfway up and draws his ladder up behind him. It all seems a little incongruous and old-fashioned remembering the Cadillacs in Bahrain and the tankers trundling up the Gulf to Sitra, Dahran and Kuwait, and the aircraft roaring overhead. But there is an age-old tradition of raiding between the sheikhdoms of the Trucial Oman and a dozen or so years ago the Sheikh of Dubai, goaded by a series of raids from Abu Dhabi territory, led a picked force out into the desert, surprised three hundred bandits in their camp and slaughtered sixty of them. On my way up to the old pirate port of Ras al Khaima I helped shovel a Land Rover out of wet sand; it had left the rutted track which was flooded and in attempting to follow a camel trail through the scrub had bedded down to its axles. The occupants appeared to be some sort of Bedou hunting party, a ruffianly-looking lot, armed to the teeth—silver-mounted rifles slung over their shoulders, brass-studded painted leather ammunition belts packed with cartridges round their waists and, tucked into them, the broad silver-sheathed *khanjar* knives which are the mark of authority in the northern deserts. After we had pulled their vehicle out, an old man, long of tooth, his hawk-like face framed by straggly beard and wild grey hair, ran after us, thanked us courteously, shook each of us by the hand.

It was Sayid bin Maktun, the old Sheikh of Dubai; the man who had been fined by the British for taking the law into his own hands. Having met him, I for one would not join a raiding party against Dubai!

Whilst at Sharjah, I lived at the fort which, despite the two iron cannon guarding the arched entrance, is no more than an airport transit hotel. For a desert hostel it is incredibly good and my guess is that Sharjah will one day

blossom as a colourful winter resort for the rich traveller—
it has beautiful sands, warm sea, all that Florida offers,
plus Arabia with its dhows and dug-out canoes, its
crumbling mud villages and the wild Bedou leading the
camel trains along the shore.

I was some days there, for rain had put the airfield out
of action and I was waiting for Foreign Office approval
for my journeys inland. My immediate objective was the
Buraimi Oasis—and Buraimi was not easy.

It is much more than an oasis where men and camels
can find water. It is the meeting place of age-old camel
routes—from Saudi via the Liwa oases in the west, from the
kingdom of Yemen far to the south, from Dubai, Sharjah
and Ras al Khaima, and from the Batina coast across the
mountains to the east. Until only a few years ago it was a
great slave market. But then it made the headlines of the
world's press, the Bedou force of the Trucial Oman Levies
moved in under a lone British major and the slave-trade
was disrupted. Buraimi had become a sort of cold war area.

The nine villages of Buraimi are frontier villages—six
belong to Abu Dhabi, two to the Sultan of Muscat on the
eastern coast and one to Sharjah. The trouble began
when Turki bin Ataishan moved into the village of
Hamasa with forty-five men in August, 1952. He was the
representative of Saudi Arabia and with lorry-loads of
foodstuffs he bribed the inhabitants of Buraimi to sign
documents of Saudi Arabian citizenship in a desperate
attempt to support his king's sudden claim to territories a
hundred miles and more beyond the borders that had been
the basis of negotiations between Saudi and the British in
1935.

The Sultan of Muscat reacted immediately to protect
his own villages and by an incredible feat of organisation
marched a large force across the mountains from the east
to throw Turki out. But the British, fearful of full-scale
war between Muscat and Saudi, persuaded him to leave
the whole affair to arbitration.

The rain cleared the same day that the Foreign Office cable arrived giving me the freedom of the Trucial Coast, and I left next morning for Buraimi with one of the political officers, headed for the mountains which I had seen from the fort roof lying in peaked confusion along the eastern horizon, stark in the livid sunsets.

Bogged by soft sand right at the outset, we turned into the dune country, past the last watch tower, and for two hours bumped and lurched from one Bedou camp to the next, a land ship ploughing through ever-increasing seas of sand until at last a clump of trees signposted the way to the first well on the main Buraimi track.

Here we joined the caravan route. Long trains of supercilious beasts moving slowly, ponderously under their burdens stared at us with contempt as we went lurching past. The cameleers—wild-looking men with unkempt heads of black hair bare to the sun, rifles slung under their arms raised their hand in desert salutation. Occasionally there were women, black bundles of clothing perched high on their camels, looking like carrion crows as they stared at us curiously through the hideous mask of the *burqa*.

We drove furiously all afternoon in a choking cloud of fine-ground sand, ploughing our way south into the blazing sun. Rust-red hills of sand-scoured rock slowly closed in on us, until at last we bumped across a gravel plain veined by dry water-courses and ahead of us rose the 200-foot ridge of the Ramlat Anej, a yellow finger of high dunes reaching out from the sand ocean of the Rub al Khali— the Empty Quarter—to the very edge of the eastern mountain ranges.

In summer, when the sand is too hot to stand on and tyres smoke with the friction, it takes anything up to eight hours to cross these three miles of soft sand. But now unprecedented desert rain had packed the surface and we took it at speed, roller-coasting to knife-edged crests that dropped away at a crazy 45°, and all to the east of us was a moon-scape of scarred mountain peaks, range on range reaching back to the hard blue of cloudless sky.

The country beyond the Ramlat was dotted with trees of camel thorn and along the western horizon lay a sea of sand, the wind rippling the dune crests into motion so that they smoked like waves breaking in a gale. The whole yellow tide seemed spilling towards us, threatening to engulf us. The sense of emptiness was appalling. The sun set and the dunes, suddenly still, turned red. Abruptly it was night and the moon stood cold and bright above the jagged mountains.

That was how I first saw Buraimi—in moonlight. There was no oasis pool of water bordered by palms. Instead, date gardens, dark and gloomy behind crumbling walls, merged with the huddle of mud villages glimpsed as black silhouettes against the stars, and then the camel thorn petered out and we drove across flat, rising ground to the fort, a solitary, square, battlemented tower, ghostly in the moonlight.

This was the home of a man who was known throughout the Trucial Coast as " the lonely Major." Peter Macdonald had been there over a year, sole guardian of Buraimi independence. He was a tall, fair-haired Scot who loved the desert and whose affection for the Bedou was matched by their affection for him.

Inside the white sepulchre of the fort, we climbed flights of dark mud steps, past a tiny cavern of a room where a radio set constituted their only contact with the outside world, up to the very top where two rooms were arranged in rough semblance of office and living quarters. We had brought a bottle of Scotch with us, but Macdonald didn't drink. " It's bad to drink when you're alone." Macdonald's sole companion was a small cat, wild as a Bedou; she was there to deal with the desert spiders that made their home amongst the palm-bole beams of the mud ceiling.

Even at night you cannot enter Buraimi unseen. Within

ten minutes of our arrival Sheikh Zeyd was there to greet us. Zeyd was the second of the four Abu Dhabi brothers, deputy in Buraimi for the oldest, Sheikh Shakbut, who ruled in Abu Dhabi. He had been in the oasis since the beginning of the trouble.

His dress was not impressive; a shapeless European jacket worn over a plain Bedou robe, barely white. His *kayffiah* was similar to those worn by the meanest of the tribesmen. But I was soon to discover that he was a man who had no need to dress the part of a sheikh. He was a born leader and in all the ten thousand miles I travelled through Arabia I never met his equal. His features were marred by the prominence of nose and teeth, but I scarcely noticed that, attracted to him by the quick smile and the flash of alert intelligence in the eyes.

He gave us just long enough to wash off the sand of travel and change into clean shirts, and then whisked us away through the moonlight to the fortified house he ocupied close to one of the Abu Dhabi villages. In a bare whitewashed room of mud lit by a single oil pressure lamp we squatted down, cross-legged, to Bedou fare of rice and chunks of mutton cooked the Bedou way over fire-heated stones. With Zeyd were his two younger brothers—Khalid, slight, almost effeminate-looking with his small pointed beard, capable of expressing the loudest satisfaction over his food that I heard from any Arab, and Hazza, thick-set, bearded, piratical.

Zeyd's quick, nervous energy dominated the room. We ate, as always, with the right hand (the left is reserved for more personal uses) and at the end a slave appeared with a pile of small, handle-less cups into which he poured sweet black coffee from a long-spouted, silver pot of exquisite workmanship.

Early next morning Sheikh Zeyd arrived at the fort in his Land Rover to take us on a tour of Buraimi. The vehicle was packed with retainers armed with rifles and again there was nothing to distinguish Zeyd from the rest

—except his bearing and the way he moved; quick, decisive, commanding. We toured the villages and the date gardens, inspected the ring of Levy posts and looked across to Hamasa where Turki was as divorced from the company of his own people as Macdonald was from his.

Close to the palmeries of the village of Jimi a field of wheat was sprouting green from water dragged up from the depth of a well by an undersized bullock that struggled down a ramp dug like the sloped entrance of an air raid shelter into the ground. And at Massidi, by contrast, a modern pump was filling a nearby reservoir that watered a once-derelict garden now green with vegetables. Shyly, one of Zeyd's bodyguards handed me a sprig of mint. The pump chugged sonorously from the depths of its well, and from the palmerie the creaking of the primitive bullock wheel was still audible.

At Al Maweigi we disturbed a group of women washing clothes at a *shireeya,* an open bathing place fed by the *fellej.* They scattered, chattering shrilly, for they should not be seen by strangers. But in a moment they were back again, drawn by animal curiosity. It was here that Zeyd produced his two proudest possessions; a pure-bred Oman racing camel and a peregrine falcon. The camel was a vicious-looking female, tall as a giraffe, her roped muzzle covered with a slavering of foam. The falcon, one of twelve Zeyd had obtained from Persia, had its head covered by a leather hood as it perched on the gauntleted arm of a bearded falconer—the same type of hood that was used back in the days of the Crusaders.

But the most fascinating part of Buraimi was the *fellej* system. This system of irrigation involves the digging of wells in series and inter-connecting them at the bottom so that the resulting tunnel line gradually builds up a sufficient flow to deliver water to the surface by gravity. At Buraimi water is brought to the date gardens from as much as thirty miles away.

Once there were as many as a hundred of these *fellej*

systems, all serving the various villages of Buraimi. But in the constant inter-tribal wars before the British came, the conqueror, as a matter of course, wreaked deadly vengeance by filling in the *fellej* wells of the vanquished village, water being above rubies in the desert. And so, now, there are only five *fellejes* left in working order.

Digging new wells and opening up the old ones is slow work. Only one tribal family has the art. It is handed down from father to son, much like well-digging in other countries, and it includes the art of water-divining. The men, mostly very old, were working with primitive implements made from the leaf springs of old motor cars. The heat and humidity in the tunnels is intense—the well-heads steam like cauldrons, and there is always the danger of a fall.

Most of the tunnels run underground direct to the palmerie they serve; but some supply more than one village, and one enterprising individual, taken prisoner whilst sniping at a Levy post at night, got back into Hamasa by worming his way through these subterranean connecting tunnels. One of these *fellejes* came out below the fort just short of the village of Ain and was carried across a shallow wadi by a mud-brick aqueduct. This was Macdonald's bath.

We came that night and lay in the shallow trough, naked in the moonlight, gossiping of home like a couple of ancient Romans. The water was tepid with underground warmth and small fish tickled our bodies as we floated luxuriously along the trough, staring up at the brilliance of the stars. But oh, the bitter cold of the desert as we got out! A small wind whispered down from the mountains, drifting sand across our feet, and, a little distance removed, a camel stood gazing at us in astonishment.

There are other sheikhs in Buraimi beside Zeyd. Sheikh Saqr, for instance, lord of the two Muscat villages of Buraimi and Suwara, entertained me to sweet tea with camel's milk, tinned pears and black coffee—tinned fruit is very much the *dernier cri* in the desert for light refresh-

ment. He was a softer, gentler man than Zeyd, with a
small, neat beard and a bad cold. When he wished to write
something down he called his secretary in, a tall, black,
finely-dressed man who wrote with an expensive fountain-
pen, the dirty sheet of paper braced against his knee as he
squatted cross-legged in front of us. Probably he was a
slave who had risen to his position by his ability.

Slavery in the desert isn't all the terrible thing that we
regard it. A slave lives under his master's roof, eats of his
master's food—indeed there are strict laws requiring the
master to be responsible not only for the man's welfare, but
that of his family as well—often a heavy commitment!
Any slave can obtain his freedom in the Trucial Oman
just by walking into the British Agency and asking for it.
But most prefer slavery, with all the security of a home and
food, to freedom to live from hand to mouth in the harsh
world of the desert; and though the British document is a
grandly-worded one—" Be it known," it says, " that the
bearer has been manumitted and no one has the right to
interfere with his liberty "—only those who are afraid of
being sold again, perhaps to a less wealthy, or less kindly
master, take advantage of it.

I cannot, of course, say much about the condition of
female slaves since the womenfolk are kept rigidly apart.
But not so long ago the Navy attempted to detain a dhow
loaded with women whom it was suspected were being
carried off in slavery. It was the *bints* themselves who
drove the sailors off with obscene shouts and rude gestures.
There was no doubt whatever that, slavery or not, they
were on that dhow of their own free will.

The courtyard of Sheikh Saqr's palace in Buraimi village was packed with his bodyguard. I never saw so much
silver wrapped round rifles in my life. It was barely possible to see the steel. But they were all old, impractical
weapons. It was the same at another sheikhly fortress ten
miles away towards the mountains but the men were
wilder, the setting more grim.

It was a medieval stronghold set on a rock circled by small, jagged peaks. A few years back it had been seized by a desert baron called Sheikh Obeid bin Jima'a who had also occupied the Toll House on the Buraimi road, a dilapidated watch tower that guarded a rock pass eighteen miles from the oasis. From there he had sniped at all and sundry, including the Levies, using soft-nosed lead bullets—one smashed into Macdonald's Land Rover blowing a hole as big as a saucer in the steel bonnet. But after Obeid had shot up one of the political officers, the Foreign Office reluctantly agreed to action and he and his men quietly faded away before the Levy advance.

Out of this stronghold, that flew the red flag of Muscat, poured a motley throng, rifles in their hands, ammunition belts gleaming in the sun. They ran towards us, shouting and waving their weapons; a disturbing moment! But it was only a boisterous greeting in a place where visitors were few, and I found myself clasping a dozen horny hands whilst teeth flashed white in sun-wrinkled, bearded faces.

The sheikh folowed them more sedately, a slave carrying a brand-new B.S.A. rifle, his pride and joy. We had come there in search of a guide to the Ramlat Anej area, for we were planning to try and find an alternative route over which a road could be built to by-pass the sands. In return he had a personal request to make, and later that day I saw him perched on an R.A.F. lorry, still clutching his precious B.S.A. but looking strangely forlorn without his bodyguard—he was on his way to the hospital at Dubai for penicillin treatment.

We found a rout round the Ramlat Anej. The sands, which seemed to pile right up against the mountains, in fact dropped suddenly short of them, leaving a 12-foot wide gap of black, fine-ground shale as smooth as a metal-led highway. Through it ambled a train of fifty camels. But the road petered out into a rock-strewn water-course impracticable for vehicles.

As we drove back to Buraimi, the wind was moving the sand sea again. Macdonald pointed to it. " That will finish Buraimi in another twenty years," he said. " I've watched it from the fort when the *shamal* has been gusting sixty or seventy miles an hour. It isn't like sand then. It comes towards you like water. You can see it moving."

Like water! Thereafter I felt the doom of it hanging over Buraimi. Already long, yellow fingers of sand had engulfed several abandoned date gardens, half-burying the palms, pouring over the camel thorn like a rising tide; the Rub al Khali—the Empty Quarter—moving in on one of the few remaining patches of green between the sand and the mountains. This is the sins of the fathers visited upon the children with a vengeance, for the camel thorn is Buraimi's only defence and for lack of the ruined *fellejes,* so clearly visible in aerial photographs, the camel thorn is dying.

Sheikh Zeyd, with his plans for digging new *fellejes* and installing pumping machinery, may save Buraimi yet, but Zeyd is short of funds. He, like every other sheikh in the Trucial Oman, dreams of oil.

I remember Sheikh Saqr of Sharjah, stocky and grave, looking much older than his thirty-three years, telling me his plans in a small, book-lined room in his palace; he wanted roads, electric light, a dredger to open up the estuary, hospital, schools. Oil was the answer. He is one of the more progressive sheikhs. But whether it is a new car, modern rifles, or roads and schools, oil will produce it. It is the panacea for all ills, their El Dorado; they talk, think and dream oil.

This pipe dream has spurred a greed for useless desert land, and territorial claims have been recklessly filed. The discovery of oil on border territory could spell trouble.

I flew to Tarif to see the third well being drilled in Abu Dhabi territory. The camp was a hundred miles from the nearest port, standing on a bluff overlooking the sea; air-conditioned living quarters, water distillation plants, fresh vegetables flown in weekly from far-away Iraq and weeks of waiting for any special equipment needed from England or America.

The camp had its own airstrip seemingly cut off by the tide at midday, for the sun produced a strange water-mirage; and in the far distance stood the derrick, a slender needle against the pastel blue of the sky, its base apparently engulfed in water. Eddie West, a little wrinkle-faced, bandy-legged man from California who looked more like a cowboy than a tool-pusher on an oil rig, had run into every kind of trouble bar fire. The rig had been idle for three months, and in the desert it costs £500 a day just to stand there and do nothing, waiting for equipment.

Out in the sea, off the coast of Abu Dhabi, another company owned the under-water rights, and Costeau, French aqualung diver who wrote *The Silent World,* was then busy on a geological survey of the sea bed.

The feeling of the sheikhs is perhaps best summed up in the words attributed to Sheikh Shakbut of Abu Dhabi when visiting Paris. On first seeing the Eiffel Tower, he is reported to have said—and this was told me by an Arab merchant in Bahrain : " No wonder your country is richer than Abu Dhabi when your oil rigs are so much bigger !"

Having seen Buraimi, my one objective now was to cross the mountains to the Batina coast that faces east towards India. But it meant transport and an escort. It was impossible. Sheikh Saqr was just back from that area. Nobody would be going there for months. They offered me Ras Al Khaima, instead, and in a mood of resignation I went north along the coast to the one-time pirate strong-hold.

It was a coastal journey through the little sheikhdoms of Ajman and Umm al Qaiwain and along the sands of the foreshore towards the mountains of the Ruus al Jibal that tower 6,000 ft. above the Straits of Hurmuz. It was all strangely Mediterranean until we came to the dhows, their curved sails reflected in the limp water, packed to the

gunn'ls with naked men, brown bodies glistening in the sun
as they sweated at the nets, laying them 200 yards out and
then wading ashore to drag them in. The scrub-covered
dunes behind were a silver sheen of sardine-like fish drying
in the sun for export to India and Indonesia, and for use
as camel fodder in the desert.

Camel caravans also used the sands, and the estuaries
that curved deep inland behind each village were a bird-
watcher's paradise—crane, flamingoes, heron, sandpipers,
curlews, terns, hoopoes as well as the ever-present bustards
and vultures.

If anywhere on the Arabian coast of the Persian Gulf
can be described as beautiful, it is Ras al Khaima—not the
town, which is the usual huddle of mud and *barasti* houses,
but the whole setting : the dhows in the great sweep of the
lagoon, the wonderful green of the Hamil valley as though
God's hand had touched the sterile yellow of the sand, and
mirrored in the lagoon, towering magnificently and smiling
in the sunshine—the mountains, a great, solid shoulder of
rock with sheer cliffs falling to blue water.

Up there live the Shihuh, small mountain men, fiercely
shy of the desert-dweller. No white man has ever been up
there. Men of the Desert Locust force tried, for it is their
job to go everywhere in Arabia in an international drive to
exterminate these pests in their breeding places, and they
came out in their underpants minus their Land Rover.
And under the dew-cooled mountain valleys of the Shihuh
lies long Elphinstone Inlet, credited as being the hottest
place on God's earth.

There is nothing in Ras al Khaima to indicate its piratical
past, but there is no doubt of the slave trade ancestry of
its inhabitants—they are blacker than in any town on the
coast. I think the only true Arabs I saw there were the
Bedou with their camels in the dusty market square and a
nakhuda and his crew building a dhow with adze and
wooden bow drill. There was a strange, almost withdrawn
atmosphere about the people. When spoken to, they

answered politely, but unsmilingly. They were incurious, unwelcoming—somehow utterly divorced from the desert.

We went back through the Hamil valley, driving for ten all too brief miles through glades of green where dainty-leaved trees grew out of a carpet of new grass. There were large herds of goats watched over by *bints* in gaily-coloured cottons who ran from us with startled bleating cries—a yai-yai-yai cry to the goats made with the tongue through clenched teeth—their faces hastily covered by a piece of cloth, for in that paradise of a desert valley the shiny, beak-like mask of the *burqa* was for some reason discarded and colours were worn in place of black. It was all part of the magic of the place, which was littered with baby donkeys, and young fluffy camels who had the surprised and tousled look of fledglings and ran with awkward gait and stiff, out-thrust neck to seek courage from their dams' milk.

Back at Sharjah, I found a message waiting for me. The U.S. Navy ship, *Duxberry Bay,* was paying an official visit to Khor al Fakhan. It was one of those lucky breaks. Khor al Fakhan was over the mountains on the east coast and the political officer would have to be there to meet the Americans. Transport was available for the Batina coast after all.

We left Sharjah next morning driven by a tattered Jehu called Mohammed Makmud who took the dune road to Dheid as though the devil himself were after him; no slowing at corners, no slowing at dune crests, the Land Rover lurching and skidding and pitching like a toboggan run amuck on the Cresta Run, and Mohammed Makmud crouched all the time over the wheel with an oil-grimed grin on his face and the ends of his ragged turban streaming in the wind. The second Land Rover piled with our Levy escort, was left far behind.

The sun was past its zenith by the time we reached the mountains. There was a Levy post perched on a bare-rock hilltop like a medieval watch tower, and then the rock-backed heat of the Wadi Khor closed in on us. Some wisps

of camel thorn amongst the loose shale, an occasional tree
clinging to a precipitous slope; that was all the vegetation.
And above us the mountains reared up on either side, peak
on peak of sandscoured chaos.

There is one tea house in the Trucial Oman, and it is in
the Wadi Khor. No Tea House of the August Moon, but
a cluster of palm-thatched shacks by a rivulet of precious
water. The owner was Sheikh Sultan, lord of the half-
dozen villages that cling to precarious life in the oven heat
of the mountains. Until recently he had levied toll on all
travellers going through the pass. Summoned to the political agency at Sharjah to be told that the practice must
cease, he drew a little silver-mounted pistol, fired two shots
over the political officer's head, and fled.

There were two trucks there as we passed, piled high
with the goods of Arabs on the move, and towards evening
we dropped through a moon-mad landscape to the sea, the
mountains behind us blue in shadow, peak upon peak like
serried ranks of dragon's teeth.

For a brief space we were in Muscat territory, the
border-keep watch towers all manned, all flying the Sultan's
red flag; then we were through to the coast, driving north
through village after village, close-packed *barastis* of palm
frond into which masked bundles of womanhood fled
hastily, to peer at us from the safety of shadowed interior
with large, brown, curious eyes, sometimes caught without
the burqa, holding a wisp of black head-dress across their
mouths occasionally a glimpse of a smile, the gleam of eyes
lit with excitement at the sight of strangers. And the men
returning from the sparsely-cultivated fields raised their
hands in sober salutation, some on camels beating them into
a shambling trot to get a closer look at us.

For this is a seldom visited coast.

Fierce village dogs sped us on our way, tongues lolling,
muzzles agrin at such easy victory. And at last, with the
moon beginning to gather lustre from the fading day, we
crossed a spur of the mountains and dropped down into a

mud village scattered along the foreshore of a beautiful, rock-grit cove. It was Khor al Fakhan and close by the water's edge stood a sheikh's palace, like a little mosque white in the moonlight with two iron cannon half-buried in the sand. We knocked at the solitary wicket gate and the black face of a slave peered at us cautiously from a little grille, and then the door was unbolted and we were taken into a bare cell of a room furnished surprisingly with a few European chairs.

Mohammed bin Sultan, brother of Sheikh Saqr of Sharjah, rose to greet us. " This not my house now. Your house. All that I have is yours so long as you wish to stay ." This said with old-world courtesy in the precise English he had learned at Bombay University.

Mohammed was a Hollywood dream of a desert sheikh. Short, dapper, with a little pointed beard and almost classical features, he would have caught the fancy of the bobby-soxers in any Western city. The slight suggestion of effeminacy, however, was dispelled immediately he moved, and one suddenly realised that under the flowing robes was a chunky hard-sinewed body, toughened by days of rock climbing in search of gazelle.

A typical Bedou meal of rice and mutton was served to us on the floor with many apologies from Mohammed " This my hunting place," he said. " I am very simple here." He was alone but for the slave who had shown us in and who served the meal and poured the coffee, his rifle slung all the time across his shoulder. Mohammed tried to tell us that the watch tower overlooking the village was manned only because it was an old custom, but the rifle slung across the slave's shoulders made his words sound unconvincing. There had been trouble in this area only a few years back and Sharjah's hold on the coast was precarious.

That night I slept on a camp bed close by the sea. A chill, niggling wind from the mountains cut through my blankets and I lay staring up at the rock shapes humped against the stars, wondering about this isolated stretch of coast. The warmth of Mohammed's welcome had momentarily taken the edge off the wildness of the place, but now I was conscious of it, conscious of the dark, curious gaze of the villagers clustered outside the palace as we left —the huddled shapes of our Levy escort curled up in their blankets and the dark silhouette of the lone sentry with his British Army rifle were suddenly very comforting.

Early next morning, as I bathed in the cool of a limpid sea, the *Duxberry Bay* steamed into the anchorage. The rattle of her chain as she dropped her hook was like a crash of cymbals in the sunlit stillness. A big crowd was gathered at the palace as Sheikh Mohammed's three-gun salute boomed out from the American ship. Every man in that crowd had a card of white string bobbing like a yo-yo from fingers that were never still as they fashioned the nets that are their chief industry.

A gleaming launch brought Admiral Beecher, descendant of the Mrs. Beecher Stow who wrote *Uncle Tom's Cabin,* to the shore. It seemed a strange setting in which to meet an American Admiral and his staff, the gleaming white of their uniform matched by the gleaming white of their host's flowing robes, two worlds meeting in a stage-set village that was unreal, even for Arabia.

As we sat in the same bare palace room sipping sweet coffee and eating tinned pears, the ship's doctor set up an impromptu surgery in the courtyard outside, watched by a gaping crowd of villagers. His patients were either the very young or the very old.

The very old had mostly lost the sense of feeling in hands and feet, symptoms of senile decay and malnutrition. They were slowly dying, and the vitamin tablets he gave them would only momentarily stave off the inevitable. Old men of the coast, when they cease to go out in the boats for fish, are of little use to a family struggling for survival in the harsh world of Arabia.

As often as not under-nourishment was the trouble with

the children. I shall always remember a little girl, all bloated belly and match-stick arms and legs, who was dying of dysentery and anaemia. The doctor insisted that she must be taken to hospital immediately. The nearest hospital was at Sharjah, back over the mountains and across the desert. "We are poor people," the father whined, " and it is far. We have not the money to send her."

We offered at once to take her in our Land Rover, but the father shook his head and—incredible statement—assured us the little girl would never agree to go without her parents, as though a two-year-old were capable of making a decision that signed her own death warrant.

Sheikh Mohammed then intervened. " It will all be arranged," he said, and I knew that nothing was going to be done. Had it been a man child, then he would have gone to hospital, but female children are of small account in the desert world. The little girl would die.

We lunched aboard the *Duxberry Bay*—Coca-Cola and ice cream within gun-shot of a village where old men and children died of under-nourishment and life had not changed since Hagar's Ishmael peopled the desert.

It was late afternoon before we were being seen off by the village dogs back along the coast again, and the mountains were dark in shadow as we turned west into the forbidding pass. It was night before we reached the tea house of the Wadi Khor. Sheikh Mohammed, who had decided to return with us to Sharjah, introduced me to a white-robed Arab seated on a bench, finely-chiselled features a vague blur in the dim-lit interior. At his command the impish small boys who served brought tea and sweetmeats.

It was only afterwards that I learned I had been the guest of Sheikh Sultan, the man who had levied toll in the pass and who had fired his pistol in the Political Agency.

At night the tea house of the Wadi Khor was a fascinating place lit by hissing pressure lamps. It was part doss house and in the farther corners sprawled the dark shapes of men sleeping. There was a woman, bundled in a tent of her own clothes, sucking at a *nargileh,* or water pipe, the coals of which glowed faintly in the darkness. The women of Arabia are great smokers. The tea house was a shop, too —and a doorway led into an Aladdin's Cave of Eastern and Western commodities. And at the back was a hell's kitchen of dark cauldrons and charcoal fires presided over by a half-naked Arab.

On our way out of the Wadi Khor we were stopped by the corporal in charge of the lonely Levy post at the entrance. Bare-footed, but moving with incredible sureness over the rocks in the darkness, he led us to the tents. "*Faddhal. Faddhal.*" There was nothing for it but to enter his tent and share the inevitable tin of pears between us, possibly their last in that week's rations.

Faddhal. Faddhal. Faddhal. You hear it all along the coast, all through Bedou Arabia. *Fadhal.* It means Enter. It means my house is your house. It means hospitality. It is a word beyond price. It can mean, as at the Levy post, simply a gesture of hospitality, a little piece of etiquette that has been handed down through generations of desert travel. It can also mean the difference between life and death to the exhausted traveller; the end of the journey, the end of a nightmare of starvation and thirst. Travel in the desert, whether it is from one village to another, from one well to another, or from one Bedou encampment to another is often dangerous, alway arduous. Whatever the circumstances of the traveller, there is always, on his arrival, the welcome word *Faddhal*—Enter—and the immediate, excited, scurrying rush to produce food.

This is carried to incredible lengths—to the length of reducing the host and his family to a state of starvation. An extreme case of this was told me by Colonel Bob Martin of the Trucial Oman Levies, and concerned an isolated post of his own men towards the Liwa Oasis. He began receiving urgent requests for rations from this post. They should have been well stocked so he flew down to discover the whole detachment crowded into one tent, whilst the big *barasti* hut was empty. Asked why they didn't use the *barasti*, he was told, "Oh, no, *Sa'id*, that is reserved for the pilgrims."

The post was on one of the pilgrim routes to Mecca and he was suddenly confronted with the certainty that as long as the detachment had rations they would feed the starving travellers who dropped like locusts into their camp, and he knew that to save the face of the Levies he would have to pump extra rations into this one post at the expense of all the rest of the force.

Our last stop that night was at Sheikh Saqr's hunting lodge at Dheid. A high, arched gateway led to a big courtyard aglimmer with cooking fires; Arab faces lit by the glow of flames, Arab tongues talking gutturally, and in the background the humped shapes of camels, chewing and belching. Men moved quickly towards us, fire flickering on the brass of cartridge belt and the steel of slung rifle, crowding round us as we were ushered through the doorless entrance of one of the barrack-like rooms that surrounded the courtyard.

At the far end two recumbent figures stirred in the lamplit gloom and one of them, clad in a white nightgown of the finest cotton with a little night-cap on his head, came forward to greet us. His huge beard was jet black, his eyes and teeth flashed in the lamplight. He looked like Captain Teach masquerading as Scrooge. Sheikh Mohammed kissed him on both cheeks. "My uncle, Sheikh Mohammed," he said, and the bearded sheikh grinned at us and bade use welcome with the warmth and old-world courtesy that is the charm of Arabia.

Whilst servants hurried to prepare us food, the two Mohammeds—nephew and uncle—laughed and chatted together with no sign of rancour. Yet this was the Wicked Uncle of Sharjah, the man who, for a brief three months, had usurped power on the death of his brother, Sultan.

When the food arrived our Levy escort was sent for and the Wicked Uncle bade them sit down and eat. Arabia is very feudal and the laws of hospitality that ruled in the medieval castles of Europe are the same laws that exist in the desert to-day.

Before we had finished, Khalid, the youngest of the Sharjah brothers, came in from night-hunting by the headlights of his Land Rover. He had seen no gazelle, but had shot six hares. His slim body was belted round with cartridges and he talked perfect English. When we left he took me to the far corner of the courtyard and introduced me to his two racing camels. They knelt before us like sphinxes, heads turned away from the light of Khalid's torch, their pale eyes glowing amber, an expression of contemptuous disinterest on their faces. As we turned to go, one of them belched loudly, derisively.

The moon came up. Thin layers of white mist obscured the dune road. It was an eerie ride, with Mohammed Makmud driving hell-bent to get back to his wife. And the next day I said good-bye to the Trucial Oman and flew back to Bahrain to join Commander John Lang on the frigate *Flamingo*.

2. THE YEMEN BORDER

Flight into Trouble

I have St. Christopher's luck as a traveller. I always have had. Even when everything goes wrong, it seems to turn out for the best in the end. I had been a fortnight on H.M.S. *Flamingo* and lulled by the Navy's kindly acceptance of me into their tight little community, I had almost forgotten my ultimate objective. And then John Lang returned from a visit to Jufair Naval Base and waved a sheaf of papers under my nose. " Sailing orders," he said, with á grin. " You're in luck. It's an Arabian coast cruise."

" Masira Island?" I asked.

" Beyond Masira—down as far as Salala to pick up the

Sultan of Muscat. With any luck I'll be able to put you ashore where the R.A.F. can pick you up."

We left next day, the routine pattern of life aboard suddenly broken. It was watch and watch about, the decks vibrating under our feet and a steady splurge of sound from our bow wave. A desert island, glimpsed at dawn, swam in the burnished water-mirror of a dead calm sea; and later the coast emerged from the heat haze, the brown, towering cliffs beyond Ras-al-Khaima.

Evening saw us anchored in the tide-torn narrows of the Khor Kuwai. The crumbling remains of an old Jarasmi pirate village stood deserted on a bare, eroded hill; and on the opposite side of the narrows, sprawled over the naked rock, were the empty barracks and rusting radio masts of H.M.S. *Hormuz,* a derelict naval base, relic of Curzon's gunboat diplomacy. It was now occupied by five wretched Arabs and whatever else besides of God's creatures can stand a climate that in high summer reaches a shade temperature of over 120° F. and a humidity of 100%.

We floated a barrel of paraffin ashore, passed stores down to the five caretakers in their boat, and left in the last of of the light, steaming out of the Persian Gulf with a full moon over the bows, out through the narrow cleft that the Navy calls the "Gates of Hell." It was a piece of navigational bravado, for the "Gates" were little wider than the length of the ship and we went through on radar alone, sheer rock walls overhanging our bows at each alteration of course and white in the moonlight.

We were in the Gulf of Oman then with whites the rig of the day and the watch on the bridge all stripped to the waist, bare brown torsos naked to the sun. And in the late afternoon, we anchored off Muscat, in an inlet no bigger than a Cornish cove, and the white painted name of every ship that had ever come there stared at us from the surrounding rocks.

We were three short hours in this little capital of the Oman crowded into the head of the cove, and I sat on a roof top as the shadows lengthened, talking to one of my own clan—Neil Innes, who was Adviser to the Sultan—talking of home and the oil camp down the coast, of local politics and the past history of the place, its age-old link with Zanzibar and the coasts of Africa. And the following morning we were in the Arabian Sea.

And what a sea that is for fish! Not in the Arctic waters of Hudson's Bay nor in tropical Atlantic waters have I seen such an abundance. There was a night I shall always remember, a night of almost unbelievable splendour. I stood on the deck, hour after hour, unable to tear myself away from a sight I felt I might never see again. Great sharks were moving round us in the midnight water, blazing a lit torpedo track of phosphorescence, curving and swirling and diving as they hunted their prey, their every movement marked and recorded like the headlight trail of cars in a night photograph. And up for'ard, beyond the incandescent splurge of our bow wave, blobs of light, luminous as nebulae, were suddenly shattered at our approach, spreading outwards and bursting on the surface like star rockets in a firework display as the fish leapt to escape. And far away, on the black line of the horizon, the gleam of a light, so faint that it was hardly discernible to the naked eye, yet undoubtedly there—the bow wave of a tanker ploughing its lonely course to Sitra or Kuwait and visible, according to the range given on the radar screen, at a distance of over 12 miles.

In the early mornings, and particularly at evening time, the fish put on a fantastical display. Huge rays would leap high out of the water, white in the setting sun, to hit the surface in a silver cascade; king mackerel on the war path —with great schools of small fry flaring out ahead of them, whipping the surface of the sea to foam and leaping clear out of the water in packs, and the Syr fish at their heels, arcing out of the sea in a dagger-curve of steel—leaping sometimes vertically to a height of almost 20 ft. to fall back with the sharp slap of body hard on water or turning unbelievable somersaults. And once two whales, huge spermaceti, sounding deep and then surfacing vertically with such momentum that all but the tail was carried clean out of the sea until they stood for a second upright like great cromlechs to fall back with the slow solidity of rock and disappear again in a mighty explosion of white water ... finally to come so close across our bows that the officer of the watch ordered both engines full astern for we were headed into one of those grey masses as though we were ramming a U-boat.

There were other moments, too. By the middle of March we were anchored off Salala and the Sultan joined ship, rowed out to us from his summer palace in a sharp-prowed surf boat, the planks of which were stitched together in the old manner. He was a short, quiet-spoken, bearded man, seemingly weighed down by the size of his turban, and he came aboard through a mist of gun smoke as we fired our salute, the ship dressed overall and the great red banner of Muscat flying from our masthead. With him came his body-guard, all armed to the teeth, agleam with the silver of curved *khanjar* knives and muskets, their bodies strapped around with cartridges. They camped on the boat deck, eating the food they specially prepared and turning to Mecca for their prayers as unself-consciously as if they were camped out in the desert.

And a visit I shall never forget—to an oil camp in the middle of nowhere, on a beachhead won from the pitiless desert shore. In twenty days they had got 500 men ashore —European and Arab— together with £300,000 worth of equipment, including 70 vehicles. It was like a military operation, for each ship-load, every vehicle, every crate had its schedule, the establishment of the camp being a race against the monsoon.

Once the monsoon broke huge seas would make the beach untenable for ships. It had taken a year to plan and organise the operation, and the man who ran it was as worried as any army comander in the face of an implacable

enemy . . . the enemy in this case thirst. They were
dependent for their water on sea water separators. They
were already boring for sweet water, but if they failed to
bring in an artesian well and the separators packed up,
then 500 men would face death.

These are the hazards and the difficulties of the oil man's
life in Arabia. The men are tough. They have to be.
They are paid extremely well. Again they have to be. They
give the best years of their lives to acting as the spearhead
in the drive to locate more and yet more fuel to keep the
wheels of industry turning. In the economic war between
East and West—and that's what it basically is, for without
motive power the struggle is lost to us—these men are in the
first wave, committed always it seems to search the most
desolate tracts of the world, for the oil lies below the ancient
sea beds, and so many of the old sea beds have become
deserts.

It was March 20 when we finally anchored off Masira
Island, and next morning, after a night of storm and stress,
with the anchor dragging, boats smashed and little sleep, I
said good-bye to John Lang and my friends of the past
month and, accompanied by the ship's mail, I was put
ashore. Half an hour later, from the control tower of the
R.A.F. airfield, I watched *Flamingo* steam away to the
north, back towards the station in the Persian Gulf. I hated
to see her go. And for a while I had the sense of having
been abandoned, the same sense that a marooned sailor
would have had as he watched his ship disappear over the
horizon, for she had been my home and now the lotus days
were over. Now once again I must work to get myself
where I wanted to go—new faces and strange beds, dust
and heat and transport problems.

The first step, however, was fairly simple. I had signalled
the Station Commander from *Flamingo* and it was arranged that I should be flown out on the next Valetta to
come up on the Aden-Masira milk-run. It wasn't due until

March 25 so that I had three clear days in which to explore the island.

It was a strange place, an almost deserted hangover of the Second World War, and I shall always remember those three days as a queer interlude—a sort of Sinbad interruption—in a long and arduous journey. A lonely handful of R.A.F. men, a thousand Arab fisherfolk, a few miles of desert, some black, eroded hills—there wasn't much else to the island. And yet somehow it had an atmosphere vaguely hostile, strangely disturbing.

It is hard to put a finger on the reason for it. Decay certainly had something to do with it. Everything seemed to be in an advanced state of disintegration. Salt and sand and wind and the everlasting humidity played hell with anything metal, and there was no shortage of metal around, for Masira had been quite a base during the war. There were railway lines, a steel jetty, railway wagons, an engine, and acre upon acre of old fuel drums and 4-gallon petrol cans, a toppling mass of piled-up containers, so fretted through rust that to walk through the sand-filled corridors between was to be lost in a scrap-metal dealer's nightmare. The 2-inch thick H-girders of the old jetty were rotted right through and the heavy bolts of the railway wagons had mushroomed into cysts of rust that disintegrated into red powder at a touch. The engine was something that only Browning could have imagined, a Tophet's tool so eaten into by the red leprosy of rust that whole sections had been blown away by the wind until it was little more than a skeleton.

And the people themselves were in not much better case. A few clung in squalor to a village that had once been a barracks built out of petrol tins filled with cement. Now rust and sand erosion had done their work, the neat blocks crumbling to ruin, so that the whole area looked like a piece of post-war Berlin transported by some magic carpet into the desert.

Here, in a little house decorated with bombs up-ended on their fins, the courtyard fenced with oil drums, I took tea with the *Wali*, the overseer of the labourers who worked at the airfield. And with me was the interpreter, a small, bearded man from South Shields whose father, a Yemenite, had sailed in British ships and had married an English girl. There were flies everywhere, and just below where we sat drinking tea there was a dhow building on the foreshore, its wooden ribs standing like the bleached remains of a stranded whale against the flat mirror of the sea.

From the *Wali* I learnt of the misery of the people. They had no money to import food from outside the island and so they were forced to a self-sufficiency that amounted to a perpetual diet of fish and eggs. Unbelievably, they still used dug-out canoes for fishing, and these clumsy craft make it a young man's work. Because it was an island, the people had no use for camels and donkeys. To see them runing wild, even on the airfield itself, gave the place a topsy-turvy, Alice-in-Wonderland feeling, for everywhere else I had been in Arabia these animals had been prized as possessions of value, the sole means of transport.

To the south of the airfield there were hills that looked as high and as unclimbable as the moon-mad mountains of the Wadi Khor, yet when I approached them they faded away into miniatures only a few hundred feet high. These little mountains stretched away to the south-eastern shores. There were gazelle there, but they were not hunted. There were even wild ass, a beast that is extinct except for this area of Arabia.

In a mood almost of despair I walked north along the island's shores. The white sand beaches crawled with the shell-backed denizens of the Arabian Sea—big spider crabs, and hermit crabs by the million, transporting on their backs whole housing estates of variegated shells. Giant blanket rays flapped their four-foot wings through the water only a few yards from the shore, and by a dug-out canoe I met an Arab ancient standing alone in a loin cloth and staring

wistfully out to sea with half-blind eyes, his long grey hair
streaming in the wind, his skin, wrinkled and burned
black by years of exposure, stretched taut over the bare cage
of his ribs—a sad skeletal figure that made me think of old
Noah.

And then at the northern tip of the island I came across
a monument that stood in a patch of scrub below some
hills, like some lone Druidical stone. And on it I read these
words : "*In memory of those of the* Baron Inverdale *who
were massacred on this spot in 1904.*" There was a baby
camel standing near, its coat as fluffy as a kitten's, and all
around me was the peace and quiet of desert island shore;
and in front of me those words. The past was suddenly
very strong upon me—a past that only fifty years ago
could murder the survivors of a shipwreck. The old man
I had greeted a while back . . . he might well have taken
part in the slaughter. The baby camel stared at me
curiously, the pale amber eyes without expression; and then
suddenly it broke and ran stiff-legged to its dam. I, too,
turned and left that spot, walking quickly back along the
western shore, down along the disintegrating railway track,
past the engine and the fuel dump and all the wind-blown
débris of a half-forgotten war, back to the world I knew and
understood, the lonely huts out on the sand by the runway's edge and the bare mess-room that was home to one
officer and one sergeant.

I never went back to that northern shore. Instead I
explored southwards, fifteen miles through the "little
mountains" of the island's *Masif Central* to a little rock-
bound cove where the sand was of powdered coral and
white shell fragments and where there were boats drawn up
above the tide level. They were larger than I had seen before, their wood bleached by sea and sun, worn smooth by
constant use, and all along the foreshore the sand was
littered with nets and lines. A little back from the shore
stood a miserable little *barasti* village. Here Sheikh Khasin
greeted me and set me down with my back against his

wife's *barasti* whilst small boys brought tea. This business of allowing the wife to overhear all that passes without in fact being seen is something of an Arab habit. Western woman may be emancipated, but I often wonder whether petticoat government isn't stronger in Arabia and other countries where the women still keep to the *harem*.

With the tea came eggs—and also flies. There were signs of trachoma amongst the children, but though the village was poor, the people were better off than any I had seen so far. There was some silver, a glint here and there on a knife and musket, and the sheikh's little daughter had a neck-halter of silver, as well as a necklace, head band and wrist and ankle bangles. The village had not the smallest cultivated patch. It lived entirely off the sea, and that I knew meant living always close to the level of bare subsistence. And yet those silver ornaments. I looked more closely at Sheikh Khasin then, at the hawk-nosed, grey-bearded face, the wily look of the dark eyes, and I wondered.

Evening stole over the cove and in the ghostly light of a full moon we drove back through the little mountains, following a sand track that twisted and turned through valleys deep in shadow and stratified by layer upon layer of white mist. And back at the camp, I was pitched suddenly into another world. A blazing fire and men of the Aden Protectorate Levies giving a display of tribal dances. These men were from the Ouliki, Andhali, Azzani, Hassani and Misuri tribes—some of them so fine-boned and beautiful as to be almost girlish. The dances were simple and direct, so that I found myself transported beyond the misery of Masira Island down into the warlike south of Arabia, a magic-carpet glimpse into the next stage of my journey, for these men were all from the trouble areas close to the Yemen border.

I was with them again next morning on the rifle range, and then I hitched a ride in a truck going to Ras-al-Haf. This village faces the mainlaind, and on the shore, surrounded by a curious chattering crowd, I held the hand of a man I had last seen mingling with the Sultan's retinue on *Flamingo's* decks. His name was Ghalani and he served the Consul in Muscat. Held there in that endless handclasp of Arab friendship I wondered how he had got himself there, and why. There were dhows standing off, but he said he was going on to Dhawah by camel, a village four hours away to the south. He was obviously a man of standing and an emissary of his master, for his bearing had considerable dignity and his voice was as soft and gentle as a poet's. Yes, he said, it would take him a month or more to get back to Muscat in one of the *Badan* dhows. I pictured him moving quietly from village to village, savouring the political climate. Such men fill the same role and have the same power as the Press in a land where there are no newspapers and where the spoken word has the impact of the printed word in other lands.

The women of Ras-al-Half, briefly glimpsed going to and from the well, were dark-skinned, almost black, a throwback to the slave days and the influence of Zanzibar on all the peoples of the coast. Some of them indeed were beautiful and I learned later that Ras-al-Half was a village much visited by men of the Levies. A background of slavery had left its dark shadow, and only recently there had been trouble there, with the master of a visiting dhow badly beaten up. "A little matter of a prostitute, I thir , sor," was how the big-boned station sergeant from Tipperary put it. And he added, "As foine a looking woman as ever I set eyes on."

Sex and disease and poverty, above all, the desperate need of food—that is the whole of life between birth and death along the Arabian shore. And the brief oil interlude will not change it. These things are endemic—like the sand and the heat and the flies.

One final glimpse of Masira; on a clear pellucid evening with dusk brightening the face of the moon, I stood on a beach of white sand and watched a small Arab boy and

his sister paddle a clumsy dug-out canoe with their hands,
out through a choppy sea. It didn't seem to matter to them
whether they were in the dug-out or in the sea—they swam
like fishes, naked and unashamed and quite beautiful to
watch, their long hair streaming behind them in the broken
water. Poverty was theirs, but so was life, too, for they
were as full of the joy of living as two puppies at play.

At 0800 in the morning I took off for Aden, and the
world was suddenly all changed. I looked down from a
few hundred feet upon Salala and the summer palace,
blurred in a mist of salt sea spray and half lost among the
gardens of coconut where the wind thrashed at the palms.
We stopped for lunch at Riyan, and then we were flying
over Mukalla, a beautiful little huddle of ivory chess pieces,
white against the crowding hills that barred the way to
the Hadhramaut. This was the gateway to the Great Wadi
and I stared down at it, fascinated, wondering whether I
should ever achieve my goal—so close now, and yet so far,
flying as I was high above the little port.

Beyond Mukalla the country changed abruptly. The
mountain ranges gave way to an extraordinary area of
craters, a black lava country, the volcanic vents looking like
the craters of the moon seen through a telescope. Here and
there a vivid, sulphurous seam intruded like gangrene, and
where the craters dropped in steps to the sea itself, there
were some that had been invaded by salt water to provide
strange horseshoe anchorages, and others that were lakes
where the sea had seeped in through the encircling lava
dust.

Then the mountains dropped away and suddenly ceased.
The clouds thickened, and close below us was flat, barren
country, with hardly a village; and this stretched all the
way to the big R.A.F. base of Khormaksar at Aden.

I was back then in the hurly-burly of civilisation. And
yet even here the past, the present and the future seemed
inextricably mixed, the primitive with the mechanised. As
we drove past Ma'ala, there were big dhows lying on the

mud and others being built the way they had always been built—the same dhows that, since long before the birth of Christianity, have run down the monsoon winds between Arabia and Java and Sumatra. Away to the left was the great Arab town of Crater, close under towering hills of black granite, where even to this day it is firmly believed that Arab children are offered as human sacrifices. And the Steamer Point, with the passenger liners and the big freighters lying off, and beyond it the R.A.F. Mess on Tarshyne Fort Hill. And away to the right, Little Aden, the huge new refinery, then still in course of construction.

The following day I visited the Secretariat and my journey into the Hadhramaut was given their official blessing. But I was warned that whether I ever got there would depend on the availability of transport and on the attitude of Colonel Boustead, British Adviser to the East Aden Protectorate. They would cable him at his headquarters in Mukalla, but . . . here a significant shrug and a final ," Well, it's up to him."

Whilst I waited for his reply I set about trying to arrange a quick visit to the Yemeni border and the trouble spots that even then were keeping troops pinned down in the hostile mountain ranges beyond the escarpment. Our obligations along this border are the legacies of Empire. Whether we should continue to fulfil them or not seems to me a moot point. So far, however, we had continued to support the Sultan of Nisbad and the other friendly sheikhdoms of the Aden Protectorate against the attacks of dissident tribesmen raiding across the border from the Yemen. The task of withstanding these raids then rested largely on the R.A.F. Regiment, supported by the Aden Protectorate Levies and by the Government Guards of local sheikhs.

A morning spent in consultation with R.A.F. Intelligence convinced me that I had insufficient time to make the journey by land. The only alternative was to fly in with one of the aircraft of the Aden Protectorate Levy Support Flight. There was a plane leaving for Nisab the following morning. Could I be at Khormaksar airfield at 0700 hours?

I was staying in the R.A.F. Mess at Tarshyne Fort, and with no transport of my own, getting to the airfield at such an early hour was in itself a problem. In fact, I didn't make it until well after seven, but as I drew up at the H.Q. of the A.P.L. Support Flight, the old Avro Anson was still standing on the apron. There was a lot of low cloud and it looked like rain.

Inside the office there was a depressing air of inertia; everybody sitting around and no sign of activity. The radio operator shrugged his shoulders when I asked what time he expected to take off. "It's bad up in the mountains," he said. "Looks like the monsoon is going to be early this year."

And then the pilot came in, a big heavily-built man, whom they all called "Pop." He seemed nervous and worried. "The weather? She is clampers already, I think." He had a peculiar accent that I could not place. And the fact that he was over forty and still only a Flying Officer didn't give me any great confidence in him. I hung around there for an hour and a half in that debilitating atmosphere, and when I finally left with the assurance that they would contact me if the weather cleared, I felt that this was one of those back-water flights into which throw-out pilots were posted. And so, instead of flying into the trouble spot of Nisab, I went goggle-fishing in the warm, oil-saturated waters of Aden.

The following day I again hitched a ride up to the airfield. Again I was late, and again the old Anson was still on the apron. The sky was clear, no sign of rain, and yet the atmosphere in the Flight Office remained one of inertia. "It looks all right, I agree," the radio operator told me, "but Pop's worried about the weather up at Am Ruseis." It was Am Ruseis to-day, not Nisab. "This damned milk-run of ours," he added; "you never can tell what will happen. It's always pretty dicey when the monsoon's due."

But I was determined not to be baulked a second time.

"Haven't we got any sort of report on visibility up in the mountains?" I asked.

Pop came in at that moment. "We wait for it now." He shook his head with a worried frown. "But I don't like it. The weather she change too dam' quick this time of the year." And he went over to the window and stood gazing out at the blue sky.

Forty minutes later the report came through. Weather good, visibility 30 miles. Even then, Pop hesitated, muttering to himself. Then suddenly the decision was taken and we hurried out to the plane. A moment later we took off.

I cannot remember ever being more nervous about a flight. We were due to make three calls, the first at Am Ruseis. When I had told a senior R.A.F. officer the previous night what my destination was, he had said, "Rather you than me, old boy. That's a very tricky one, that is." Apparently Am Ruseis airstrip was in the bottom of a narrow ravine, requiring a tight descent inside the rock walls and a sudden turn on to the landing field. "It's under attack, too, right at this moment," he had added.

As we headed east, climbing steadily, I was wishing I had my old-Etonian daredevil of a pilot of the pirate-coast flight at the helm, instead of this over-aged and worried man. It was still clear overhead, but in front of us I could see great cotton-wool clouds of cumulus-nimbus standing up out of the desert as though we were headed into a dozen atomic explosions. And then, suddenly, above them I glimpsed the dark knife-edges of the mountain tops.

We crossed the escarpment at 9,500 ft., dodging between the mushroom growths of cumulus, and only a few hundred feet below us volcanic ridges, as bare and black and empty of life as the day they had been created by some huge re-adjustment of the earth's surface, stood like the gates of Paradise Lost.

I barely had time to take stock of this utter desolation before the plane gave a violent lurch and tipped over on to one wing. Imagination instantly pictured what it would be like to crash amongst those knife-edged ridges, so impossible of access on foot; and then we were in a side-slipping descent that left my heart in my mouth. Turning and twisting through long corridors between the clouds, we came suddenly out into the bright sunlight, and there below us, as we did a sharp banking turn, was a steep ravine—the airstrip of Am Ruseis.

We were below the level of the mountains then and almost imediately we seemed to be enclosed in walls of red rock, with barely room to turn. I had a brief glimpse of a vertical wall of rock sliding past my window, and then we had done a tight turn and there was rock again, close beyond the opposite window, now high above me. We were side-slipping again now, sliding on one wing tip down the whole face of the ravineside, with the hard, flat sand-stretch of the airstrip rushing up to meet us. And straight ahead of us was another rock face, with the stone walls of a fort perched on the top of it.

I was convinced then that the pilot had left it too late. We were going to crash. And then, unbelievably, he skidded the aircraft round on its tail, pivoting on one wing tip, and in one side-slipping rush slammed it down on to the airstrip.

Before we had taxied to a stop two Land Rovers were driving pell-mell across the sand towards us. They were full of R.A.F. Regiment officers, sun-reddened, tired and a little jumpy. Their three hundred Levy troops, scattered along the walls of the ravine and in the fort, had been in action all night. "There's a shower of bastards called the Abhudi up in those hills," one of them told me. "They're firing on us all the time." One Levy corporal had been killed during the night, they added.

We had mail for them. And there was more mail to go out, and despatches. As we waited for these, Pop paced up and down, constantly glancing at his wrist-watch. I could feel the nervous tension in him building up, and every now and then he stopped his pacing and glanced up at the sky. But there was no cloud there; only an eye-searing humid sun haze.

I doubt whether we were there more than five minutes, but Pop couldn't get out of the place fast enough, lifting the old Anson up the face of the ravine walls in tight turns, standing her on her tail at such a crazy angle that I clutched the arms of my seat, nerves taut with the fear that he was going to stall the plane and go into a tail spin. Up and up we climbed, and then back across those vile volcanic ridges until the scene changed back again and we were dropping down into another world. The mountains had vanished. Ahead was nothing but sand.

We came in to an easy, straighforward landing. No fort this time. No sign of habitation. Just a broad belt of sand and gravel, with a little camel thorn dotted about. We came to a standstill and Pop came aft and opened the fuselage door. He was sweating.

A camel was grazing close by, and seated beside it, cross-legged on a brightly coloured carpet, was an extremely fat Arab—a eunuch I was convinced—dressed in turban and flowing robes and smoking a water pipe. With him was his black servant, a brass-bound trunk, a carpet bed-roll and a chromium-plated pressure lamp. It was such an unbelievable sight, there in that lonely stretch of desert, that I would not have been in the least surprised if there had been a genie attached to that incongruous pressure lamp!

On the carpet, close beside him, lay a dirty bundle of clothes. Closer inspection revealed it as a child, its eyes dull with sickness. The sick child proved to be the reason for our landing. It was as though that pressure lamp really did have magic powers, for I never discovered how the fat Arab had managed to conjure an R.A.F. plane out of the sky to take the wretched boy to hospital at Aden.

There now began an interminable argument, whilst Pop paced nervously up and down. It appeared that the Arab would not let the child make the journey alone. He must

accompany him. Not only that, but he insisted that he
must take with him the carpet, the bed-roll, the brass-
bound trunk, and the pressure lamp. I felt that for two
pins he would have insisted upon taking the camel and his
servant as well!

In the end we achieved a compromise. He would accompany the child, and the pressure lamp would go with him.
" He can sell that at Crater," the radio operator said. " He
hasn't any money, only goods."

Once that was settled, we bundled them both in and took
off in a hell of a hurry. As we climbed, I could see the
mountains all round us again, rising up from the sand,
which must once have been the bed of a great river. We
kept fairly low this time, crossing a few small volcanic outcrops and then winding our way through the wadis of dry
river beds until we came to a wide sand plain scattered
with the dusty green of crops and a few villages. Each
village was centred about a *dhar*, or fortified house, some of
which were three stories high.

Baïhan, our last stop, appeared suddenly through a gap
in some bare hills, and we skimmed a dry river bed, made a
tight, low turn and dropped on to an airstrip of soft sand
close below the *dhar* walls.

Here we were to pick up an appendix case, a local
Government Guard, due to be evacuated to hospital. We
were met by a hook-nosed, effeminate-looking Arab, clad
in an American shirt hanging loose outside a green skirt.
His Land Rover announced that he was part of the Locust
Control. With him was the Captain of the local Government Guard, an impressive, ramrod figure in black Arab
head-dress, the curved-bladed *jambia* knife of authority
stuck in his belt.

Though both the Captain of the Guard and the officer
of Locust Control had come out to meet us, they had not
thought to bring the sick private with them. With many
shrugs they intimated that he would be along in a few

minutes and we knew that that might mean half an hour, an hour, maybe more. Time was of no object to them. Pop was livid. With one eye on the clouds that were now beginning to gather overhead, he told them that if the private wasn't there in five minutes, he would take off without him.

In the end, it was a quarter of an hour before we at last got him on board, a small dark man, dazed by the pain that had stricken him and moving like a sleep-walker, but still resolutely clutching his rifle, which at no time would he relinquish even for a moment.

We took off for Aden then, climbing steadily again to 9,500 ft. The clouds had built up considerably whilst we had waited at Bahrain. They stood in thick, piled-up masses over the escarpment, and as we headed south-west and they closed about us, the sun vanished and it became very dark.

Leaning forward I could see into the cockpit, with Pop seated at the controls and the radio operator's head bent as he held the earphones tight against his ears, their stillness and concentration suggested tension and an unpleasant sensation of uncertainty was communicated to me. We were turning and twisting through narrowing corridors in the cloud, and every now and then white wisps enveloped us so that we were flying momentarily in a void until we found the next corridor. And as we climbed up into the thicker clouds, these corridors became fewer and fewer, the blank white walls closing in on us faster. I kept on glancing at my watch, trying to work out in my mind the moment when we would cross the escarpment and those grim, eroded ridges would be behind us.

Unsure of my pilot and completely helpless, I sat there with the Government Guard, the eunuch and the sick child. The eunuch began to complain in a high-pitched, frightened voice. He had never been in a plane before, but though he did not understand what was going on, he, too, had sensed the tension. I gripped the arms of my seat as the plane was tossed about in a violent eddy. And then suddenly we were in cloud again and it was dark.

It was at this moment that the radio operator turned round and caught my eye. He gave me the thumbs-down sign, using both thumbs in an urgent, stabbing movement, and I suddenly felt empty inside. I knew that we hadn't crossed the escarpment yet.

The plane lurched again, and then suddenly rolled over on to the port wing-tip. It was lighter then and looking down through my window, I found myself momentarily suspended over a long, funnelling gap in the clouds. It was like looking down a plastic tube, and at the bottom was a small, dark patch of volcanic mountain top, and right in the centre, looking very small, the silver shape of a crashed plane lay spreadeagled against the rock.

I only caught that one brief glimpse of it before we were back in the cloud and my body was thrust hard into my seat as we made a tight turn, side-slipping all the time, a sickening sideways plunge that seemed to go on and on, endlessly.

The light increased again as we came out of the cloud, but still we plunged down like a dead duck on one wing, with the ground and that crashed aircraft slamming up towards us at a fantastic rate. At the very last moment, just as it seemed inevitable that we should go on falling until we smashed ourselves into the ground, Pop dragged the plane round by its tail in a complete 180° turn, the nose lifted and the wheels slammed down on to a water-logged airstrip. Sheets of mud flew up on either side as we bounced; down again in another back-breaking jolt, another bounce, and then we were on the deck and plunging forward through mud and water towards a little hut.

We stopped close beside it, and as the engines were cut, I sat back, dazed and exhausted. Pop came back down the fuselage. For the first time during the whole trip I saw him smile. " Why am I so good to you boys, eh?" he said, and the smile spread into a broad grin.

I couldn't help it. I had to give vent to the tension that still gripped me. " I thought we were going to crash," I said. He patted my shoulder in a fatherly way. " I tell you something," he said, " there was a moment when I think so, too."

He went aft and opened the fuselage door. Outside, it was pouring with rain and bitterly cold. We were 7,000 ft. up and wearing nothing but tropical kit. Dark clouds streamed low overhead, and from what looked like a little mud fort, a battered Land Rover came flying through the mud towards us. It drew up close beside us and an R.A.F. Regiment officer got out. " You've brought reinforcements, have you?" he said.

" Reinforcements?" Pop laughed. " I haven't brought you any reinforcements."

The Flight Lieutenant's face fell. " Then why are you here? I was expecting reinforcements."

" I am here because I am a lucky chap. We are just coming up to the escarpment when we get a radio message from Khormaksar to say the monsoon has struck and we cannot land there."

" There's a hell of a storm raging over Aden," the radio operator put in. " Visibility about a hundred yards, the cloud base right down on to the deck and raining buckets."

And Pop added, " I do not think we make it anyway, against those headwinds. Not enough petrol. And then I looked down, and there is the old Valetta and your air-field right below me, and I remember that I have stored two cans of petrol in this hut here against a rainy day. And this is a rainy day all right," he added, sniffing at the mountain downpour from the open fuselage door like a dog unwilling to leave its kennel. " I'm a dam' lucky chap to find this place, I think."

But I knew now that it wasn't luck. It had been gradually dawning on me that this man Pop was no ordinary pilot. Any man who can side-slip an aircraft 3,000 ft. down a funnel through storm clouds and land on a water-logged airfield without tipping the plane up on to its nose must be good.

" Well, now that you're here, I hope you can all handle small arms." The Flight Lieutenant's eyes were fixed on me. " We're expecting to be attacked at any moment."

The place where we had landed was Mukeiras. It was only three miles from the Yemen border, a tiny airfield perched on the very lip of the escarpment. Until recently it had been a summer leave camp for the R.A.F., but now the grey little stone-walled Rest House was a sandbagged fortress with a Bren gun mounted on the roof, and scattered around it were the tents of the Levy troops, who were all busy erecting small circular redoubts of piled-up rock, ready to withstand the expected attack.

After the humid heat of Aden, it was unbelievably cold. The rock walls, the little patches of green grass, the sudden glimpses of country far below seen through ragged gaps in the clouds—incredibly it was like the English Lake District. We had barely reached the Rest House when cloud enveloped the whole area in a white mist. A startling clap of thunder reverberated round the hills, lightning stabbed the dark interior of the house. In shorts and sleeveless shirts we shivered from the dank chill of stone and concrete walls.

We borrowed pullovers and greatcoats and sat pretending to read magazines whilst listening and waiting for the expected attack. It was then that I was able to solve the mystery of Pop's lack of seniority when he was so obviously a first-rate pilot.

He was Polish, the son of an anti-espionage officer killed by the Russians in 1936. In his own country he had been a ski instructor to the Alpine Regiment. He had also flown for an Air Circus, which accounted for his ability to side-slip an Anson, a thing which I was told later is no ordinary feat. He had joined the Polish Air Force, and after the defeat in 1939 he was in no less than four prisoner-of-war and concentration camps, and one by one escaped from each of them. He eventually got out through Roumania and joined the Polish Air Force in Britain.

Now, all he seemed to worry about was the poor wretched Government Guard. He kept on staring out of the window, which showed visibility nil and the rocks streaming water. " If we do not get out of here to-day," he said. " then maybe I have to operate myself. An ignorant man like me!" And he shook his head. " I do not think that would be very good—either for me, or for that poor devil!"

But by now I was quite convinced he was capable of anything—even to removing an appendix under radio instruction from Aden.

In fact, he was never put to this last test. In the middle of a hot curry lunch, the clouds lifted, the sun came out, and after topping up with the two jerricans of fuel he had cached in the hut, we took off from Mukeiras in a hurry. My last impression of that grim little fortress perched on the lip of nothing was of three unveiled native women carrying water in two-gallon cans to the roof of the Rest House to feed the flush lavatory and of the Flight Lieutenant, a lonely figure, waving us good-bye, whilst behind him his Levy troops oiled their guns or carried stones to increase the height of the walls protecting their tents.

And as we flew back to Aden I was no longer worrying about the plane and whether we should land safely— instead, I was thinking that here we were riding high in the air on our way back to Base and behind us were those poor devils, cut off absolutely from any contact with the outside world, except by plane and radio, and expecting hourly to be attacked, in what strength they did not know. Would it come that night? And when it did and they had beaten it off, there would be another night, and another attack.

It was only a glimpse that I had of the ceaseless vigilance

of our men along the borders of the Aden Protectorate. But after that forced landing at Mukeiras, I understood the danger and the tension that constantly faced these men—and the sense of frustration, for the raiders came always from across the Yemen border and no retaliation was possible.

3. JOURNEY INTO THE HADHRAMAUT

Back in Aden, I checked with the Secretariat. Still no word from Colonel Boustead. All next day I waited, hoping for news, wondering whether I should be able to get into the Hadhramaut or not. But nothing came through, no message, no cable, nothing. I began to feel desperate then, for time was getting short and the twice-weekly R.A.F. flight along the coast to Mukalla left on Saturday.

Friday I was down at the Secretariat again. " The only thing for you to do," the told me, " is to take to-morrow's flight and hope for the best. Just turn up and if he likes you . . ." It was left like that, with a slight shrug of the shoulders.

I was not very happy about it, therefore, when I took off on Saturday. I had no idea what lay ahead. Nobody had invited me. I had virtually invited myself. Slumped in the sun-drenched, sweaty heat of the crowded transport plane, I felt nervous and ill at ease. We bumbled along the coast, following the white line of the surf where it broke against the sands of Arabia, until at last we came to the lifeless craters and the volcanic outcrops. Then I could see the mountains that sprawled across the route I must take to get into the Hadhramaut. They were 6,000 ft. high, a sepia mass that ruled a straight line across the brilliant blue of the sky.

And then, suddenly below us, there again was the dainty ivory chess set of Mukalla. Twenty miles farther on we touched down on the drying mud of Riyan airfield and the

Station Commander came bouncing out in his Land Rover to meet us. "Mr. Innes? This came for you this morning —from Mukalla." He handed me an envelope. "Don't know how the fellow managed to get through after the rains we've had. But he did, and he said it was urgent."

My heart sank. It must be to tell me that there was no point in my proceeding to Mukalla. Why else should it be so urgent? And then I opened the envelope. *This is to welcome you to Mukalla,* Boustead began. And he added : *I am leaving at eleven o'clock to-day for the interior by the West road to attend an important tribal gathering in the Wadi Duan and if the R.A.F. can get you here I should be delighted to have you accompany me. I could send you on to the Hadhramaut.* . . .

I couldn't believe it. It was just too good to be true— the Hadhramaut, and a gathering of the Bedou tribes. And he was leaving at eleven o'clock—to-day. I glanced at my watch. It was already nine-thirty. An hour and a half to cover twenty miles. It should be enough. But when I raised the question of transport with the Station Commander I realised that it wasn't going to be as easy as that. His jeep couldn't make it, he said. The track was axle-deep in mud after the night's rain. He was even doubtful whether the three-ton truck would succeed, but he'd tell the driver to "have a bash at it."

The next hour was one of the most exasperating I have ever spent. The three-tonner acted as fire tender at all landings and take-offs; it couldn't leave for Mukalla until the aircraft that had brought me in took off again. This it didn't do until after ten. In the little wooden control tower I listened to the Station Commander chatting to the pilot as the plane dwindled to a speck over the sea, spoke to him myself and thanked him for the flight. Then at last I was clambering up into the open cab of the battered old three-tonner. Even then we were not away. There was the fire equipment to be dropped off, petrol to be taken on board— precious minutes lost whilst I sat and fumed.

"Do you think we'll make it in time?" I asked the driver as we finally left the airfield.

"I'll try, sir." And I saw him glance at his watch and frown.

He certainly did his best, crashing and pounding that aged relic through the gullies, slithering it through seas of mud. Twice we screamed to a standstill, wheels spinning a black liquid spray, and all the time I watched the clock, knowing we couldn't make it, knowing I was going to miss this heaven-sent opportunity by a matter of only thirty minutes perhaps.

Battered and bruised, we were on the outskirts of Mukalla at eleven-fifteen. But there was still a flood detour, and then the final straw, a long train of camels that we could not pass.

It was eleven twenty-five when we ground in through the archway and up the main street of the dainty, bone-white city. The Residency looked deserted, the servant who answered my knock surprised to see me; and the Englishman who finally came to greet me was not Colonel Boustead. "I suppose the Colonel's left?"

"Good Lord, no. We never get away on time. Always so much to do, you know." He took me through to the courtyard at the side of the Residency, and there to my relief were the trucks of Colonel Boustead's caravanserai piled high with baggage, his bodyguard of Bedou troops clustered about them, a gay splash of colour in their green and red *kufia* headgear; I felt at that moment the same sense of reprieve that Jules Verne's character had felt when it suddenly dawned on him that, in travelling round the world, he had gained a whole day.

It is difficult to describe my first impression of Colonel Boustead, for in the next few days I got to know him well and that has clouded the impact of that first meeting. He belonged to that select group of men who keep the peace over large tracts of wild country through the force of their personalities. I had met his counterpart down in the Sahara amongst the French *Officiers des Affaires Indigènes*. Men

of the desert and the *bled,* they represent the élite of colonial powers, the men who make colonialism work and
justify it as a stage in the development of backward territories. His manner was abrupt, almost hostile at that first
meeting, which was hardly surprising considering that a
stranger had wished himself upon him at a time when he
was going north, to the yearly fair of Qaidun, to persuade
three thousand Bedou tribesmen not to go to war.

That night we camped at 4,000 ft. in a rock gorge through
which the boulder strewn track that they called the West
Road climbed steeply. High above us the cry of the baboon
was an unearthly human shrill that merged as evening fell
with the harsh calls of cave-dwelling Bedou summoning
their goats, and camel boys gathering in their charges. Conditions had not changed since Freya Stark came through
this country some twenty years before, but she had been
alone with her Government Guard and her drivers, travelling by donkey, whereas we had mechanical transport and
were a much bigger outfit, almost an expedition, so that
we had no fear of robbers.

It was a strange encampment, and in a sense typical of
the country, for whatever a man's position it reduces him
to the Bedou way of life. Colonel Bousted had with him
Captain Ellis, his military adviser, and Abdullah Rais, a
captain of Jordan's Arab Legion. The four of us made
camp in the usual Army fashion. Sheikh Qaddal (the Q,
as always, hard like a G—Gaddel), however, lay sprawled
in splendid isolation in the tent his servants had hastily
erected. State Secretary of Mukalla, he was making a
royal progress through the land that would culminate in a
formal state visit to the Hadhramaut states of Qaiti and
Kathiri; a huge man from the Sudan, whose face, in contrast to the spotless white robes and turban, seemed blacker
than any face I had ever seen—a man of immense dignity
and, as I was later to witness, a born orator of great
persuasive powers. With him was Sheikh Ali Hamid,
Minister of Education in Mukalla; he had been in the

Sudanese police, spoke English and was much more approachable. To complete the entourage were a dozen or so servants and guards, some of them with faces of quite feminine beauty.

At this camp we were joined by the *Qaim* of the Wahidi tribe in a rickety truck, a magistrate and a man of importance whom the Colonel always referred to in affectionate tones as " that bloody Bedou." He, too, was bound for the great meeting at the Qaidun Fair; but now, his magisterial importance discarded, he sat against a rag of a windbreak slung on four sticks, waited upon by his only servant; one eye was blindly white in the dark, piratic, hawk-nosed face, and his thin lips were clamped round the stem of his waterpipe, which burbled liquidly like a baby's stomach. The Colonel and I lay on our camp beds and watched the stars come out one by one.

With darkness the camp came to growing life. Oil lamps and torches moved like fireflies and a goat, bought by Ali Hamid from a nearby Bedou encampment, was a grisly silhouette against the glare of a cooking fire, strung up by its legs from the back of a truck, its slit throat dripping blood into a pot. Bedou men, attracted by the glare, slipped shyly into the camp like wild animals—unkempt, skinny old men, blue-black as printer's ink, only the ungainly *jambia* stuck in the wrinkle of cloth at their waists winking silver in the firelight.

We fed that night on a pile of rice soaked in a spiced sauce of goat's blood and on strips of goat's meat frizzled over stones that glowed like coals. The fingers of our right hands dripped fat as we huddled close to a roaring blaze, our backs cut by a freezing wind that whipped down the gorge. And then to be with the stars brilliant and cold above the limestone cliffs; and in the grey dawn our bedding was so soaked with dew that it looked as though a bucket of water had been poured over us during the night.

The track that morning wound upward through the gorge; sometimes the loose bed of a watercourse, sometimes built up, bend above bend, across steep slopes of rotten rock. Twice it had been almost obliterated by the rains and all of us were out ahead heaving stones to rebuild the road-bed.

And then at last we were out of the gorge, speeding through an open valley of bare hills to the village of Mala Mattar. An isolated detachment of Qaiti Armed Constabulary were drawn up for inspection, and beyond the village was the last escarpment and the narrow gorge leading up to the *johl*. We breakfasted on the stone verandah of a little porticoed house built like a Greek temple. It had been erected by Harold Ingrams, the British political officer who brought peace to the warring tribes of the Hadhramaut —a sort of halfway house for his journeys up from Mukalla.

The gorge up to the *johl* was narrow and steep, widening out to sheer slopes of loose rock up which the road twisted and turned. It was there in that gorge that I first learned the reason for the Bedou conference in the Wadi Duan. A camel train was coming down, picking its slow way through the debris. "There you have it—the old and the new," Hugh Boustead said as the camels swayed past our trucks. "That's the problem I'm supposed to resolve. And I can't resolve it. Only time can do that.' And then he nodded towards the barefoot tribesmen, small, blue men with their long, antiquated muzzle-loaders gleaming with silver. "Twenty of those bloody Bedou could close this road— sniping and throwing rocks down. That's what worries me." And again the "bloody Bedou" was a term of affection.

A few years back there had been famine in the Hadhramaut. To save the wadi people from starvation vehicles had been brought in and relief foodstuffs trucked up from the port of Mukalla over camel tracks hastily widened to take them. A minimum of seventy trucks were needed to keep the Hadhramaut supplied in case of emergency, but once acquired they had to be kept running to pay for their

keep. And that was the problem, for the Bedou of the *johl*
with their camel trains were the age-old carriers for the
Hadhramaut. It wasn't only their livelihood that was
threatened, but their whole way of life that had not
changed over countless centuries.

"You cannot suddenly destroy a people without their
fighting back. And if they decide to fight . . ." Hugh
Boustead shrugged his shoulders. The eastern route into the
Hadhramaut, like this western one, climbed to the *johl*
through precipitous gorges. The budget to maintain those
two roads was little more than £8,ooo a year. It would need
an army of labourers, as well as an army of troops, to keep
them open in the face of hostile Bedou tribesmen.

And the odd thing was that at the time of the famine
the whole thing nearly resolved itself, for the Bedou had no
fodder with which to feed their camels. The animals died
like flies and were only saved from complete extermination
by the R.A.F. who mounted an airlift to drop fodder to the
desperate tribesmen. Now, after several good years, the
camel herds were as numerous as ever. And though much
slower and slightly more expensive than road transport as
carriers, they were indigenous to the country, whereas road
transport had to be subsidised, for the Hadhramaut exports
little with which to acquire the foreign currency necessary
for the petrol, oil and spares to keep the trucks going.

A last hairpin, a final slope and we were suddenly out on
top of the world. All behind us the land fell away in
craggy steps towards the sea. Ahead was a flat, level
plateau of gravel—brown, endlessly brown against the blue
of the sky. This was the *johl*; flat as a board except for
small hills that went up in ledges as though it were only
yesterday that the seas ceased to break against the steep
beaches.

At Muscat I had been shown big fossilised oysters that
had been found a hundred miles inland. And on the *johl* I
found further evidence that at some time in geological
history all this part of Arabia had been tilted skywards.

There were sea shells amongst the gravel, and pebbles rounded by waves.

I say it was flat. That was how it looked to me as we travelled across it. But we could glimpse the shadowed beginnings of gorges dropping away on either side. Later, coming out of the Hadhramaut, I flew over the *johl* and it was unrecognisable—a table-land, true; but so veined and cut by gorges, water-eroded out of the limestone base, as to be unrecognisable. Those gorges ripped out of solid rock meant volumes of water—a considerable rainfall at some period of the land's history. But now it was dry—bone dry, despite the unprecedented rains of recent weeks.

And here is another problem. We began to pass black heaps of charcoal by the roadside; charcoal waiting for the camel trains to carry it down to Mukalla. Once perhaps the *johl* had borne a forest of trees. But, unlike the rest of Arabia, it was the charcoal-burners, not the goats, that had denuded this upland country, and now it was bare and tree-less, except in a few sheltered declivities.

For half the year great cloud formations build up over the *johl* and hang there, rainless. "If there were trees here," Hugh Boustead said, "it might lower the temperature sufficiently to produce precipitations." He had persuaded the Sultan to rule certain areas out of bounds to charcoal burners. But the trouble was that charcoal was Mukalla's only fuel. Afforestation, which might solve the problem of famine in the Hadhramaut, was just a dream.

Besides the charcoal burners, we were now meeting up with groups of Bedou squatting down amongst their camels. The blue of their bodies looked a colder colour up on this roof of Arabia. They say it protects the skin against cold. Certainly the poor devils needed protection, for in winter the nights are wretchedly cold up there and they have nothing but the cloth bundled about their waists with which to cover their bodies. At each group the Colonel stopped the car and got out to talk to the tribesmen. At first their faces would be blank, animal-cautious, and then suddenly there would be a flash of teeth as they laughed, their faces lighting up with childish delight at being taken notice of, and the clash of hands on wrists as he gave each man the Bedou grip of welcome.

"Come and meet the Secretaire," was his stock introduction, and they would crowd round the car, wild blue faces pressed excitedly to the glass of the windows, to peer in at Sheikh Qaddal; and soon the palms of my own hands were blue with clasping the sinewy wrists of these strange, attractive people.

Colonel Boustead had a magical touch with them. A stocky, leathery-faced, hard-sinewed Englishman from the Sudan, he had given his life to the East. He was a bachelor but he treated these wild men as his children, and they loved it. He cast the spell of his abundant energy and vitality over them. I had heard of Boustead as far away as the Pirate Coast of the Persian Gulf and having seen him at work amongst his people I know him to be one of the élite of colonial administrators.

We lunched in a field of mud and new-sprouting corn beyond the poor mud hovels of the only village in that part of the *johl,* resting on a patch of fresh green grass in the shade of an 'ilb tree that was sucking up such a wealth of water from the sodden ground that it rained down little drops of moisture on to us. The tree was laden with small cherry-like fruit that had the consistency and taste of bread; it was part of their staple diet in Arabia, but Sheikh Ali Hamid, who also came from the Sudan, said that in his country they made a sort of chocolate from it.

One final memory of the *johl* : By piled-up heaps of charcoal we came upon two lorries packed with Bedouin Legion troops. Excited shouts of welcome, a sudden swirl of armed men intermingling, dark hand clasping dark wrist, white teeth flashing, tongues clattering in a flood of news. For these men were a patrol back from the Rub Al Khali, back from the Empty Quarter where everlasting sand of piled-up dunes stretches to horizon after horizon.

There had been a raid into Aden Protectorate country and they had fought a battle with the raiders and sent them fleeing back into the desert from which they had come.

On again along the tree-less back of a promontory of the *johl* thrust out like a tongue between the shadowed gashes of gorges closing in on either side. And so, as the shadows began to lengthen, I came at last to the threshold of the land that I had promised myself and I looked down through a limestone cleft, all brilliant yellow in the slanting sun, and saw the Wadi Duan, blue in shadow; a broad rift cut in solid rock by a now-vanished river, a sunken highway half a mile wide running north to the Hadhramaut.

The moment was precious to me and I got out of the car and stood there, staring down at the flat white of the dry stone watercourse and the bordering grey-green of dusty palm and olive, with here and there the brown of mud villages piled like battlemented fortresses against the steep cliff faces. It was the last day of March and I had come ten thousand miles through Arabia, a fantastic, unbelievable journey, with this my final objective; it was a dream come true, so that I stood like Moses, or " stout Cortes," drinking it in.

A dirt road had been cut in the face of the cliff, turning and twisting as it dropped more than 2,000 ft. in a mile and a half, and as I walked slowly down it with Hugh Boustead, the mud-baked town of Jahi came into view below, piled on its broken limestone hill, and all the irrigated side-wadi of the Leisar, with the dusty green of its date gardens, was laid out before me as in an aerial photograph.

Behind us lumbered a train of a hundred camels, their bulky cargo swaying and lurching as they picked their way with soft, sure, padded feet down the precipitous slope, their Bedou cameleers walking tirelessly beside them, the indigo-blue of their half-naked bodies gleaming in the sunlight. White teeth flashed in greeting as they passed us; blue-black faces, wild with an unkempt mass of blue-black hair, matching the blue of hard-sinewed body and legs. Even the cloth at their waists was blue with the dye, and the only relief was the white of the teeth and the glitter of silver—the silver of the fantastically U-shaped sheaths of the *jambia* knives stuck in their waist cloth; the wild Bedou of the high *johl* carrying merchants' trade goods down to the Qaidun fair; blue of men and tawny brown of camels picked out in the evening sun against the brilliant yellow of towering limestone buttresses.

And behind them, our own caravan, first the gleaming Plymouth with the huge body of Sheikh Qaddal, sprawled in the back, swaddled in white robes, white turban above heavy, black, Sudanese face; then the Land Rover with Ellis and Sheikh Ali Hamid and Abdullah Rais; and behind that our two trucks laden with our escort of Hadhrami Bedouin Legion—camp kit, cooking gear and bearers; and finally the *Qaim* of the Wahidi in his overladen truck that now swayed crazily on ancient springs as it negotiated the hairpin bends above us.

It was dark before we reached Sif, where we were to spend the night, and Bedou cooking fires flaring among the olive trees lit us to the outskirts of the town, dark like a fortress and crammed against a hulking rampart of cliffs outlined against the stars. Mud buildings piled up on us in the glare of the headlights, closing into narrow lanes, a maze of sheer-sided gullies barely wide enough for the car; faces peering curiously at us from the dark mouths of doorways, litle squares with people waving, children running beside us. All Sif had been up since dawn, dressed in their best to greet us.

The school where we were to be billeted was white, with arches and pillars and a tower—a little piece of almost Moorish architecture, brash amongst the sober brown of plain mud. Inside, the tiled courtyard was open to the stars and sloped to carry off the water, for when it rains, it rains heavily. Here we sat against the wall, drinking tiny cups of sweet tea and talking with the elders of the town, whilst our baggage was taken in to the little school rooms that opened off one side of the courtyard. The *Naib*—the local governor, who was responsible for entertaining us—bustled about; a tall, thin, harassed man, wearing glasses and looking like a schoolmaster.

Here in the Wadi Duan I was conscious suddenly of ancient civilisation. The world of the Bedou had been left behind on the high *johl*. Here the people were organised, a community with all the problems of a small town—drainage, water, education, law.

It was a world apart, different from anything else I had seen in Arabia—even their dress was different; bright colours and strange little round hats like the Persians wear, and the *futa*. The *futa* is a circle of cloth that you step into and fold about the waist like a skirt, very comfortable to wear in the dry, searing heat of the wadis. The Colonel and his military adviser, Captain Ellis, changed at once into their *futas,* and soon Sheikh Qaddal in his white robes and I in my khaki trousers were the only ones without a splash of colour—even that "bloody Bedou," the *Qaim* of the Wahidi, had abandoned his travel-stained rags and blossomed forth in green *futa* and gold and green headscarf, though the same precious water pipe of battered wood stood beside him, gurgling its protest as he sucked at it.

The meal was a roof-top *kouzi,* a dozen of us squatting round a gaily-coloured cloth and dipping the fingers of our right hands into mounds of rice; still basically a Bedou meal, but more elaborate, more seasoned—more dishes, too.

As I was unlucky with rain, I was lucky with the moon. That night we slept on the roof and all the mud pile of Sif was white in moonlight, tower upon tower reaching back into the quarry-bay of cliffs in which the town had been built, an Arabian Nights' spectacle—bleached to the purity of a sepulchre, remote, unearthly; empty and without lights like the ghost of an ancient city. And in the morning, life returning—the bray of a donkey, the bleat of a goat, the sudden, eager cries of children, the soft voices of women, the splash of water. The sun lipped the limestone cliffs across the wadi and all the hundred traceried towers of Sif's houses flushed suddenly rose-pink in the dawn.

It was the first day of April; April Fool's Day in the West, but in the Wadi Duan, it was the day of the fair— the *ziari*—opened at Qaidun. Sif was bursting with life at the thought. The women had put off their black and were dressed in a motley of colours; a gay, orange-red predominated with the mask of the *burqa* in a matching colour and a silver line to mark the nose, and wrists and ankles a-clatter with silver bangles; painted and bedecked as though they were going to a dance. And the children— boys in their brightest *futa*, little girls gay with paint, a teardrop of gold fastened to pierced nose, collars of silver and pretty, coloured necklaces of beads and tinsel glittering on pretty, coloured clothes.

From our roof we looked down on to a cistern filled with sweet water piped in from a cliff spring. Donkeys jostled and bit each other as they waited in a bunch for boys and women to fill the water-skins and then, loaded with the dripping bags, their dainty little hooves would pick a delicate way over the stone and up into the town. There was a goat-herd fattening his flock for the fair sale with rope-like skeins of green, wiry grass, and every now and then a passing train of Bedou camels would whip him into a frenzy by filching the long skeins with their thick, prehensile lips. And in an open space nearer the town a crowd gathered around paraded ranks of Armed Constabulary, banners fluttering in the morning breeze, a gay medley of colour through which villagers straggled with their camels and donkeys on their way to the fair.

By eight o'clock we, too, had joined the throng. The Colonel inspected the Constabulary, and then we removed our shoes to sit cross-legged on carpets and listen to school children—a speech of welcome from one, a piece of oratory from another and then two of them giving a demonstration of the intricate etiquette of a host greeting his guest; all done with a wealth of gesture and complete assuredness that was not to be disturbed by the braying of donkeys or the laughter of Bedous and villagers passing through the throng. The art of speech, so precious to the Arab, was born in them.

We breakfasted on our own carpet under a giant 'ilb in the middle of the wadi bed a mile from Sif. And then we entered Qaidun by a road that was no more than a dry watercourse. The place was packed with people, crowded around an open reservoir. More speeches of welcome and, of all things, a demonstration of P.T. by the children, whilst at a distance the women were gathered in a tight huddle—one half black and the other half in orange-red, like two denominations of nuns. One small boy had trouble with his *futa*—it kept slipping, and finally he let it fall. Naked? Not on your life; he had proper P.T. shorts on underneath!

And then up through the fair market, little stalls crowded against the houses in a narrow main street that climbed up and up until it finished in a great square, a camel caravanserai, above which the yellow limestone cliffs shimmered in the oven-glare of the midday sun.

We had been allocated a house in a side street. The owner was away and the elders had simply borrowed it. It was a fine house with a blue, iron-studded door and smooth-polished plaster stairs that led up to rooms lined with cedarwood intricately studded with pewter; rooms with fine lattice windows that opened on to roof-tops where shady arbours nestled against the mud walls of towers. A rich man's house, and yet even here in a town nomadic ancestry governed the way of life. When the owner left he simply moved out with his cooking pots, clothes and carpets —all you would need in a tent, and it was all he had in the house.

It is so simple to go visiting in Arabia.

At the entrance to that house we had stopped to speak

to an old Bedou. He had blue-grey hair and a tufty little beard, his face weathered to a thousand wrinkles by the hard sun of the *johl,* his body gnarled like a desert tree that had battled for years with the sand, the blue-ed skin stretched taut over hard bone and the stringy sinew of old muscles. Slung over his bare shoulder was a modern service rifle. There was no silver on it. He had four men with him, big fellows for the *johl,* tough and surly-looking. They, too, were armed with service pattern rifles. There was no wrist-clasping, only a flood of words poured out by the old man.

" He's a fine old chap, but a trouble-maker," Hugh Boustead said as we climbed the stairs to our room. The man led a gipsy life, wandering from tribe to tribe across the *johl.* He owned a camel or two, but that was all, for he spent all his energies talking politics amongst the *johl* people. More than once he had had to flee the country, but there he was, walking openly through Qaidun with a bodyguard armed with purposeful, modern rifles.

Nobody bothered to inquire where the rifles had come from.

I saw him again and again that day as we moved from room to room through that beautiful, furniture-less house, drinking cloying-sweet tea out of tiny cups and listening to the arguments of a dozen Bedou groups. And our own room had no privacy. There was a constant movement in and out of men from the *johl.* They would come in unannounced, not shyly, but with the confidence of free men who went armed and had no fear of any man. They showed no deference to Colonel Boustead or to Sheikh Qaddal. They met them, man to man, hand clasped to wrist.

They would stand their long, silver-decorated rifles by the door, solemnly make the round of everybody present, clasping each by the wrist, and then slip to a squatting position in one easy movement. The talks were serious, but there was much laughing with black eyes flashing and teeth gleaming. And each with that incredible *jambia* knife at his waist. And the strange thing was that though their blue bodies were almost naked and they had come many miles to the conference through the heat and sand of the high *johl*, they were devoid of the human smell of sweat. I have sat with as many as forty of them crowded into a small room and wondered at their incredible cleanliness—or was it that the indigo dye operated as a deodorant?

The middle of the afternoon saw us seated in the open space by the mud-brick reservoir, seated cross-legged and shoeless on carpets in the shade of a big tree. This was the big conference. The *Naib* was there and the schoolmaster and a lot of merchants and truck owners, a mixture of European and Arab clothing, and mingled with the crowd, conspicuous by their tousled heads of blue-black hair, were large numbers of Bedou, all armed.

I was a little apprehensive at first, for there were so many Bedou, and they stood all round us and behind us, and I knew that in this battle of trucks versus camels their very existence was at stake. But I might have known that decisions would never be reached at a public conference. Indeed, this wasn't a conference at all. The British Adviser spoke and then Sheikh Qaddal heaved his bulk up and stood there, talking quietly to them, quoting learnedly from the Koran, his black, heavy features kindly and fatherly, a very impressive man. He even made little jokes. "You do not relieve yourself against your neighbour's tree, then why cut down God's trees?" He was pleading the case for afforestation. Sheikh Ali Hamid spoke and then the *Naib* and then the schoolmaster.

And that was that. Nothing had been decided. Just speeches. And then we returned to our house to more cups of tea and more Bedou coming in and out, silent blue shadows in bare feet, blueing our hands as they greeted us and talking, talking, talking.

A sudden bustle and we were hurried out to our vehicles and driven back to Sif, to a house on the outskirts where thirty of us packed the walls of a finely-rugged room, shoulder to shoulder on silken cushions whilst cigarettes and water pipes and cups of sweet black coffee were passed round. At the entrance to the room Sheikh Ali Hamid had turned to me and whispered in English. "Do you like money, Meester Eenez?"

"It's a useful thing to have," I said, cautiously, wondering what was coming.

His black, beardless face twinkled at me. "There is plenty here in this house. You know what a millionaire is? Well, our host here is a millionaire—in sterling, you understand."

Our host was a good-looking Arab of about thirty, neat-featured with a dapper little pointed beard. His robes were of finest cotton and he wore the black *agal* of Saudi Arabia. Near him sat a ruffianly-looking old man with sharp, beady eyes, a hooked nose, his body a bundle of old rags. His uncle, I was told. And then I heard his story. Twenty years ago he had been a camel boy driving pack beasts down to Mukalla. He had gone to Saudi Arabia, and now he was one of the biggest contractors in Jedda and had made a fortune.

Night found us sitting in the packed courtyard of the school listening to plays acted by the children. It was a little Moorish piazza, and all around us the flowing white of Arab robes. The curtain of the stage was a white cloth on which had been painted historical scenes. It sounds incredible, but they had pictured St. George killing a dragon and there was a Saracen slashing the head off the chain-mailed figure of an undoubted Crusader.

The play seemed an extension of the scene I had witnessed that morning from the school roof at Sif : a goat-herd, driven to desperation by camels stealing his fodder he had fought for his goats, drove them off with stones, and one stone had hit the cameleer and killed him. The man was accused by the elders of murder. It all became very complicated then, and my head nodded. All our heads were nodding. The play went on and on, and it had been a long day.

And when it was finally over, we made a midnight tour of the crowded market streets. They were packed with Bedou and the Colonel stopped each group, asked them where they came from, guessed at the tribe they belonged to, told them who he was. His vitality, his interest in them —it worked every time. Animal suspicion and shyness vanished in flashing teeth and hands clasped to wrists. Our progress became a triumphal procession as group after group followed us, dog-like, to see him greet the next lot of Bedou, to see if he guessed their tribe right.

Usually he did, for the tribes were quite distinctive in bearing and features. Some of the youths were strangely beautiful, their hair cut in a girlish bob, their smooth faces delicately shaped with long lashes, arched black brows, finely-chiselled nostrils and prettily-moulded lips. But though they had faces of young girls, their foreheads were low and there was no doubting their manhood as they swaggered in the *suk* alley with their guns and *jambias*.

At the far end of the main street was the square where the camels were laagered, kneeling bulks that chewed and belched, black shapes against the glow of cooking fires. The mud towers of the houses with their whitewashed, pinnacled tops glowed richly in the firelight and overhead the moon shone out of a starlit sky and the circling cliffs of limestone were smooth ivory walls.

We slept that night on the roof-top that opened off our room. The noise of the *suk* came up to us from the alley below, and the mud walls of the house opposite, with its multitude of little head-sized window-openings, was lit by a ruddy glow. But neither the noise nor the light, nor fear of malaria from the mosquitoes released by the recent rains, could keep me from sleep that night.

I woke to the stillness of dawn and watched the sun warm the mud of the house across the street and flush pink the cliffs that towered above the town. A hand moved in a

mud-latticed window hole, wrist with a gold bangle on it.
I lay on my camp bed and watched. There was movement
in the house across the street. A child's head peeped
through a hole only just big enough for it, peered down at
the street below which was beginning to murmur with life,
and then stared at us lying in our camp beds, fascinated.

We were opposite the women's quarters.

A little girl appeared on a terrace higher up. Already
her face was painted and she wore the gold tear-drop at the
end of her pierced nose. She was excited and very pretty.
Then women's faces appeared, peeping out of the head-
sized holes, already masked by the gala *burqa* of ochre red
with silver nose line, but visibly painted.

The *suks* had spread that morning to neighbouring streets
and though we were abroad early, the narrow alleys were
packed with people, women mingling with the men—a thing
I had never seen before in Arabia. There were sweetmeat
stalls, haberdashery and grocery stalls, rolls of coloured
cloth hanging in the sunlight, cafés where cauldrons
bubbled and men sat smoking communal water pipes,
stalls of brass, and in a side street the silver market, packed
with Bedou haggling excitedly, for no Bedou would dare
return to his wife from the Qaidun fair without a piece of
silver jewellery.

There were no stalls of silver. The merchants sat cross-
legged in the alley, their box of gleaming trinkets open on
their laps, a pair of scales in one hand, bracelets and neck-
lets held up for view in the other. Each silver ornament
was weighed in the scales against 1 oz. Maria Theresa
thalers. Throughout Arabia the Maria Theresa dollar is
the recognised currency. They are not the original thalers,
but are minted in London and Switzerland to the old
design, even to the date—1780.

Muhammad Sayid, the *Qaim* of the Wahidis, was with us
and he wanted to visit some of his tribe who had established a caravanserai on the other side of the town. We
picked our way cautiously down narrow alleys, watchful of

the palm gutterings that stuck out from the sides of house towers like dripping gargoyles. Sanitation in the mud towns of the wadis is primitive but effective. It drops from the palm gutterings to the alley below to be rendered innocuous by the blazing heat of the sun. It is of priceless value, often the only manure the land ever gets.

The Wahidi were gathered on a stony slope with their camels. A camel auction was in progress. All camels have to be sold through an official auctioneer, for there is a sales tax. In any case, he invariably gets a better price, and he certainly earns his 3% commission.

It is a painful business buying and selling camels. The auctioneer is a paid bully. " Buy it, you fool!" he screams and seizes an old man who wants a camel by his beard. "Buy! Buy! Buy" And when the old man agrees a price, he turns on the seller, seizing him by the ear or by his hair, "Now sell! The price is right. Why do you shake your head? Sell, you wretch!" And he brings the two together, assisted by the laughing crowd. "Sell! Sell!" And when the sale is accomplished hands clasp wrists and the crowd relaxes.

Everybody loves the auctioneer. It is such fun to watch others going through the mill. "Buy, you fool! Buy!" And another man is thrust bashfully into the outstretched hand to have ear or hair or beard if he has one tugged and tugged until he either agrees or is obviously unwilling.

Breakfast that morning was constantly interrupted by Bedou braves, coming to pay their respects, coming to argue, coming to bring their problems to the Adviser, or the State Secretary, coming perhaps merely so that they could say to doubting relatives back on the *johl* that they had shaken the White Father by the hand down in the wadi at the Qaidun Fair. It was open house.

And then we heard that the *Mansab*, the religious leader, had arrived and we went to greet him outside the mosque to the staccato din of rifles being fired into the air. Great crowds swarmed in every open space and after I had shaken the old man's hand, Hugh Boustead said, "This is where we part. I'm leaving now. You'll go on with Sheikh Qaddal in the Ford. He'll look after you."

I had barely time to thank him before he was swallowed up in the crowd. The battered Ford drew up beside me. "*Faddhal, Mister Eenez,*" Enter! The door was opened. My kit was there. Everything had been organised despite the air of chaos. We got in and my last impression of Qaidun was of solid banks of womanhood massed above the road—the black-draped ones with the black *burqas* looking as though they were just out of a nunnery and those in ochre-red, painted and bejewelled, looking like a bank of brilliant flowers.

We took the trackless wadi bed, going downstream, northwards towards the Hadhramaut—Sheikh Qaddal, Sheikh Ali Hamid, the Arab driver and myself, and behind us a Land Rover carrying their baggage and their servants. The glare from the limestone cliffs was eye-searing, the heat intense. But every minute the cliffs were falling back, the wadi widening out as we approached the Hadhramaut; and ahead of me at the journey's end was Shibam, the New York of the Hadhramaut, the skyscraper city where we were to spend the night.

But the Arab does not travel like the European. He has to live his life out with the desert's heat. On the very threshold of the Hadhramaut we turned aside into a branch wadi, to the town of Haura. It was more open, much less of a fortress town than Qaidun and the buildings were slightly more elaborate. The elders, somehow warned of our coming, met us in the square and conducted us to the town hall. We lay on rugs in a bare room where flies buzzed wearily, fanning ourselves with the little palm fans provided. It was oven hot. Yet this was only April. What a hell of a furnace heat these sunken wadi-beds would be in August! My dehydrated body was already soaking up water, mug for mug, with Sheikh Qaddal.

Though they were travelling, my two companions still observed the hour of prayer, preparing for it with much sluicing of water in the lavatory down the corridor where a big butt-full was kept for the purpose. After a meal I lay and dozed, thinking of Shibam, wondering what it would really look like, where I should sleep. Ali Hamid had said, "It is all arranged. Everything is arranged." But he hadn't been able to tell me what had been arranged.

By four o'clock we were in the Hadhramaut, driving through the mounds of crumbled mud villages whose walls had been obliterated at some period of time by flood waters pouring out of the Wadi Duan. A deep wadi-bed, a wretched little village and then we were ploughing through soft sand. To our right were the familiar limestone cliffs. But away to the left the ground was flat like a piece of desert, and the wadi cliffs on the far side looked no bigger than a boundary wall of yellow mud.

The sand merged into cultivated fields and the green of sprouting corn. The track leapt a series of irrigation channels, humping itself so steeply that stones scraped the engine sump of the car. The channels extended for miles across the flat bed of the Hadhramaut, water running swiftly from the mountains to grow two, sometimes three, crops a year. Men and women were working in the fields, dust-covered bodies bending and stooping, tall witch-hats of palm nodding to the hoe; the farm peasants of the Hadhramaut, serfs who were lower than slaves, a poor, wretched people by comparison with the free Bedou of the *johl*.

Towards evening a wind rose, drifting sand across the fields, drifting sand across the track until the sunset was blotted out by brown clouds of swirling dust and the sky vanished. That was how I first saw Shibam, through the sepia miasma of a sandstorm. It burst suddenly upon us like one of those Italian towns that are built facing inwards and present a rampart wall of houses to the outside world.

There were no towers, no arched gateways—just a solid
façade of windowed buildings that looked like a line of
tenement dwellings.

It was only when we were close to them that I realised
their height—ten or twelve stories and built of mud, shoulder to shoulder.

The road swung in a wide detour, past white mud villas
each in its own walled garden, and we entered Shibam
up a ramped road through a great archway into the public
square. Filthy with sand and sweat I stumbled out of the
car to be met by the whole city council, all in spotless white,
with finely woven little Persian hats. No chance to wash or
change or even brush the sand out of my hair; they took us
straight up into the great council chamber and there I was
forced to sit in a position of honour beside Sheikh Qaddal
while the council went into session over little cups of coffee
in silver holders, each with its slender, delicate silver spoon.

To understand my feeling of discomfort I must tell you
that Shibam is like no other city in Arabia. The Shibami
have the Midas touch. These men seated around me in
their immaculate *futas* or spotless robes were the equivalent
of the Aldermen of the City of London; immensely rich,
highly conservative, rigid in their observance of all the
complex etiquette of the Arab. But I think they were
accustomed to travel-stained guests, for the sands blow at
dusk across the road to Shibam almost every day of the
year.

At last the conference was over and we were taken up to
our rooms. This was the city hall, a twelve-storey mud
building piled up in tiers and white like a wedding cake.
My camp bed was already set up in the largest bedroom I
have ever slept in—there was even some furniture; chairs
and an odd sort of dressing-table, and the place was so big
the roof had to be supported by numerous wood pillars.
And in the lavatory across the passage I was actually able
to have a shower.

This lavatory was similar to all the lavatories in the

Hadhramaut, except it was bigger, the drop longer. It was a pleasantly cool room, the smooth hard plaster surface of the floor sloped towards the outer wall and channelled down the centre. At the upper end was a big butt full of water with a metal scoop. Close against the outer wall was a little platform with a hole in the middle and beside it a trough full of mud stones. The pan of the lavatory dropped away twelve storeys to the ground beneath, to a corner that got the full sterilising blast of the sun. That night hot water had been brought up for us, a rare luxury.

Cars whisked us through the city gate and out into the country, along dusty, mud-walled lanes, to a whitewashed villa bright in the moonlight. It was so like Italy it was unbelievable—except that the people were different, the food different. It was a really elaborate banquet this time— curries and a dozen different spiced dishes, crisp fish wafers that are a special delicacy, all sorts of nuts and fruits.

The Javanese influence was strong—the faces of the men squatting around me, the food they served, the clothes they wore; all stemmed from that two-way monsoon trade that developed centuries ago across the Indian Ocean. But the rice, the nuts and fruits, many of the spices were local produce. Agriculturally the Hadhramaut is rich—given sufficient rain.

Given sufficient rain! That was one of the things Sheikh Qadal had come to see them about : more financial support for the installation of pumping equipment. It was a scheme the British were fostering to combat famine that is inevitable every time there is a drought.

In all Shibam there is only one European—Eva Hoeck, a woman doctor from Germany. She came to the Hadhramaut by way of the Yemen where she was physician to the king's household. She was tall, rather severely dressed like a schoolmarm, and the breast pocket of her blouse bulged with the monstrous wooden Arab keys that look like toothbrushes with pegs instead of bristles. The pegs are the wards that lift the latch.

In rusty English that she had somehow managed to pick up in Arabia she told me about the lot of the women in Shibam. Many of them are high-born—*sharifas* or descendants of the Prophet. And so rigid and conservative are the men in their observance of the rules of behaviour that a woman is regarded as no better than she ought to be if she so much as crosses the main square opposite the city hall, even though she is heavily veiled and wearing the *burqa,* for the main square is the off-loading place for trucks and camels. Moreover, it is guarded by police and overlooked by their headquarters.

Now Shibam's mud skyscrapers all lean against each other and that square with its big arched gateway and ramp is the only way in or out of the city. It is, of course, permissable for a woman to be driven out in a heavily-curtained car. But there are only two cars in Shibam, elderly vehicles packed in piecemeal by camels years ago. The result is that few of Shibam's wretched women ever go outside from the day they are born until the day they are carried out feet first to the cemetery to be buried. They are prisoners of a rigid conservatism, birds in a gilded cage.

And in Shibam, where the men traditionally depart as youths to the four corners of the globe to make their fortunes, there are two or three women to every resident male!

There is one other way in which a woman can get outside the narrow, shadowed alleys of Shibam. If she goes on the *Haj*—the pilgrimage to Mecca—then it is permissable for her to cross the square. For many the first and only journey made outside the walls is by plane, the only quick means of getting out of the Hadhramaut.

All that night the wind whistled through the wooden shutters of my enormous eyrie of a bedroom and in the bright morning light I drove away from Shibam, watched it fade into the distance, a lonely, white fortress mass in its desert of sand—one of the most Alice-in-Wonderland cities in the world. For there is no reason for Shibam. It is not an agricultural centre. It is purely residential, maintained by the wealth of its sons who always, always return to it. Why, I never discovered.

We had now reached the limits of Qaiti territory and Sheikh Qaddal heaved his bulk out of the car to inspect the Qaiti Customs Guard. A hundred paces farther on he had to get out again to inspect the Customs Guards of the next state. We were then in the little sultanate of Kathiri, and outside the wedding-cake palace at Seyun we met the political officer.

It was the end of my journey, my last day in the Hadhramaut—or so I thought. A hectic tour of Seyun, which is more open, less claustrophobic than Shibam, with dainty white mosques and old, towered buildings with whitened crests and lovely villa-like houses set in their own gardens; a drink before lunch and a bathe in the villa's cool basement pool; and then we were driving out through the dust of a rising sandstorm to Gharuf airstrip fifteen miles away, heavy storm clouds building up over the *johl*. An R.A.F. plane was due to pick me up at 3 o'clock.

But it never came. It had been reported flying over to the oil company's geological camp at Thamud and once we thought we heard it, but all the wadi was filled with swirling clouds of dust, and though we sat for three hours in the sand-scoured heat of the mud airport building, we knew it was hopeless. The clouds were thickening over the *johl*, black menacing clouds piled high into the sky, and all the world was a sepia wretchedness of moving sand.

As it happens, I was glad, for something occurred that evening that I wouldn't have missed for the world.

About seven o'clock the wind suddenly increased. The palms that surrounded the political officer's villa were whipped to a roaring frenzy and sand spilled through the house, millions of sifting grains spilling forward like water. It was an open house, built for great heat—there were no doors, only archways, and there wasn't a window in the place, just openings—and all the rooms led out on to flat, walled roof-tops.

It was suddenly dark as night. Great flashes of lightning struck at the *johl* high above Sayun, momentarily illuminating the whole city and the side-wadi and the cliffs, and the thunder reverberated incessantly, the noise of it caught and held in the sunken depths of the Hadhramaut.

And then the rain came. It came with the roar of a waterfall, swept through the house by the tornado force of the wind, and in an instant the spear-like shafts of water had cut into the basic material of which the villa was built and sprayed a film of liquid mud through every room.

It went on for perhaps twenty minutes, so violent that I expected to see palms uprooted and wondered whether mud houses could stand such a battering. Then it ceased abruptly and there was a sudden stillness; no rain, no wind. A glimpse of the moon and some stars through a ragged gap in the clouds, and then wind again, thrashing at the palms, more rain—this time from the opposite direction. The vortex of the storm had passed right over us.

Gradually the rain slackened and as it died away, a new sound took its place—a distant, rushing sound : the sound of water pouring down the cliff crevices and into the wadi. And then above the sound of rushing water, a slowly increasing tide of human voices—women's voices shrilly giving tongue to their joy, a sort of ululation, a wild wailing of delight; and all through the city lanterns appeared like will-o'-the-wisps as the whole population turned out to protect the channel banks and keep the water flowing to gardens and fields.

For this was the *sael,* the flood that would fill the wadi-bed, fill the wells, reach out to all the farthest fields. Praise be to Allah, the All-bountiful; this was Life itself, flowing down in a thundering river through the middle of Seyun. It meant fat goats and cattle, things growing, and no children crying with distended bellies for want of food. It meant the end of famine fears for another year.

It meant, too, that both roads to the coast would be washed out, probably impassable for weeks. There was no going back the way I had come. All through Arabia that winter and spring I had been dogged by rain. But it is a small thing to be inconvenienced by rain in a land where water is the breath of existence.

As it happened, a plane came in from Aden two days later and I just got out before another storm water-logged the runway. By then I had seen the third great city of the Hadhramaut—Tarim; a strange place, wholly Javanese, and slowly crumbling to decay.

Once Tarim had main electricity, a telephone exchange, too; the broken wires hung in festoons, the bulbs of the street lamps were covered in sand. Great mud palaces of painted Victorian splendour stood half empty, forlorn and peeling. There was an air of disintegration about the place. It had all happened in two generations. Selfish fathers had kept their sons at home and, with their properties in Indonesia requisitioned, the once powerful Javanese families were now dependent on rents from Singapore and spent their days playing Javanese music—soporific and monotonous in the faded grandeur of the empty halls.

Tarim was essentially a city of the Hadhramaut. So was Shibam. Both enclosed cities, like the wadi in which they were built—both useless, both doomed. Flying out, I was glad to see again the mud towns of the Wadi Duan, to remember the gaiety and colour and excitement of the Qaidun Fair, and high up over the *johl*, flying between towering masses of cloud, I thought of the Bedou; their wildness, their freedom. Were they doomed, too, or would the crevassed emptiness of that uplifted sea bed preserve for them their centuries-old way of life?

II. NORWAY AND WHALING

I. LAND OF THE VIKINGS

Viking means the dweller in a *vik*—a bay or inlet. The translation is too soft. *Viks* are sudden gashes in precipitous mountains; the homesteads little patches of emerald green, crevice-tucked at fiord head among towering crags capped with snow. Glimpsed from the air, the men of the *viks* are dwellers in a moonscape half submerged in sea; barren, glacial land with ragged fingers deep-thrust in Arctic waters, scattering from their tips rock islands like drops of molten lead congealed. And yet, somehow, a fairyland country.

The clouds were breaking up below us as we crossed the Svartisen, that black ice glacier whose dirty, frozen skirts have only recently been drawn back from the sea. We were barely two-thirds the way up Norway, yet already inside the Arctic Circle. North from Bodö the sun shone in a clear blue sky and the coast of Norway smiled up at us. Beyond the flapping corrugated wing of the old JU52 seaplane, the Lofoten Islands emerged from the horizon's haze, a serrated, alpine outline of incredible brutality. Below us the mountains of the mainland hefted the sea aside into narrow strips with rippling, ice-worn shoulders that rose 2,000 ft., their snow patches gleaming white in the sunlight only a little below the bumbling course of our aircraft. Away to port the sea was littered with skerries; islands of rock, white and bald from a million years of glacial polishing.

Three-quarters of Norway is barren, uninhabitable. Surely this included the land below us? Yet here and there the gleam of a white-painted wooden house proved the contrary. Man was here, clinging precariously to the scree skirts of the mountains, building on barren rock and harvesting the sea in default of land that bore any trace of life-giving soil. Occasionally, glacial deposits provided root purchase for crops and here the fresh-cut hay showed a tiny carpet of green marked by the sun-shadowed bars of the hay hung to dry on wire fences.

Directly below us the islands seemed to float in patches of livid green as though rimmed by mineral discoloration; the sun colouring the water in the shallows. Elsewhere the water had the flat, black look of great depth. Flat, with no corrugation, for we were over the Inner Lead, that maritime highway that runs a thousand miles almost uninterrupted from North Cape to The Naze, a salt-water river protected by island banks. Boats like toys arrowed the mirror stillness, ploughing the water throughfare that has cradled the sea's toughest sons.

The men of the *viks,* originally Teutons from Asia, were in Norway almost before the glacial ice had receded. Long before Christ was born the Land of the Midnight Sun was a legend; Homer had heard of it and Herodotus wrote of a people who slept like bears six months of the year. In the search for whale and walrus (the hide was used for ships' ropes) and in the crossing of the Folda, that forty-mile break in the Lead where the gale-torn might of the north Ocean has been as effective as an Iron Curtain separating North Norway from the south, the fishing "coracles" underwent a sea change and emerged as ships.

The Viking as we knew him—the trader, the marauder, the explorer, the settler—was born.

Ohthere, a trader to England with furs and walrus tusks and rope, and the down of the *aerfugel,* the eider duck, reported to Alfred the Great of a voyage he had made eastward to Russia's White Sea. This was in 875. But already the longships were farther field, thrusting out into the ocean to establish colonies in Iceland and Greenland. They were in America, called Vinland because of the grapes, more than five centuries before Columbus.

But for all their reputation as raiders and seamen they

were, and still are, fishermen. The warmth of the Gulf
Stream brings them a silver harvest and fish dominate all
my memories of the Inner Lead. Oksfjord, typical of a
thousand tiny *vaags,* or wharfs, seen at two o'clock in the
morning with the sun already high and blazing bright in
the translucent air; a trailer of blue smoke hangs over the
sheds and oil tanks of the fish factory, drifting vertically
against the shadowed bulk of a mountain whose scree slopes
support a dozen wooden houses. Nothing else but the silence
of the mountains, bare, ice-scarred, devoid of living thing.
The stillness of the fiord, the harshness of the unnatural
sunlight has a frozen quality. And as we touched the *vaag*
and our warps were looped over the hooks of mooring
chains run through hawse holes in the wooden quay, we
could smell the fish oil.

The reek of fish hangs like a cloying mist over almost
every *vaag* the length of Norway. " It is a good smell," I
was told once, and the Norwegian rubbed his hands and
his salt-wrinkled face cracked in a grin. " It smell of
money."

In the far north, round Nordkapp (North Cape), where
the villages face the Polar seas, I climbed between the
houses of Mehann to a headland and looked across acres of
drying cod to the burnished brilliance of the fiord and the
midnight sun. The cod were tied two-by-two, hung by their
tails over a framework of poles. I could have walked for a
long time beneath a canopy of drying fish; a piscine version
of a hop field. And at Baatsfjord it was the same, only the
sun was gone and in the black gloom of a midnight mist, so
sultry that the bald, scarred rocks of the fiord looked like
the Gates of Hell, we met the fishing fleet going out : solid
chunky boats wallowing to an oily swell, their varnished
bows, clean and clearly numbered in black, headed north
into the Barents Sea, their engines stabbing the silence with
the toc-a-toc that is as much the modern theme song of the
fiords as the oar chanties of the longboats were in ancient
times.

Once I saw the Lofoten Islands at midnight, a black silhouette against the flame of the sky, as though a giant had sowed dragons' teeth along the rim of a molten sea. It was July, but I was thinking of March when more than twenty thousand men and two thousand boats gather for the cod harvest. One wonders at the hardiness of man that he can wrest a living from this torn wilderness of sea and rock. The mountains and the fiords, the moods of the weather and the startling appearance of the little settlements in their wild surroundings dwarf the people themselves, so that it is almost with the surprise of discovery that one realises they have become fairer and gayer as one has gone north. There is something about the midnight sun, or maybe it is their remoteness from the world; they have a childlike quality.

At every stop they pack the *vaag*. It is almost as though they were the tourists, and the passengers the curiosities to be gaped at with wonder. Week days, women and children predominate the girls tall, strongly built, with flaxen hair and rain-washed, sea-washed features—the most clean-scrubbed complexions in the world—flirting with the un-inhibitedness of all girls in lonely places. Red is the prevailing colour—coats of the girls, ski suits of toddlers with toddlers' rucksacks, colour bands of the men's woolly caps —red to beat the dead black and white of winter's landscape, red to frighten away months of night, red to cheer the drab grey of mist and rain. But on Sunday it is different. A little incongruous in neatly pressed store suits of blue and black, the men then bring their wives down to watch the pageant of the world go by their village and the *vaag* is so jam-packed with people that it is almost impossible to fight your way ashore. And at each *vaag* a dog meets the ship, a dog who bears himself with the dignity of a harbour master.

Still splashed with the raw yellow of new wood, there is a pioneer atmosphere about this northern country. The Germans, in their scorched-earth retreat before the Red Army in 1945, razed everything to the ground. Houses and fish factories are all post-war buildings rushed up without form, so that they are not an expression of the people, only of their haste at that time to get back home.

What brought these people back from the comfortable south to which they were evacuated, back to this hard north? The tourist sees it as the Land of the Midnight Sun. The inhabitants know it as a land where it is dark twenty-four hours a day two and a half months in the year. "If you sit by the window and it is a good day, then maybe you are able to read some words in the paper at midday." And at Tromsö, from a man who had had big jobs offered him in the south and yet remained : " You know how far north you are? You are so far north that if this were the Antarctic you would be standing on the Great Ice Barrier." This sent me running for a map of the world. He was right. We were a long way north. The 71st parallel—and Nordkaap is above this—leaves Hudson's Bay far south, just tips the north of Alaska and skims along the northern shores of Siberia.

Were they "bushed," these people who came back? Were they a little in awe of the big world outside, hankering for the remote solitude of the fiords, the isolation of island strongholds? But they are of the sea, open to all the winds of thought that blow. They and their sons have sailed the world and they stand on the precarious threshold of one of the only two direct frontiers between the Soviet Union and the Western World.

Strong individualists, with no particular feeling against the Russians, they harbour communists with even greater tolerance than other European countries. The frail barrier of wood and barbed wire that marks the Norwegian side of the frontier by the road at Storskog and the one-man patrols along the Pasvik River are symptomatic. Mention Russia to people in the iron ore town of Kirkenes—and they shrug their shoulders. They know the North is wide open to a sudden attack, however much strategists in Oslo may bury their heads in the sand and say, "We'll open our country to Allied forces as soon as we feel ourselves threatened."

At Honningsvag my wife and I once sat, waiting, in the front seat of a bus, near the door. A short, dark man stood on the step and stared at us. As people moved in and out he made way for them, but always he returned to his point of vantage, a sharp-featured face with high cheekbones and narrow eyes that stared at us unwinkingly from a distance of two feet with the straightforward animal curiosity of a child.

No village idiot this—his face was too alive with interest. He was in fact a Laplander. Shy, troll men of the High Plateau, they follow the reindeer to the coast, across river, lake and fiord for the lush summer pasture. In winter they retreat to the solitude of remote wastes where their herds burrow down through the snow for the reindeer moss on which they live. The men are withdrawn, curious, slow to smile—shy as mountain deer. The dark, gipsy faces of the women smile more easily. Legs swathed in reindeer hide, carrying bone-handled knives and thin lariats, with strange four-pointed caps, the predominant colour of their clothing is black and red. Some, like the man on the bus, have come to the ports to stay and the mingling of their blood can be seen here and there on the *vaags*—a darker colouring, black hair, the slanted brown of eyes and lifted cheekbones.

"Do not be surprised if you find children playing in the streets in the north at midnight," I was told in Oslo. "They don't sleep much there in summertime." But to the people of Oslo the North is as remote as Iceland. As we approached Kirkenes late in the evening the birch tree country took on a queer, rose-tinted glow. The colours were soft, incredibly beautiful; the air had a summer warmth and mist rose like smoke from all the lakes. The *multe* berries—a sweet, golden loganberry-like fruit—were an unripe carpet of red in the clearings.

It was midnight when we reached Kirkenes. The long

streets of wooden houses under the shadow of the ironworks were utterly deserted. Blinds were drawn in all the upper windows. Kirkenes was asleep. No children played in the street. The place was as dead as any lamplit town of the south. Yet the sun blazed high. Late afternoon you'd think : except that it shone straight out of the north and you were somehow conscious—the clarity of the atmosphere maybe, or the feel of the air—that the Polar pack-ice was very close.

Another fallacy : " You'll never get tired in the North." I was more tired than I have ever been. Twenty-four hours of sunshine daily is too much. And in Tromsö I met a man who said his wife couldn't sleep in the wintertime, nor could his little boy. I suppose the uncanny, eclipse-like darkness has its compensation—the brilliance of moonlight on snow at midday, the incandescent, flickering curtain of the Northern Lights. But the longing for the sun sends men to the mountains in January in the hopes of a midday glimpse of its red rim lifting for a moment above the southern horizon. An airman told me how he's flown north in winter and for a short time at five thousand feet had seen the wings lit by a red glow, whilst all below him the people were in utter darkness.

Give me normal daylight hours. Going south in summer there is relief in the sight of the first lit buoy, sign that the boat is leaving the latitudes of total daylight.

I was south of Bodö then, just across the Arctic Circle, on the bridge of the *Ragnvald Jarl,* picking out the marks of the Inner Lead with Karl Rafsnas, an apprentice pilot of the Nordenfjedske Line. Karl was tall, pale-faced, a youngster until you saw that eyes and face were already marked by years at sea. He smoked rolled cigarettes, only a few puffs at a time. He had no pay and his wife worked as a stewardess. " When you see the face of a man in a mountain peak clear beyond the shoulder of that headland, then we shall turn. Come now. I will show you.'

There are more than 4,000 such navigational marks be-

tween Kirkenes and Bergen, and a pilot has to know every
one by heart. In a four-day examination these boys have to
take an imaginary ship through the Inner Lead from
memory.

Karl had been five and a half years in the Norwegian
navy, six years in the merchant service. He held his mate's
certificate, had done his captain's school, and with another
eight months tramping the world would have had his
master's certificate. Yet now he wore no uniform, only a
neat white sweater and peaked cap set at a jaunty angle.
For a whole year he would get from the company only
cabin and food.

"It is all right here in summertime," Karl said. "But in
winter it is not so good. All snow and fog, and dark as
hell all the time." I could picture it, for only the day
before we had run into fog after leaving Harstad. For
more than an hour we held our speed at thirteen knots, our
siren blaring and a bow lookout searching the white void
ahead for the fishing boats that litter the coast. Then the
captain rang for half speed. Through glasses he searched
the fog on the port bow. Several minutes passed. And
then he nodded, lowered his glasses, and rang for full
speed again. Close along our port side a slender iron
marker post emerged from the writhing smoke trailers of
the fog. We turned then and entered the Risyund Strait.

"It is a difficult piece here," Kaptein Bolling said. For
this gruff, sixty-five-year-old sea dog, who had sailed the
world at the beginning of the century in square-riggers, to
admit a place was difficult made it sound something unusual. The fog suddenly lifted, revealing a wide sound.
"Now you will see," Karl said. "Look! There is the
Risysund—the deep-water channel they dredge thirty years
ago." It stretched ahead of us like a street, barely fifty
yards wide, flanked by markers that looked like lamp
standards. "You must watch the tide here. The depth is
shown on the first marker. We need fifteen feet, one more
than we draw." The marker showed seventeen.

The insurance companies insist on a pilot's certificate for the men who con these ships. Hardly surprising, for Norway's 2,150-mile coastline is stretched to 12,500, taking in all the inlets and fiords, and you can count more than 150,000 islands. In winter it is an obstacle race in black night that would turn a man not born to the coast grey in a single voyage. Yet the Vikings sailed the Lead without radar, charts or compass. They named the rocks and as they smelled their way through the tortuous channels they invented stories about them.

Best of these sagas concerns four islands whose towering rock shapes have obvious personality—Hestmannen, Lekamoy, Somna and Torghatten. Hestmannen, the Horsemen, angry with his sweetheart, Lekamoy, shot an arrow at her. But the Somna King threw his hat into the sea to save her and the arrow passed through the hat. At that moment the sun rose and all were turned to stone; and there the four of them stand. The most spectacular is Torghatten, almost 1,000 feet high, shaped like a great hat and holed through the centre by a tunnel 500 feet long, eighty feet across and 240 feet high. More modern is the statue of Queen Victoria on a pedestal of rock at the entrance to Nord Fjord where the wind blows icy cold off the Jostedal, Europe's biggest glacier, and the ships run the gauntlet of towering cliff masses that lean outwards, perpetually toppling as the clouds drift across their summits.

When I first came to Norway just after the war, I came by sea. To wake up and find your 9,000 tonner gliding into the heart of Stavanger, into what would be the market place in most other countries, and mooring at the very doorsteps of the gaily painted wooden houses of this old town, is to be put into the mood of adventure from the start.

From Stavanger the boat proceeded to Bergen, and from there I went out to the islands, to a little place called Bovaagen. There was a hotel, a warehouse, a fish factory, all wood and all clustered round the *vaag*. A little street of

Sheikh Zeyd shows me the underground water system of the Buraimi Oasis

Sheikh Zeyd's falconer with a new peregrine from Persia; in the background is his racing camel

Outside the walls of Buraimi village, once a slave market

The view from the house where I stayed in Qaidun

Lunch with the Qaim of the Wahidi

Two of the blue warriors of the johl

Shibam; the skyscraper mud city

Tribesmen on the Yemen Border. Half an hour later we were waiting for tribesmen to attack us!

wooden houses ran out into a country road that led no-where, except to scattered farms. In the evening the sun shone down the silver silence of the north-facing inlet to pick out the white-painted wooden spire of the church on its green knoll and colour the rowan trees clinging to their precarious hold in the rocks. I was told there might be some language difficulty. "Maybe the manager at the cannery speaks a little English."

The first person I saw in the clean, scrubbed-looking lounge of the hotel was reading the American edition of *Forever Amber*. Small, dark, alert-featured, he might have been the manager of the cannery. But no. "Gor'blimey. Oi'm a doiver," he said in almost too-good-to-be-true London Cockney.

There was no language problem. We were thirteen for *aftens*—the evening meal—and with only one exception they all spoke English while consuming the usual large quantities of cold board—fish of all sorts, fresh and canned, *laks*, which is salmon, wafer-thin *flatbröd*, and a variety of other bread eaten with that rich, brown goat's-milk cheese that comes from the *saeters* or summer farms—all washed down by glasses of milk.

The English language comes easily to the Norwegian, for there has been a two-way trade in words between the two countries since very early days. On the bridge of any Norwegian steamers you can hear the officer of the watch ordering *starboard; midships, steady*. Some speak it with an American accent, some with an English, dependent on where their ships have taken them or what nation has hired them as crew. The people of Oslo speak it with the sing-song of the Welsh. But apart from school-taught English—young-sters mostly have a good command of the language—the biggest single influence has been World War II and the trek westward across the sea to fight for the king they loved.

This was on the scale of a migration. A few went over-land via Sweden and Finland, some to Russia to fight with the Red Army—there is a statue at Kirkenes near the

Russian frontier to commemorate twelve Norwegians killed by the Germans after being captured in Russian uniform. Others, like Attlee Torgelsen, who accompanied me from Aurlandsvaagen on a three-day trek across the 5,000-foot Sankt Paal Glacier, to circle the globe by way of Siberia and China and finish up back in their own country with the British-trained commando unit known as the Kompanie Linge. But the majority moved across the sea, to Iceland, the Faeroes, the Shetlands and Scotland, mainly by fishing boat, but some by rowing boats with nothing but oars and the strength of their arms with which to fight the westerly winds. Many were lost. But many got through.

Still others, like Peterson, the Cockney-speaking diver's partner, stayed to fight in the resistance. He told me stories of train wrecking and gun duels high in glacial wastes as he fed air to his partner from a boat moored off Bovaagen's inlet. These two were disentangling a big diesel marine engine from a Dutch barge blasted by a bomb and sunk between two rocky islands. A local man had bought the wreck for a few kroner just for the engine.

Like all maritime nations, the Norwegians love a salvage job. More than eight years after the war I saw them at work on the *Tirpitz* just to the west of Tromsö Island. A floating crane and several small ships were anchored beside what looked like a skerrie of rust-red rock uncovered by the tide. Trygvie Sundt, stocky and dapper, owner of a local steamship company, told me he had seen the British bombers come over on November 14, 1944. " I saw it all. I saw the *Tirpitz* roll over." The salvage company, he had been told, had bought the wreck for Kr. 50,000. Tombed up with the bodies of over a thousand German sailors was a fortune in machinery, insulated from the corrosive effects of air and water by the fact that the hulk was submerged.

Norwegians have an innate business sense. What other country with almost half its length inside the Arctic Circle has turned barren mountain and icy glacier to capital account and exported it as scenic beauty? The towns they build are business towns, centring round the ports—quiet, almost self-effacing, yet bursting with civic pride. Dating back about a thousand years—to the days, in fact, when the Norsemen were spreading out into Europe—few of the old wooden buildings have survived the flames of successive fires.

History in these cities is local, not national. Thus the statue which dominates the pleasant square in Trandheim is not of a king of Norway, but of Olaf Trygvason, the man who founded it in 997. The booklet on Bergen—every town issues invaluable little guides for the visitor—states only that King Olaf Kyrre founded the city in the year 1070; no mention that he was the nephew of King Olaf Haraldsson who spread Christianity with the sword through Norway.

But though they are proud of their towns, their hearts are in the mountains and the fiords. All but the poorest have some little country place. Their wooden cottages, each with its flagpole, dot the islands and the shores of the fiords, climb the mountain slopes—" summer places." They start work at seven-thirty and finish at three or four in the afternoon, go home for *middag,* the midday meal, and then out, ski-ing or boating. Even their most popular restaurants are out of town, by a lake, a fiord, a ski jump, or, like Floyen, which has its own mountain railway up from Bergen poised high above the town, an eyrie with a fantastic view.

A fish country, they cook fish best. *Laks* dishes are a poem in even the humblest restaurant. Memories of salmon served with a horse-radish sauce, of *multe* berries or wild strawberries served with cream, of *flatbröd* and thin slivers of brown goats'-milk cheese crowd upon me as I write. Salmon is such a commonplace in Norway that in the old days servants stipulated " salmon not more than five days a week." And one hotelier just north of the Lofoten Islands assured me that he considered fresh-caught cod a greater delicacy !

Only four per cent of the total land area of Norway is

tillable, and though their mercantile fleet is huge and the tourists swarm, this is only jam to the bread-and-butter business of fishing. And the big game here is the whale.

Picture a *vaag* with a derrick and a lot of oil drums and the sea all round flat and black with a scum of oil. Ugly iron chimneys dominate a clutter of corrugated iron sheds built round a wooden deck full of saws and winches and with an oil-and-blood-soaked ramp slithering down into the sea. A cinder path leads up to neat, dolls'-house quarters beside a small black lake. All round the rocks are dotted with the bones of apparently prehistoric monsters. Sea birds rend the air with noise as they fight for flesh amid the clatter of machinery, and over all hangs the deathly, cloying, unbelievable stench of whale.

From Blomvaag Hval, with its catchers, grey and slim like fast minelayers, the boots of the flensers have blazed a white trail over the island's rock face to their houses in the cheerful little port of Blamvaag, where the sea is still like a mill pond in the shelter of the islands and there is no smell. Here are the *mink* whalers—big toc-a-tocs with a *tonne*, or barrel crow's nest, at the masthead.

I was ten days at Blomvaag Hval and I can still see Alfred Höjem, round-faced, smiling, bubbling with excitement, as he listened to the radio, waiting for the reports from his catchers up beyond the Arctic Circle. The men's union doesn't allow them to work on Sunday and if a whale comes in, then the ship's officers with the directors and their friends turn out to save £1,000 worth of meat from turning bad. Thus I found myself, equipped with big, curved flensing knife and ex-German jack boots, wading deep in a whale's intestines, hacking out the richest, tenderest meat I have ever seen. And at two one morning, I sailed with *Skud 2* in a howling gale to hear the cry of *Blaas! Blaas!*—age-old tally-ho of what is still the biggest of big-game hunts.

It was Alfred Höjem who first introduced me to the work of Norwegian artists. Individualism is strong in Norway, and though painting and sculpture have thrown up no names like Greig or Ibsen, it is in art that the people find an outlet for their latent urge for self-expression. No town is complete without its local statuary, no house without at least one painting. Often they are mere daubs, more concerned with colour and mood than with brush work.

Norway, with its little *vaags* and its boats and its old log houses and colourful national costumes set against backgrounds of towering beauty, is one of the world's most photogenic countries; the artist is undoubtely conscious of this and searching for something to express what he sees in a way the camera cannot. The result is boldness, and an experimentalism that doesn't always come off.

My personal preference is for the simplicity of the painted altar backs of the little wooden churches, often caught in slanting sunlight, and in particular for the painted stone chancel of Aalesund Church with its sea motif woven in colour and form into the story of Christ's birth; this is something as individual as the town itself with its ancient warehouses huddled, shoulder to shoulder, round the island's perimeter, piled feet mirrored in still waters.

And for modern architectural beauty, the cool, stark serenity of the building that houses the three Viking ships in Bygdy, Oslo's open-air museum. Norway is proud of her ships. *Fram,* which carried Nansen on his great Arctic drift and later took Amundsen to the South Pole, has a house of its own with its interior arranged to show how these great explorers lived. And now Thor Heyerdahl's *Kon-Tiki* raft has gone to join the Vikings and the Polar explorers.

There is a civic pride as well as individualism, stemming from the isolation of the towns. At one point—near Narvik —the country is only a few miles wide. It is cut by numerous rivers, deep-gashed by as many fiords, so that only in the softer forest-and-lake country of the south and east has it been possible to establish communications with relative ease. Even on the coast the open sea stretches of Stad, Hustadvika, Folda and Nordkyn have split the country over the centuries. Not only do the citizens of the larger towns, both in their private and public buildings, support their own artists but they each have their own folk museums.

They are proud of their fish, too, and while you might reasonably expect to find an exhibition of local fish at the big port of Trondheim, it was with some surprise that I was taken across Tromsö Island to look at a neat little aquarium built on the rocks facing the midnight sun. Below these examples of local fish was a wire enclosure invaded by the tide in which two Polar bears—they call them ice bears— paced with unending, restless tread.

Serving villages and homesteads widely scattered through large areas of mountain and fiord, the number of hospitals and schools in the provincial capitals is astonishing. They have their own civic anthems, too, and once on a mountain trek I listened to a dozen hikers from almost as many towns competing in singing their own town songs before the blazing log fire of a *saeter* hut.

Alas, the old way of building is gone now and, I think, the art is dying out. In the mountains and the far north you still come across barns and a few old houses built of log, dovetailed at the corners and thatched with turf. Apart from the few fabulous stave churches, the best of this architecture is preserved in the open-air folk museums, particularly at Oslo and Lillehammer.

Sogne Fjord is six hours' steaming from Bergen and as the longest and, in my view, the most spectacular of the fiords it will serve for all of them. Here no sailing boats are seen. Indeed, there is little sailing now on the west coast. The wind is fickle in the Inner Lead, and near the fiords sudden downrushes of air from the cold, snow-capped mountains produce squalls of intense violence. Sogne Fjord is one of the more awe-inspiring waterways of the world. It cuts inland for 106 miles, its subsidiary fiords curving far to the north and south; it is said to be as deep as the mountains that engulf it are high—over 5,000 feet. All the superlatives that Hollywood has ever used to describe an epic—colossal, stupendous, awe-inspiring, breath-taking—barely do justice to this monstrous glacial trowelling of the earth's primeval rock.

The climate of the Outer Sogn is damp, and the people, like the Bergenske, have a certain stolidity. But as the sheer slopes of the enclosing mountains rise to greater heights and you approach the narrower, wilder fiords and the ice, the climate becomes drier and the people gayer. It seems a characteristic of Norway that the tougher the conditions the happier the people.

Balestrand, half-way up the fiord and dominated by the great rambling wooden bulk of the Kvikne's Hotel, is where the subsidiary fiords begin to radiate out and it is in this broader hub of water that the steamers have their "conferences," when connections are made simply by tying up alongside each other in midstream. The sun is hot here in summer and fruit is grown, yet a few hours' simple climbing will bring you on to the roof of Norway, a snow-white world that often smiles in blazing heat where the narrow fiord below is shadow-chilled.

Up past Balestrand runs the Fjaerlands Fjord, a narrow slash of water the colour of which changes from black to icy green and then to the frozen milk colour of glacier water as it cuts right to the very fringe of the Jostedalsbre. At first the steep mountain slopes are clothed in firs, but gradually the tree line descends and then, suddenly, everything is wild and bare, almost terrifying, as though you have been swept back into the Ice Age; and round a bend you come face-to-face with the glacier that made this waterway, its frozen fangs lipping ice-green over the black, shadowed bulk of the mountain ahead.

A local farmer took me up this mountain, across the green ice crevasses, on to the broad white highway of the glacier which stretches, with barely a rock outcrop, back into the central mass of the Jostedal. I cannot now recall his name, but everything else about him I remember vividly.

He was an oldish man, tall and fair, hard-muscled as a mountain goat, and he climbed like one. His eyes had a faraway look—remote, blue as ice. We talked of Shakespeare and Browning and Charlotte Brontë! He wrote stories for his own amusement. One had been published in an Oslo paper.

" On Sundays I do not farm and I do not take anyone up the glacier. I climb for myself then and if the weather is good I come up here and lie naked on the rocks above the snow. It is so peaceful and the sun is hot. I write here— stories, letters. I feel near to God."

If he'd no family to keep and the mountains had been kinder, he would have been a hermit. And yet I remember the boyish glee he took in rolling boulders over a precipice down on to the tumbled ice of the falling glacier stream —just for the hell of seeing the sparks fly. Through the mist we glimpsed the green of Mundal and the colder green of the fiord bright in sunshine. The swirling mist and the cordite-harsh smell of the clashing rocks remain in my mind as something out of Milton. He danced and sang down 5,000 feet of mountain to a *saeter* hut where girls making cheese gave us milk warm from the cow. Back at his farm he changed into the gay jacket and breeches of national costume and drove with me back to the hotel to dance folk dances as exhausting as Highland flings until midnight.

The mountains are the Norwegians' playground. In summer their sturdy legs carry them and their piled rucksacks far into the wild hinterland of rock and snow, following the course of mountain torrents from one tourist hut to another, some to fish the trout and salmon-full rivers, the majority just to breath God's good air and feast their eyes on the beauty of Nature. Nature is their God. And if it is a simple, uncomplicated God, those of us who take advantage of the hospitality provided by the many tourist hostels established through all the finest mountain country will admit that it is a God that harms nobody and makes for a clean-living, friendly people. To eat trout as I have done, fresh caught in a mountain lake high up in the great solitudes and cooked in a sour-cream sauce, and to listen to the youth songs of boys and girls uninhibitedly tramping the mountains together, is to be as near to the Elysian Fields as one may get in an Atomic Age.

And in winter they don their skis, again to face the mountains for the exhilaration of the clean swoop down through virgin snow, the feel of freedom and the cold oneness with Nature. At the age of two a boy gets his first pair of skis. At four he tries his first small jump. Grown up, he'll ride the air with whirling, balancing arms as he swoops from the springboard of one of the tall ski-jump platforms that stand at the back of every town. Trekking on skis and on foot his tough body quarters the mountain ranges winter and summer and he is as astonished as any ardent fly-fisher at the sedentary "salmon-looking" visitors to Sogne Fjord, who sit all day on a scaffold platform of pine poles under a black umbrella, staring down through the waters of the fiord, waiting for a salmon to cross the white board and enter the net.

As for the sea : this is to Norway what the fields are to any agricultural community; it is only a playground for the townsmen and the people of the rich forest lands of the south. Indeed, on the coast, from the great whaling ports of Tonsberg and Sandefjord in the south to Alesund and Lofoten, where the toc-a-tocs gather to harvest the herring and the cod, there is little talk of playing, summer or winter; nor along the steamship highway in the shelter of the islands, nor on the high seas carrying the world's goods. This is the real Norway. These are the real Norwegians. The ships may have changed down the ages, but the sea hasn't, nor have the men. They are still the men of the *viks*—still sailors, traders, fishermen, whalers—still Vikings.

The road forked and there was a signpost with a single name painted black on buff yellow. The left fork swung away to Jarfjord in a fine-ground curve of dust; the right fork, down which the single-fingered signpost pointed, ran straight for three hundred yards and then disappeared abruptly into the wooded slopes of a hill. It was blocked by a crude barrier of wood and barbed wire that wouldn't have stopped a child, and for all its visible length it was grass-grown with disuse.

That road once led to Finland. Now the word *Sovjet-samveldet* was painted on the signpost.

Half-way down the road there was another, even flimsier, wire barrier and a yellow sentry-box, and a little to the right two white flagstaffs stood above the shimmering flicker of the silver birches.

There were no customs officers or immigration officials. No sentries. Nothing but the trees and the lake on the right, and the hills ahead, all shimmering in that everlasting glare of northern sunshine. The country beyond the barbed wire looked exactly like the country bordering the dirt road to Jarfjord. Yet this was a frontier; the most northerly frontier in Europe. And all beyond it was Russia as far as the Pacific.

It was hot and peaceful when I was there, an evening for a picnic. It reminded me of Surrey's woods; the red flag fluttering from one of the flagstaffs might have been a firing range flag near Pirbright. A car stopped and four Norwegian tourists got out. They went to the wire barrier and read the notice pinned there. The notice was in Norwegian and English and it warned that under a Royal Decree it was forbidden to enter the Military Zone, to fire into the Soviet territory or make rude faces or be the owner of a camera within 1,000 metres of the frontier or point it into Russia. They read the notice and then stood and stared down the disused road. The girl suddenly slipped round the side of the barrier and stood for a moment on the forbidden ground. She came back quickly, giggling nervously, a little tensely. The father and mother and the boy stared with set faces. Then they turned and got into their car and drove off.

We stayed there waiting because of the red flag that flew from the flagstaff in the woods. This was Storskog and the flagpole marked the place where the Norwegian and Russian Border Commissioners met to settle incidents.

An old mad woman came and walked a little way down the disused road mouthing nonsense to herself. But she didn't go beyond the second barrier. An old man joined us and talked hate of the Germans who had ravaged this northern country. And then at last what we had been waiting for: three Norwegian soldiers marching smartly along the dirt road, rifles slung, their boots ringing with Guards' precision. The middle one of the three had a heart-shaped shield of metal on his breast that bore the Ging's crest, marking him as a courier. They went through the wire and down the road, turning right by the lone sentry-box and disappearing into the woods where the flagpoles stood.

A few minutes later they returned, carefully closing the frail barriers behind them, the way a cowman closes a field gate after him. Their footsteps died away down the dusty road and we stood by the barbed wire and stared into Russia. Nothing moved. There was no sign of life.

Yet, a moment later, the red protest flag came fluttering down, the halyards operated by unseen hands. The Russians had received Norway's answer to their latest protest.

There was something uncanny about that fluttering flag and the hot stillness of the woods—a sort of menace.

We had just seen one instalment of a frontier incident that would probably drag on for days. The incident? Two British girls—one Australian and one South African—had crossed the frontier at Boris Gleb and had unscrewed a shield from one of the Russian border posts; Number 214. They had taken it the way youngsters remove the " Penalty £5 . . ." notices from railway carriages— as a souvenir. To the Norwegians it was just a silly prank. To the Russians, however, it was a gesture of insolence, an incident to be reported to Moscow and for which full retribution was to be demanded.

The incidents were all as petty : the cow that has strayed across the Pasvik River, the boat that has drifted to the opposite shore, young men who have crossed the border on skis in error, the pictures of tree-covered slopes in a foreign paper that are described as Russia and which the Russians choose to regard as an attempt to photograph Soviet military installations.

I asked if there wasn't one serious incident; didn't anybody ever slip across the border escaping from Russia? The answer was Yes, there had been one man. " And what happened?" I asked. " Did you send him back?"

" No. The Russians never raised the matter."

Were they glad to get rid of him? Or were they just unwilling to admit that they didn't know who it was? Odd, for the Norwegians made no secret about the man's arrival on their territory, though they refrained from disclosing his name.

This border would be sheer comedy if it weren't so disturbing.

From Kirkenes I took a drive down the Pasvik River, 40 miles to Skogfoss. By the beauty of the falls there I stood and looked into Russia. I could have tossed a cricket ball into Soviet territory—and so doubtless caused another International Incident. The river is narrow here. The red and black border posts on the opposite bank showed bright and fresh-painted in the slanting sunlight, their metal shields winking brightly.

There was nothing else to be seen there—just the trees and the swirling white of river rapids and a Norwegian fishing for salmon. It was a scene of complete and absolute peace, made strange only by the fact that the sun still shone brilliantly though it was past ten in the evening. But I was conscious all the time of the white observation towers I had seen on the drive down, the big barracks in a clearing in the woods and the sprawling mass of Nikkulahti—the big nickel town with its faint buzz of machinery and its one tall chimney drifting smoke into the translucent air. All this, of course, on the other side of the river.

There was something a little bizarre in sitting peacefully in the tourist hotel, feeding with Norwegian holiday-makers and looking so casually out through the open windows into Russia. And as we drove back through the blinding glare of the midnight sun, I saw again the white watch towers (" If you look through a pair of good glasses then you can see the Russian soldier inside ") and the barracks in the distant clearing and the tall chimney of the nickel town. I was thinking that on this side of the frontier there was nothing; just one Norwegian soldier who lived in a cottage with his family and did an eight-hour border patrol daily, just to see that tourists didn't take pictures and didn't make rude faces.

Maybe NATO'S frontier isn't on the Pasvik River. That's what the Norwegians in Kirkenes think. There are Communists up in the North in key positions and the people themselves are not ill-disposed towards the Russians. The Red Army carried through a model occupation when they poured south and west across Finnmark, following the Germans' scorched-earth retreat through the winter of '44-'45.

The people of the North—those that think—know that under the present policy of non-aggravation the North cannot be defended. There is a tenseness. But that is all. Nature provides them with problems enough without worrying about this strangest of strange frontiers that has been foisted upon them. They shrug their shoulders when you question them and their only comment is that life was simpler when the Finns were across the Pasvik River. And it irks them that for want of twenty-odd miles of road where it crosses the long finger of Russian territory, they have to journey seven hundred miles by boat via Hammerfest to meet up with the land route down through Sweden to the south. They are thinking, too, that Kirkenes has big iron ore mines, crushing 10,000 tons of ore a day, and that they have ice-free fiords that their big neighbour might covet as naval bases in certain eventualities. Yet life goes on, with less fear than is shown by countries buffered by satellites or separated by sea.

3. THERE SHE BLOWS!

Blaas! Blaas! This cry, echoing from the masthead, is worth almost £2,000 of anybody's money. It is the Norwegian cry for a whale sighted, the huntsman's tally-ho for the biggest of all big game hunts; cruel, commercial and highly mechanised, but at the same time fascinating. That cry has largely replaced the Anglo-Saxon "There she blows!" just as the Norwegian ports of Tonsberg and Sandefjord have replaced the British and New England ports of a hundred years ago as the centres of modern whaling. Even the English factories, of which there are three, now sail from these ports, crewed largely by Norwegians.

In the clatter of publicity that surrounded the various Antarctic expeditions of the International Geophysical Year, one is apt to forget that thousands of men go down into the Antarctic pack-ice every year as a matter of course. They sail from their home ports in the autumn, arriving in the whaling grounds early in December when the season opens, and it is perhaps significant that each unit is called an *expedition.*

The equipment of a single expedition runs into hundreds of thousands of pounds, for each is a fleet in itself comprising, in the case of the larger British and Norwegian expeditions, a factory ship of anything up to 26,000 tons, as many as a dozen catchers from 300 to 700 tons each, buoy boats and tow-ers, a tanker to supply fuel and carry the whale oil back to the world's markets, and a refrigerator ship in which to store the meat.

The season of 1957-58 saw nineteen expeditions gathered in Antarctic waters—one Dutch, one Russian, five Japanese, three British and nine Norwegian; a total of more than two hundred ships. And in the latest Russian Five-Year Plan provision has been made for the building of three factory ships, the nucleus of three additional Russian expeditions.

These factory ships are nothing but giant abattoirs, and at night, under the arc lights, their flensing decks have the nightmare quality of an inferno; the winches clatter, the saws rip, the long, curved blades of the flensers flash, and the decks run red with blood; and all the time the blubber chutes steam and the hoses swill the filth of giant intestines into the scuppers.

These decks can swallow a 100-ft. fin whale weighing eighty tons or more in less than forty minutes; and a big factory ship with her flensing deck going full blast round the clock can consume anything up to seventy of the smaller whales in twenty-four hours. Besides the vats for converting the blubber of the whale into oil, there is machinery for producing animal feeding stuff, huge cold rooms for storing the meat, even in some cases plant for the manufacture of meat extract.

And in addition to all this, the factory acts as mother ship to the catchers, supplying them with fuel and stores, providing workshops for repairs, a foundry for the reforging of damaged harpoons, a magazine for the explosive war-heads of the harpoons, sick-bay and recreation rooms for the crews. It is also the fleet's headquarters, equipped with every navigational aid, often even with aircraft to scout ahead for whales or search for leads through the pack-ice. There are scientists on board, doctors, fishery inspectors, as well as all the necessary officers, crew and engineers to run a big ship. And by long tradition, everyone from the youngest apprentice to the most experienced gunner, gets his allotted share of the value of whale caught.

Because of this, the whaler remains a highly superstitious man. When my Antarctic whaling book, *The White South,* was being filmed, the unit was barred at first from taking shots of the flensing decks and virtually confined to one small area of the ship that was quite useless for their purpose. The reason given by the Norwegian captain was that the men would put the finger on them as the cause of any failure to find whale—a clear case of the Evil Eye.

It sounds a little fantastic against the background of a factory ship's mechanisation, but luck still plays a big part, even in modern whaling. And time is against the unlucky ship, for the season is a race. In order to prevent the Antarctic grounds becoming denuded of whale, the way other sea areas have in the past, the season is limited by agreement—an agreement to which all the nations, except of course the Russians, adhere. Even the Japanese have been forced to accept limitation, realising that it is in their own best interests.

Thus the season opens to the starters' pistol of a given date, and it finishes the instant the overall number of units already agreed upon has been caught. The limit is the aggregate of whales caught by all the expeditions. There is no allocation to each separate expedition, and so it is vital to each that they get off to a good start; from that moment competition is intense, each expedition wrapping itself in a cloak of secrecy, even to the extent at times of radio silence, and always the catchers report back in code.

In this highly competitive atmosphere, it is hardly surprising to find superstition strongest amongst the catcher captains. They are the prima donnas of the fleet. They are not only captains who, by long experience, have developed a nose for whale; they are also the gunners. They go down the long catwalk to the bow platform and, standing there in the icy blast and spray, they fire the harpoon. All the huge organisation, the equipment, the crews, all the expenditure of vast sums of money to gather a fleet in Antarctic waters, depends finally on them—on their luck and their skill.

To quote again from the experience of this film unit: Not unnaturally, they wanted shots of the catchers in action, but it was a long time before they could persuade one of the gunners to ship a camera-man. This was the fleet's crack gunner, and I imagine he only agreed as a gesture of bravado. The catcher then had a run of phenomenally good luck and the unit experienced great difficulty in getting him to release their camera-man, who had come to be regarded as something of a mascot, a sort of good-luck charm.

Before writing *The White South*, I lived for a time—and occasionally worked—at a Norwegian shore station on the islands off Bergen, and it was here that I first experienced the thrill of the chase. You may think, as I did, that the result is a foregone conclusion. Here is a 240-ton ship powered by 1200 h.p. engines capable of driving it at 14 knots, with a gun mounted in the bows, firing a heavy harpoon armed with a $1\frac{1}{2}$-lb. explosive charge. What possible chance has a defenceless whale against such powerful armament?

But though man no longer risks his life with hand harpoon and lance in an open boat, no longer pits his strength and cunning against the monster in mortal combat, it nevertheless remains a battle of wits. It is a case of the rifle having replaced the bow and arrow and, as in other forms of hunting, the quarry has still to be brought within range. Herein lies the excitement.

We left at two in the morning, with a full gale blowing and heavy seas. Twelve hours later we were on the edge of the Arctic Circle and from the crow's nest came the cry " *Bla-a-as! Bla-a-as!*" and with the lookout pointing his arm to starboard. " *Go an! Go an! Der Blaaser den!*" I could see nothing. But Captain Schulstok could and as the telegraph rang for full speed and the throb of the engines quickened, the little catcher heeled in a sharp turn. Soon even I could see the whale wallowing lazily in the aftermath of the gale with a thin plume of vapour rising from its vent, and then abruptly it vanished.

The engines were stopped as soon as we reached the spot where the whale had sounded and we lay, rolling heavily in the waves, watching and waiting. Ten minutes passed and then the cry from the masthead sent us off in pursuit again. We came up on the whale quickly, driving it under before it had time to expel all the stale air from its previous dive and fill its lungs with fresh. This is the object, to drive the whale under faster and faster until it lies helpless on the surface, gasping for breath—for the whale is not a fish, but a mammal, and it has to breathe.

Now Schulstok took a chance and stationed the catcher well to port of the point where the whale had dived, relying on that instinctive sense that every gunner acquires. But in this case he guessed wrongly. The whale outwitted him by doubling back underwater, and we lost it in a rainstorm.

Half an hour later we sighted a second fin whale and this time Schulstok's sixth sense didn't let him down. It was almost uncanny. Each time the whale dived, the catcher was waiting for it within a cable or so of the spot where it broke surface, and each time the dives became shorter, the whale more blown.

I cannot now remember how long the chase lasted; I was too absorbed, the atmosphere of tension on the bridge too electric. And then at last Schulstok went down the cat-walk to the gun, and after that the mate was on the wheel, manœuvring the catcher to the gunner's hand signals until at last the whale was wallowing helpless just right under our bows, Schulstok swung the gun and fired.

To hit a whale, even at fifty yards, is not easy. The gun platform, being right up in the bows, is never still, and the weight of the harpoon makes it necessary to aim it high above the target. I saw the harpoon leave the gun and fly out in a great curve, the forerunner line snaking after it. I saw it strike the whale. And then everything seemed to happen at once.

The whale was a big cow; ninety tons I was told later. As the harpoon struck, the water seemed to burst into spray all about her, and in the instant of her frenzied plunge forward, the forerunner tightened, the deep-bedded barbs of the harpoon were pulled outwards and the grenade exploded.

In theory, the grenade is supposed to break the whale's back and kill it almost instantly. But more often than not it merely injures, instead of killing, for how can the gunner, firing from such an unstable platform, be sure of striking the vital spot? It was so in this case. Lumps of flesh and blubber flew up from the whale. Pain and terror sent her off in a wild rush—a crazed dash for freedom.

Then I was witness to a tragic spectacle, a long-drawn-out struggle in which courage and endurance and a vast, unbelievable energy were merely the prelude to a cruel and protracted death.

For the whale now had to be played like a fish on a rod. As evidence that whalers do not really expect to kill outright, catchers are fitted with two powerful springs capable of withstanding a strain of 20 tons each. These springs are connected to pulleys fixed to the foremast and the heavy 3-inch manilla lines run from the steam winches, up over these pulleys and out through fairleads in the bows.

Now, as the whale ran fast and straight away from the bows in its efforts to give death the slip, the port hand pulley was dragged down to the danger mark and Schulstok, back on the bridge, increased speed, watching intently as the winch drum screamed and the heavy line went pouring out over the bows. There was upwards of 1,000 yards of that port line, more than half a mile of rope, and she took nearly the whole of it before her first frenzy of energy was exhausted and the engineer was able to start taking it on

the winch. Gradually we came up on her as she breached
and thrashed and the vapour from her vent turned to blood,
and when finally she lay exhausted and dying, the engines
were stopped and she was pulled in on the winch alone.

Even then, she made a last, desperate, dying effort, and
for a moment she was actually dragging the catcher through
the water. Finally we hauled ourselves up to her and in
pity Captain Schulstok went for'ard again and fired another
harpoon into the bloodied mountain of dying flesh. The
carcase was then deep-lanced, filled with compressed air to
prevent it sinking, the wounds plugged with cotton waste
and the flukes attached by chains to the catcher's side for
towing back to the factory.

That description is typical of what goes on, hour after
hour, day after day, down in the Antarctic during the
season—the thrill and excitement of the chase, followed by
the sickening cruelty of the death struggle. And though the
permitted number of units gets smaller every year as the
fear grows of fishing the hunting grounds bare, the number
of whales killed is still prodigious—a total of almost thirty-
three thousand in 1956-57.

As far as I know, Britain is the only nation involved
whose conscience has been stirred to the extent of attempting to lessen the cruelty of this method of catching. We
have spent thousands of pounds on the one method that
would ensure instantaneous death—electrocution. But,
despite all the money poured into the electrical harpoon,
there are still snags that make its general use impractical.
It will come—but not yet.

Why all this expenditure of money and effort to alleviate
the whale's death, when methods of fishing just as cruel
raise no word of protest?

The answer lies in the nature of the whale. It is a warm-
blooded creature, a mammal that mates and then suckles
its young the way animals do ashore; in the case of the
cow we killed on the edge of the Arctic, for instance, it had

in its womb a two-month-old embryo, a complete and perfect replica of itself that we cut out and stared at with an uneasy feeling of guilt. The fact is that the whale has all the qualities we find endearing in animals, and its behaviour is often so human as to wring the heart.

There is no point in my attempting to describe this human quality when Frank Bullen has done it so perfectly, and from his own experience. He was a Cockney who had run barefoot in the docks of Liverpool, and at the age of eighteen, after six years of seafaring, he shipped out of New Bedford in an American whaler in the year 1875. Here is a description, taken from his *Cruise of the Cachalot,* a book of which Kipling wrote : " This is immense—there is no other word."

The first mate has just harpooned a humpback whale— a cow :

But for all the notice taken by the whale, she might never have been touched. Close nestled to her side was a youngling of not more, certainly, than five days old, which sent up its baby-spout every now and then about two feet in the air. One long, wing-like fin embraced its small body, holding it close to the massive breast of the tender mother, whose only care seemed to be to protect its young, utterly regardless of her own pain and danger. . . . Once, indeed, as a deep-searching thrust entered her very vitals, she raised her massy flukes high in the air with an apparently involuntary movement of agony; but even in that dire throe she remembered the possible danger to her young one, and laid the tremendous weapon softly down upon the water as if it were a feather fan.

So in the most perfect quiet, with scarcely a writhe, nor any sign of a flurry, she died, holding the calf to her side until her last vital spark had fled, and left it to a swift despatch with a single lance-thrust. No slaughter of a lamb ever looked more like murder.

Nor, when the vast bulk and strength of the animal was considered, could a mightier example have been given of the force and quality of maternal love.

Needless to say, there were then no regulations governing whaling; the killing of a cow with calf is prohibited now.

But the behaviour of the cachalot is not so gentle. The whaling ship *Essex* of Nantucket was battered and sunk by a lone bull in 1819, the enraged animal twice ramming the wooden hull with its head. This may well have provided Melville with the basis for the end of *Moby Dick,* though the *Essex's* crew went on to a ninety-day ordeal in open boats with the survivors sustaining life on the flesh of their dead comrades. "A dead whale or a stove boat" was one of the shanties whale men sang, and the old adage, "Beware of a sperm's jaw and a right whale's flukes," is a clear indication of the fighting qualities of these animals, and incidentally of the courage of men who faced these creatures in open boats but a quarter of their length, for the right whale's tail can be as much as 15 feet across and the sperm whale's narrow jaw is a snapping 20-foot line of teeth designed for the destruction of giant squid in the twilight deeps of the ocean.

One final quote from Bullen, who escaped alive from an experience as dreadful as that which caused the death of Captain Ahab. The whale he had attacked had just destroyed his boat with one blow of his tail, and then: "Towering above me came the colossal head of the great creature, as he ploughed through the bundle of debris that had just been a boat . . . nor to this day can I understand how I escaped the portals of his gullet, which of course gaped wide as a church door." Half-drowned in the bloodied froth of the water, he finds himself thrown against the whale and in desperation pulls himself up the sloping slippery bank of blubber until he has hold of the harpoon iron. "Then I remembered the flurry. Almost at the same moment it began; and there was I, who with fearful admiration had so often watched the titanic con-

vulsions of a dying cachalot, actually involved in them. . . .
Then all was lost in roar and rush, as of the heart of some
mighty cataract, during which I was sometimes above,
sometimes beneath, the water, but always clinging, with
every ounce of energy still left, to the line. Now, one
thought was uppermost in my mind—'What if he should
breach?' I had seen them do so when in a flurry, leaping
full twenty feet in the air. Then I prayed." But, in the
event, the whale died without breaching.

That intimacy of contact experienced by the old-time
whalers has been lost. Bullen learned more about the
behaviour of the sperm whale in a single voyage than a
modern catcher skipper could hope to learn in a lifetime;
the pity of it is that more of these rough, courageous men
were not gifted with the same inquiring turn of mind, the
same vivid imagination that could see the fascination of
their daily contact with this leviathan of the sea. As it is,
Bullen's book is a classic—to my mind the greatest book
that will ever be written about whales and whaling.

I was talking recently with a director of one of our
whaling companies and he admitted that, even now, we do
not know how long a whale lives, how many years are
required to reach maturity, nor do we know much about
their migrations—this, despite the fact that scientists sail
regularly with the Antarctic expeditions. It is an immense
field for study that includes, with the smaller Dolphin,
Porpoise, Killer and Narwhal, more than twenty different
species.

All are of the order Cetacea, and they fall into two main
categories—toothed and baleen. The toothed range from
the small dolphins and porpoises and the speedy, wolf-pack
hunting killers, through the various beaked or bottle-nosed
whales, right up to the big cachalot, or sperm whale. The
feeding habits of all these creatures are much the same as
land animals and because it is the sperm whale that men
like Bullen went after, we know more about the habits of
this creature than we do about most of the other species.

The behaviour of the male is not unlike that of the elephant. Until he loses his virility and his ability to fight off the younger bulls, his sex life is based on the harem. When finally defeated he becomes a lone bachelor, a potential Moby Dick. It is one of the strangest things in creation that this animal, dependent on air for life, is forced to seek its food in the depths of the ocean. The cable layer *All America* found a dead sperm whale entangled in a length of cable lifted from the ocean floor off the coast of Colombia. The cable had been at a depth of around 3,500 feet! It would appear that the purpose of the ton or so of spermaceti oil secreted in the huge tank of the head is primarily to counteract the enormous pressures to which this deep-diving species is subjected.

The feeding habits of the baleen whales, on the other hand, are quite different. The sub-division *baleen* refers to the fact that the mouth is fitted with whalebone in place of teeth—a close-packed series of plates edged with bristle. The baleen whales have only small gullets—not the type to swallow Jonah—and they feed on plankton and krill, those tiny, shrimp-like creatures that in their millions colour whole patches of the ocean. These whales feed by gulping in a ton or so of sea water and expelling it out through the baleen plates, the bristles retaining the plankton and krill. In short, whereas the toothed whales are hunters, the baleen are grazers of the sea. They are gentler, their home life tending towards monogamy. They breed in the shallows with a gestation period of up to two years, and the biggest, the blue whale, is the largest of all the whales.

But though the baleen whale forms the bulk of the Antarctic catch, little is known about the reason for its presence there in such abundance. What urge sends it south into those cold seas? They are now marking whales at the end of each season, but even so it may be decades before any real picture of their migratory habits can be built up. There is thus no real knowledge or scientific direction to these huge and costly expeditions. They have simply followed the whale blindly into the Antarctic the way other whale men followed them to the Arctic right back to the days of Ohthere, the Viking, who, after his first voyage in King Alfred's service, reported on the northernmost limits reached by the Norse whale hunters.

Indeed, the history of whaling goes back to the Stone Age, with the earliest hunters of recorded time, the Indians, Eskimos, Japanese and Norsemen. The Basques were fishing the right whale systematically in the twelfth century, and by the sixteenth century they had followed it across the Atlantic to the Newfoundland coast. With the demand for whale oil for illumination, the industry grew and at the start of the nineteenth century the British and Americans had ships ranging the seven seas on voyages of incredible length, and whole fleets of whalers fished out the Greenland seas and followed the whale to the ice-bound waters of the Davis Straits and the Arctic Sea.

And yet, in less than a century, these fleets had disappeared and what had been virtually an Anglo-American monopoly became largely a Norwegian venture. There were various reasons for this. But in each case disaster started the decline.

The first was largely a British disaster. The year was 1830 and a fleet of fifty sail passed through the Davis Strait and ran into heavy pack-ice at the entrance to Melville Bay. Twenty-three penetrated a lead, and of these, twenty were crushed in a gale that piled the pack-ice up in layers and lifted ships bodily on to the ice. Nineteen British ships lost and twelve damaged, a financial loss of £300,000 to be borne by the ports of Hull, Aberdeen, Leith, Dundee, Peterhead, Whitby, Montrose, and Greenock, besides the death of many of their menfolk. It was a crippling blow to British whaling so carefully and venturously nursed during two centuries and the industry never recovered. By 1849 there were only fourteen whale ships sailing out of British ports.

But America still had nearly six hundred vessels engaged

in whaling. Then came the Civil War, and shortly afterwards the industry suffered a disaster even greater than the British. In 1871 thirty-nine vessels passed through the Bering Straits and, with an apparent disregard of danger, fished a narrowing channel between the pack-ice and the Alaskan shore. Despite the warnings of the Eskimo, they continued on these grounds until they were beset by the ice and overwhelmed. There were twelve hundred people then on the floes and every one got out alive in the boats. But thirty-two ships were lost.

This was the beginning of the end of American whaling. Steam, with its prospects of more profitable trade, and the switch from animal to mineral oils for lighting finally killed it. Moreover, whaling was shifting from the fished-out grounds of the Arctic to the great unfished waters of the Antarctic, following in the wake of the explorers and the more venturesome whale men who were establishing stations on the recently discovered islands of South Georgia and the Falklands. To be away from home for long periods did not suit the American temperament. The British might have followed the lead of their great Antarctic explorers and re-established their whaling industry, but both their merchants and their seamen were finding sufficient scope in the rapid growth of trading that followed the introduction of steam. And so it was left to the Norwegians.

And with them, it wasn't only a matter of temperament born of a harsh home climate. They had Roald Amundsen and a dozen other lesser explorers to lead them on, and in Svend Foyn they found the man to give them the tools of a new industry. Until he invented the harpoon gun with the explosive warhead nobody had considered going after the big fin whales. It had been observed that these whales were plentiful in the cold southern seas, but they were fast and when dead, they sank almost immediately. The invention of the big Svend Foyn-type harpoon gun—as opposed to the primitive and somewhat dangerous hand gun that had been in occasional use for over a hundred years—had to wait upon the introduction of steam, for the whole principle of this new form of whaling was that the gun should be mounted in the bows of a fast catcher requiring better means of propulsion and manœuvre than by oar and sail.

The new principle was used first on the Finnmark coast of Norway. But as the supply of rorquals diminished, the hunting area was extended until it covered most of the northern seas. The first Antarctic station was established at Grytviken in South Georgia in 1905. Others followed and ships were used as floating factories at convenient points. Finally, in 1923, Captain C. A. Larsen with the *Sir James Clark Ross* and five catchers entered the Ross Sea, operating successfully for a whole season, independent of any shore base.

This was the first pelagic expedition, the forerunner of the huge fleets that regularly hunt the pack-ice. It is a big industry now, but how long can it go on? The huge blue whale is already scarce. The fin whale population is declining, despite control and the limiting of catches. Man, in fact, is busy creating another area of devastation. If you presume the necessity for the slaughter of these remarkable creatures, still the method does not bear examination. It is as though ivory hunters were permitted to go out in fleets of lorries, firing harpoons into the elephants and then letting them drag the lorries, blood pouring from their entrails, until finally they drop with exhaustion, still not dead.

I have given an instance where two harpoons were used; but sometimes more are needed. The bomb, that in theory should break the whale's spine, often bursts in its intestines; the harpoon line, which in theory is to enable the catcher to winch in the kill, more often acts as a tow rope for the creatures to expend their last energies on the dead weight of a ship, hauling it through the water in agony, their guts torn to shreds and blood filling their bodies and bursting out through their vents. The agony of the whale's end must be indescribable, for as I have said, they are not fish.

It is far worse now than it was in the old days, when the boats they hauled through the water were light and the culmination of the whole operation was a lance thrust into the vital spot, bringing a quick death. Whale men are not exactly soft, and the fact that we in Britain have been spending a small fortune in trying to perfect an instant-killing, electrical harpoon, shows that the whalers themselves are revolted by the cruelty of it, even though they have not the same affinity with the whale as the old-timers who hunted it as close quarters.

The end of it all is the flensing deck, a sad place—far sadder than a slaughter house. Stern-first, this largest of all God's creatures comes slithering up the ramp under a white cloud of scavenging sea birds, winches clattering, the steel hawser taut as a bar. The first time I saw it done was on a Norwegian island, and I could hardly believe that the eighty-ton mass of inert flesh and blubber was the thing of grace and beauty I had so recently seen moving with such power in Arctic waters..

Slits were hacked in the sides of the mouth whilst flensers walked the corrugated belly, cutting and cutting. Tackle was fixed to the jaws, the winches clattered, a long strip of blubber was peeled off. Chains wrapped round the carcase were used to roll it over under the power of the winches. The pink mass of the tongue was ripped from the throat, the lower jaw peeled off. And then the flensers were into the carcase itself, knee-deep in blood, slithering on the slippery flesh as they cut and cut and hauled great junks on hooks to the meat racks. Somebody hacked into the bladder and several tons of urine gushed out in a yellow wave. The womb was opened to reveal a perfect replica of the mother. The torn and already putrefying intestines were cut out and lay in slimy piles, and the gulls wheeled and dived, ripping and tearing, filling the air with their raucous noise. And over it all hung that smell, that rank, cloying smell of dead whale and bubbling vats—the smell of money.

This then is the finale, industry swallowing the whale piecemeal, bloody chunk by bloody chunk. And yet, so few hours ago, the grey ugly mountain, that cannot even breathe when stranded because of its great weight, was a gliding shape seen through green water, a shadow moving to the flick of a fluke, to the whim of a living brain, to the demands of nature—food and procreation. Gentle and unobtrusive, a menace to nothing but the plankton that litters the seas, it has the misfortune to possess something man needs, and so the mechanical skill, the money and industrial power of maritime nations is concentrated upon its destruction; and because only those who do the killing see the cruelty of it, the whale has few champions. It is of the sea, and man still fears the sea, so that his conscience is not stirred by anything that happens to the creatures that inhabit it.

III. MOROCCO

SOUTH OF THE ATLAS

A flat brown plain, dusty in the sun, and at the end of it a sudden wall of mountains towering against blue skies—a fairy wall, all crystal-gleaming and white like sugar icing. That was how I first saw the High Atlas, from a roof-top in the *kasbah* of Marrakech. Thirty miles away and fourteen thousand feet high, they reared up above the great red-walled Berber city, a fabulous natural barrier barring the way to the south.

Those were the mountains we had to cross, for we were going south into the Zone of Insecurity, down into the Sahara in the hope of meeting the illusive Camel Patrol.

But first we wanted to see those mountains at close quarters. We chose Amizmiz in the foothills. I can't remember why, for it proved disappointing; all olive groves and well-fed sheikhs, and the white peaks lost to sight behind drab hills. But we had an introduction to the French Controlleur Civile and for three days we waited there, our hopes pinned to the fact that he was due shortly to make his yearly tour of some of the mountain villages. And then suddenly it was all arranged and we left next morning by car, up past the piled-up heaps of black olives on the outskirts of the village, up past the shrine of a local Berber saint, up and up the muddy hairpin bends, until after half an hour the dirt road ended abruptly.

Here we were met by mules brought down by barefoot Berber men from the villages of the Haut Atlas, and we started up a mule track precariously poised a thousand feet above a torrent bed cut deep by the melted snow. "*Deux heures*," the Controlleur said. "*Deux heures seulement.*" But we were an hour and a half getting to the first village; a group of mud houses huddled above the ravine and the women lining the track, ululating with their tongues a greeting for us—the same sound that they use to urge their men to battle. The *chef de village* met us, coffee with cinnamon proffered. Throughout Morocco etiquette demands that the guests leave only after the third cup. But this village's idea of hospitality was to serve their guests in tumblers—an embarrassing prospect!

An hour later and another thousand feet up the dose was repeated at a second village whilst we admired the art of a potter puddling clay in a pit and turning the wheel with his bare feet. Now the torrent bed was coming up to meet us and ahead the valley was blocked by a huge mountain peak, a pyramid of snow rising seven thousand feet above us. Another hour and we had forded the torrent and had climbed the valley side to come out suddenly upon a grassy plateau where sheep grazed. An old Berber chief, greybearded and wearing steel-rimmed glasses, spurred to meet us on a snow-white mule. Hands were kissed and touched to the heart in greeting, large bowls full of goats' milk were proferred by his attendants.

We entered a village, but it was not our destination. "We ride another kilometre," the Controlleur said, "to the *source d'eau,* a sacred place where the water comes out of the mountain. There the *difa* will be held and there will be dancing and music." Three villages had combined to provide the *difa,* which is the traditional feast. "They will have been cooking all night." And he added, "They have killed a sheep and examined its entrails—they hope the weather will be fine." And he glanced up at the sky and shrugged his shoulders. There was cloud now and it was bitterly cold. A few flakes of snow began to fall.

As we rode on, up towards the foot of the great *cime* of snow that now seemed poised above us, he told us the story of the old man on the white mule and how he got his glasses. For many years he had been blind, a pitiful figure led about by a small boy. And then the Controlleur, on one of his yearly visits, had brought a friend with him, an eye specialist from Algiers. "My friend said he could cure him of his blindness if he would come to Algiers for an operation. *Le pauvre vieillard*—he had never been farther than Marrakech. And an operation . . . it was much to ask of a man born and bred in the mountains here."

"And he went?" my wife asked.

"*Oui.* He went—alone to Algiers. It was an act of faith." And he added. "I think I was more frightened than he was, for it meant much to me in my work here."

We topped a rise amongst great rocks like houses and suddenly we were faced by a cliff wall from the base of which a great stream of water flowed. There was a fire there and a mass of villagers, and as we came into sight the band, crouched round the flames, began to beat their tambourines and the women formed a tight circle and sang, hands and feet moving slightly so that it was a constantly shifting pattern. And on rocks below some caves bright carpets were spread and brass braziers gleamed, the charcoal glowing red as bellows were pumped. Wisps of blue smoke rose into the air.

Pack mules arrived as we seated ourselves cross-legged on the carpets. They were loaded with dishes for the *difa* —*mechui,* whole roasted sheep; *pastilia,* that wonderful pie filled with pigeon and vegetables; *tagines* of chicken cooked in oil with orange and almonds. And as we ate, there was the persistent sound of singing, the constant shuffle of movement, the beat of the tam-tams, and the fire blazing and smoking, the silver head ornaments and bangles of the women glinting as they danced.

It was a fabulous, wholly Biblical setting. High up on the cliff opposite, spectators sat, leaning over the edge— Berber girls in gay colours, men in turbans. And the water pouring silently out of the base of the cliff, swirling down the valley bed, and all to our left snow—snow piled up to the sombre sky in one solid, towering sweep. So might an artist who saw things larger than life have painted the affair of Aaron's Rod.

We had barely finished the *pastilia* when it began to snow in earnest and we moved into the caves. The snow came sweeping up the valley, half-veiling the scene, and yet still the villagers went on dancing and the sound of their singing echoed back to us from the cliffs. I attended many *difas* in Morocco, but none like that.

And after the *difa* we went down to meet the dancers. Encouraged by our interest, the tempo of the tam-tams increased, the women formed a circle and two men came out to dance. It was the dance of the pigeons, a mime of the courting of two birds. And after that a man and a girl, and the silver gleamed as she moved. And then we were back on our mules again and riding down the valley, leaving that lost, lonely world of the Haut Atlas behind us.

Back in Marrakech, there were still two things we wanted before we went south across Atlas Mountains; we wanted to meet the Glaoui—the Pacha of Marrakech—and we wanted to see the New Year in at the Mamounia, a last fling at the fleshpots before the hardship of the desert. But it all went wrong. I was struck down with amoebic dysentery and saw the New Year in from a bed on the rooftop, staring in agony at the white wall of the mountains, now suddenly remote, and unattainable.

But for a French doctor, straight out from Paris to study tropical diseases, I doubt if I should ever have crossed those mountains. He came each morning in his little car, driving the mile of twisting, teeming streets that separated us from the nearest European, to prod and prescribe and leave me again, utterly exhausted, staring at the mountains and wishing I were dead. Five times a day the muezzins called the Faithful to prayer, the sound of their voices reaching me faintly through the city's persistent, tumultuous roar; tam-tams beat a bridegroom to his wedding feast, and through the long night I heard the sound of revelry and dancing as men from the desert tasted forbidden pleasures in the houses where small boys and their sisters plied their trade. All the viciousness of this City of Delights rose up to

me as in a bad dream so that I felt as though I were separated for ever from my kind, for we were living in the Dar
Jackie, one of the only two French houses in the old part
of Marrakech. It was cold at night, hot during the day,
and I was worried about my wife who had to walk alone
through the crowded Arab streets to shop in the great square
of the Djemaa el Fna. But it didn't seem to worry her.
" At least I'm not pestered by small boys as you are."

Convalescent at last, the future was suddenly brighter. A
cable from England, addressed simply : Dar Jackie, Marrakech, came as an almost unbelievable contact with the
outside world. And then at last a message from the French
to say that we would be received at the Dar el Glaoui. We
made our plans to leave for the south the following day and
clip-clopped in a hired fiacre through hot dusty streets to
present ourselves at the gates of the Glaoui's palace.

The gatekeeper in *djellaba* and turban greeted us with a
salaam, led us through a mud archway into gardens where
oranges hung on the trees like Chinese lanterns. We entered
a big circular building through carved cedar-wood doors,
and in the dim interior of a great council chamber we sat
and waited. I had asked to see Hadj Thami el Glaoui himself. But the Great Caid, Pacha of Marrakech, was then
seventy-six. He was seldom seen by Europeans. Probably
it would be one of his sons who received us, one of those
who had been educated in England.

We spoke in whispers, for the place had a cathedral
atmosphere. It was a lofty building with three entrances.
The walls were a delicate tracery of plasterwork, ivory-
coloured and hard like marble. Big pouffes, green on one
side of the chamber, purple on the other, were arranged in
a semi-circle around a central pouffe. We kept our eyes on
the dark cedar-wood entrance doors, not knowing what to
expect—servants with the silver impedimenta of the tea-
drinking ceremony probably.

After half an hour we became restless. It was then a
quarter to six and our interview had been for five o'clock.

Our guide finally signalled us to follow him and we climbed to a sunlit balcony that circled the outside of the council chamber. Another cedar-wood door of beautiful pattern was opened for us and we were invited to inspect the couch where the Glaoui rested from his labours in the Council. Other cedar-wood doors were opened and we slowly circled the building, our guide pointing to the lion statues in the garden that faced both ways, and the view of the Katubia and other buildings of Marrakech.

Then finally we were taken down into the gardens again and led up a flagged path, flanked with orange trees, to a much less imposing building with a small French car standing in the driveway outside. Here we were met by a short, alert man in a European suit with a muffler round his neck; the Glaoui's personal secretary. From a cool, dark corridor we were ushered into a small room; it was gloomy and rather bare except for a clutter of nondescript chairs and many longcase clocks that stood like sentries, shoulder-to-shoulder, round the walls.

From his seat behind a small desk a man in a spotless white *djellaba* of purest wool, his head hooded, rose to greet us. His only adornment was a beautifully-carved silver dagger hung on his left hip and suspended by a shoulder cord—the curved dagger that all Berbers of standing wear.

He was tall, and in his quiet dignity he gave an impression of absolute power. His features were aquiline and I was reminded of a tortoise—the same ageless look, the same suggestion of remoteness and patience. Perhaps I sensed a certain cold-bloodedness, too. The guttural Arabic tongue came softly from his lips. A slight movement of the hands to emphasise a point; otherwise, his body remained motionless as he talked to us through his secretary. The desk in front of him was entirely bare, except for a small model of a tank.

This was the Glaoui himself, the man who, shortly before his death two years later, was to play the kingmaker once again, to advance with ten thousand Berbers to the very walls of that great sunken city of Fez, and proclaim the aged Moulay Mohammed Ben Arafa as Sultan in place of Sidi Mohammed Ben Youssef, whom he had originally placed on the Sultan's throne. This victory, however, was to be short-lived, for the French Government lacked a decisive policy; expediency, taking no account of loyalties, was to leave him deserted by his French friends to kiss the dust at Ben Youssef's reinstatement and to die in the bitterness of disillusion.

But when we saw him he was still the Great Caid, playing his hand adroitly—the French against the Sultan and Nationalism, with his Berbers the trump card. It was my wife who told him how impressed we had been by his mountain Berbers and how we had seen the dancing high up on the edge of the snow line. He nodded and spoke quickly to his secretary, whilst we waited, hoping, for next day, when we crossed the 7,000-foot pass of Tizi n' Tishka, we should be close to his mountain stronghold of Telouet; it was to this *kasbah* that the favoured few were sometimes invited to see Berber dances. A unique spectacle, we had been told, and one usually reserved for diplomats, a gesture to impress and win powerful friends.

With a sudden smile of great charm, the Glaoui turned to my wife and made a short speech. His secretary interpreted: " It is all arranged. You go first to Telouet . . ." The Glaoui was offering us not only the hospitality of Telouet, but, as contrast, a dancing display of a different kind, at night in one of his feudal strongholds in the south.

It is something now to have seen the *kasbah* of Telouet from which the Great Caid came, the springboard as it were of his feudal power. It was eight thousand feet up in the mountains, a robber baron of a stronghold gleaming white amongst bare brown peaks at the end of a long dirt road. A big mud village, brown as the arid land around it, huddled close to the *kasbah* as though for protection in the immense solitude of the surrounding mountains. A glimpse of girls in their fineries as we drove through the village and then our driver was sounding his horn as he squeezed the car through a formidable gateway. It seemed unbelievable that a message could have reached this remote place and that we should be expected; but in the courtyard beyond, the Glaoui's *khalifa* was waiting to greet us and to escort us up to a cool, couched room, walled with a tracery of plasterwork as intricate as the marble reredos of a cathedral.

Here servants brought us course upon course—*mechui, pastilia,* a whole series of *tagines,* conical-lidded earthenware dishes containing first chicken cooked in olive oil with almonds and grapes, then *couscous,* the national dish, a pile of millet garnished with meat, and then with a variety of vegetables. In all, there were thirteen courses, and we ate to the distant beat of the tam-tams and the sound of singing. And when at last we had finished, servants came with ewer and bowl of beaten silver, and we washed the hand with which we had fed ourselves.

The *khalifa* returned again to escort us to a balcony overlooking a sun-drenched courtyard, and there we took our seats like royalty to see a sight that few Europeans have been privileged to witness. There were sixty-four dancing girls in that courtyard, weaving a pattern of gentle and persistent rhythm around the hub of a blazing fire where twelve men sat in a circle beating the time out on their tambourine drums. And as we seated ourselves they sang to us a song of welcome—of how the motor machine had come to Telouet from afar bringing us on the visit they had longed for, etc., etc.

These girls were not professional dancers. They were women of the village that lay sprawled about the *kasbah,* and their dances were the traditional dances of the mountain Berber people, a slow, rhythmic movement of hands and feet, a constant glitter of silver ornaments as the pattern changed and changed again to the accompaniment of a monotonous, almost hypnotic chant. For an hour we sat there, and it seemed like a moment, so fascinating to our senses was the sight and sound of the pattern they weaved. Mint tea was served to us, and after the third cup we rose as the etiquette of the country dictated, and as we rose the tempo changed, a new song, a song of farewell.

It was then that our driver broke the spell and brought us down to earth. He approached my wife and in harsh, determined French demanded of her: "*Madame, vous avez besoin du water-closet, oui?*"

This is something so seldom offered in a Muslim community that my wife seized gratefully on the opportunity, prepared for the worst and not expecting for a moment what she got.

As she was led away, I was asked the same question. And when I, too, said Yes, I found myself being directed to follow her. Because she ate with me—a thing no Berber wife would dream of doing—it was presumed by our hosts that we were quite prepared to share other functions.

At this point, I dug in my heels, and made it clear that we, too, had our customs.

My wife came out, her eyes dancing with delight. "It's a complete bathroom," she told me breathlessly. "All in pale green porcelain. There's even a bidet. And everything works."

It was true. Both, bidet, everything had been ordered from Paris by one of the Glaoui's sons, transported up into the mountains and installed as a demonstration of their enthusiasm for Western plumbing.

Very different was the scene that night at Taourirt, when we were entertained to a second display of Berber dancing. Another mud fortress, but this time pale, almost ghostly in the moonlight, and cavernous black pit of the entrance lit by naptha flares that added to the menace of the fierce, hawk-faced men who awaited our arrival. Dark mud passages, a dark mud staircase, and then suddenly a flat roof above a glaring courtyard filled with flame and smoke. The tam-tam band squatted round the blaze, stretching the skins of their tambourines in the fire's heat; the girls stood motionless around the walls, their headdresses brilliant in the firelight, their silver earrings, all their beads and necklaces a-glitter.

And then, suddenly, the throb of the tam-tams, and instantly all was movement, the silence shattered by the singing, that montonous tongued *Aiya* that combines with the rhythm of foot and hand and drum to produce an incessant assault upon the ear that is somehow more primitive, more insistent than jazz.

And as I sat there, spellbound by the scene, I could not help a feeling of embarrassment that in the course of one day two large villages had been disrupted and half their female population requisitioned to give an English author a glimpse of Berber music and Berber dancing. But the following day, when I saw them still wearing their dancing finery, I realised they enjoyed it; they regarded it as a fête. Nevertheless, it revealed the feudal nature of the Berber system. We were back in the Middle Ages, with the *kasbahs* like Norman keeps, and the dogs that wandered freely in and out of the firelight, between the dancers' swaying skirts, were big, rangy animals straight out of the Bayeux tapestries.

The girls and the tam-tam band were merged now, throbbing to the weird music, faster still and faster. The heat from the courtyard was overwhelming. Every now and then a Berber boy on a battlement threw a pile of desert furze down into the holocaust, and each time smoke and flame roared up into the chill, velvet night, where the stars stood like jewels above *kasbah* towers bone-white in moonlight.

Next morning we found ourselves looking at the southern face of the snow-capped Atlas, looking at it across ten miles of flat desert sand. Seventy miles of red, tortured rock had brought us to the military post of Ouarzazate. Between us and the Sahara there now stood nothing but the Anti-Atlas, a range of round and eroded hills, blackened by the perpetual shadows of their stony slopes. *Le Pays Noir*.

There is wealth down here, riches deep-buried and as yet

barely scratched by man. There are a few mines—cobalt
and manganese—but it is a day's journey in dust and heat
and difficult driving to reach them, and when you do, they
stand like infernoes of Dante's imagination against a background that might be the surface of the moon.

The minerals and the products of the valleys, the dates
and the almonds and the figs, all have to cross the mountains to Marrakech. To the visitor, Marrakech is the *souks,*
with their miles of palm-thatched market shops, and the
great colourful square of Djemaa el Fna, where story-
tellers and snake-charmers entertain the crowds. But to the
people of the south, it is their market. It is the source of
all luxuries, even the wood with which to make a fire.

That same day we crossed the Anti-Atlas and entered the
Valley of the Draa, where the palmerie stretches uninterrupted for nearly two hundred miles till the river disappears,
swallowed up in the sands of the Sahara. Here the *kasbahs*
crowd one on top of the other, a legacy of the country's
history, which has been one of successive waves coming in
from the desert and of inter-tribal, even inter-village, war-
fare, until the French brought peace and a stable government to the area.

Twenty years is not long in a history of pillage and
massacre that goes back beyond the Muslim invasion of the
African coast, beyond Christianity which once captured
the imagination of the Berbers, beyond the Vandals and the
Romans, back to pre-history; and the story of a thousand
years of birth and death and misery is writ there in the
sands of this crowded ant-heap, each death marked by a
head stone, and the stones so close they cover the sand like
shale and stretch almost uninterrupted from one *kasbah* to
another. Twenty years of peace have not persuaded the
inhabitants to move out of their unhealthy *kasbahs,* but
the mud walls are beginning to crumble, neglected in the
absence of danger.

Some of these fortress villages have a population of
several thousand, but though they suffer from tuberculosis

and sometimes die of pneumonia—for it can be desperately cold in winter—trachoma is the chief disease. It is carried by the flies that swarm at the time of the date harvest in September and there are few children whose eyes are not infected at an early age. Hospitals for treatment are not enough; the French had to combat the mental torpitude of the people that is summed up in their oft-repeated *Inshallah* —it is the will of Allah. This, and the shrug that accompanies it, is the Muslim's acceptance of each fresh calamity as inevitable, a fatalistic attitude encouraged by their religion and born of the need of fortitude in a hard world.

Contrary to what I had been led to expect at that time, France was not holding Morocco in thrall by weight of arms. The Foreign Legion and the *Goums* were fully committed in Indo-China. Five hundred officers of the A.I. (*Les Affaires Indigènes*) held the south for France by sheer force of character and training; not only the south with all its mineral wealth, but the Sahara, too, the oil potential of which was just beginning to be realised. And from the Atlas to Lake Chad the only force they could call on was the Desert Camel Patrol—two patrols of thirty Taouregs, each under a *sous-officier*.

As a guest of the A.I. I had an opportunity to study their methods. Their responsibilities were much the same as those of our own D.C.s, but their standing was somewhat different since they were not responsible to France, but acted in *loco parentis* to the Sultan's Government. Tough, self-reliant, they were a ten per cent picking from the volunteers of the North African colonial regiments, an élite corps of officers imbued with the ideals of France's greatest coloniser, Marshal Lyautey. They gave their lives and usually their health to the job, amoebic dysentery being an occupational disease necessitating ever more frequent recuperative periods at places like Vichy as they grew older. When I was there they were slowly making headway with schools and hospitals and improved methods of agriculture against the *inshallah* mentality of the people.

Has all that gone, I wonder, now? Driving south into the Sahara we came upon two muleteers, leading their caravan along the *piste*—the dirt road. This was forbidden because it breaks up and destroys the track. Capitaine Gauthier, who was driving us in his jeep, stopped and a vociferous altercation followed; the result, a four-days' prison sentence and instructions to report to the next post.

" But you haven't got a prison," my wife said as we drove on.

" No, but they will work on the *piste*."

" And if they don't report?"

" But of course they will report. I have ordered it."

It was impossible for him to entertain for a moment the idea that they would not obey. Muslim communities are essentially patriarchal, a social structure based on the family with the son giving unquestioning obedience to the father—and in the years he had served them he had come to be regarded as their White Father. Besides, where would they go if they disobeyed him? Into the Sahara? But then the bush telegraph of the desert would inform him of their whereabouts, for he had word of every traveller in that inhospitable zone.

In Tagounit there is a big concrete signpost. It directs the traveller to the various *pistes,* showing the place to which each leads, and all the distances are marked in kilometres—all, that is, except one. A single line points south and against it is written : *Timbouctou 50j*—fifty days across the Sahara by camel !

That to me is the most exciting signpost in the world, for we had been coming south a long time, *kasbah* after *kasbah, difa* after *difa,* and always with one object in mind, to meet the camel patrol in from the desert on one of their infrequent visits. We stopped two days at Tagounit, held up by torrential rain and wondering all the time whether we should make our rendezvous at M'hamid in the Sahara in time.

A guest room was put at our disposal. It was in an annexe to the foreign legion fort, a huge walled parade ground of a place covering several acres and utterly deserted. It was cold in that room at night, but the French had done their best to make it comfortable, even to installing a bathroom, and in the morning *café complet* was brought by a huge, bearded Taoureg dressed in turban and blue-dyed cloak.

The third morning the sun was shining and we left for the south. The Camel Patrol had arrived at M'hamid. With Capitaine Gauthier, in his jeep, was a ruffianly-looking young Frenchman in a blond beard and sandals. This was the *sous-officier* of the Patrol. We dropped him on the outskirts of Tagounit to pick up his camel and then slithered and floundered through thick, red desert mud the sixteen kilometres to M'hamid.

M'hamid was just a fort in the middle of nowhere, a small desert outpost familiar to anyone who has ever read *Beau Geste*. And as we drove in through the twin-towered entrance, a wild blue figure—blue face, blue-black hair, blue desert robes—stood stiffly to attention and presented arms. The *sous-officier* on his racing camel was close behind us, and before we sat down to lunch in the spartan mess, he had shaved off his beard—a gallant Gallic gesture to the presence of my wife—and now appeared as a smooth-faced youngster barely old enough to have left school.

It is a strange life these officers lead and right from the start they play it tough. This boy had been posted to the Patrol straight from the safe haven of regimental life, with no knowledge of Taoureg and no experience of the desert. He had been given a camel and the map reference of a waterhole in the Sahara and told to meet the Patrol there in so many days. There was no other officer with them when he reached the rendezvous. He found himself in command, yet a probationer, for the Taouregs themselves would decide whether he continued as their leader. Either

he made out on that first patrol, and was accepted by them,
or he would be sent back to his regiment with his tail
between his legs.

And *les hommes bleus* so like the men I met on the high
johl of southern Arabia, with long hair, often curled close
to the head, and features as classic and beautiful to look
upon as Michelangelo's statue of David in Florence. Wrapped in their blue desert cloaks they stood amongst their
fabulous racing camels, small, virile men, remote as the
Sahara and as independent as the Bedouin, with the same
quickness of mind, the same flash of dark eyes at a joke
shared, the same self-assurance based on the certainty that
all men are equal before God and the cruel fire of desert
sand. They are a warrior people, born to the life of the
nomad, as thoroughbred as the camels they ride, utterly
contemptuous of all those softer peoples who live outside
the Sahara's sand.

This handful of men and that young boy were policing
an area larger than France. What are they doing now,
I wonder? And Capitaine Gauthier, the White Father,
who entertained us with a distillation from dates and
cheese laced with cognac dug up from beneath the sand—
is he still there, keeping the peace over a thousand square
miles or so? And if not, who has replaced him, and is there
still justice in the land?

IV. THE LOW COUNTRIES

I. EUROPE'S CROSS-ROADS

I first saw Belgium as a light winking in the darkness at the end of a North Sea race. We were driving in under full canvas and the seas were breaking on the banks of Rhineborne silt spilled out from the German hinterland. Six hundred years before, square-rigged sailing ships ploughed this same route, bringing England's wool harvest to the weaving factories of Ypres and Ghent and Bruges. Nothing had changed out there in the North Sea, but as the dawn came we raised a coastline vastly different. Gone were the featureless flats that must have made landfall a nightmare for our ancestors and in their place buildings stretched to the limits of the horizon, presenting a cliff-like face to the sea, for we were coming into Ostend, summer playground of the Belgians.

It is worth coming into Belgium from the sea, for water is the key to this thriving little kingdom. Sitting with your beer at a pavement café on Ostend's Visschers Kaai you look across a forest of gaily painted fishermen's masts at ships gliding through the Voorhaven to the lock that will take them to Bruges. There are yachts moored almost in the centre of Ostend, and at night the streets are blazing arches of coloured lights, jam-packed with a laughing, chattering mob of holiday-makers, and the huge Kursaal is full of gaiety. But out along the sea front you could find houses with their windows still bricked up, relic of the days when all the coastal strip was *verboten*. And farther along the coast road, towards Middelkerke, the grey concrete gun emplacements of Hitler's North Sea Wall still crouched in the dunes, staring blindly at the sea.

All along this coast you are conscious of the sea. Sometimes it has been a friend, as it was for the British when they crowded the beaches just west of Belgium's borders in the great evacuation of Dunkirk. Sometimes it has been an enemy as in the disaster of January, 31, 1953, when northerly gales and unprecedented tides breached the defences of the Lowlands and Zeebrugge's towering mole was swept by giant waves that rolled across the *avant port* to fill the fish harbour, where the shrimpers lie, and flood the half re-built town. But always the sea has been a means of trade, linked with the great inland towns of Flanders by a network of waterways.

Sail up the Scheldt to Antwerp and your eyes are suddenly opened to a whole new world; the world of the barges. Belgian barges, Dutch barges, German barges—barges from Rotterdam, Bremen, Hamburg, Dusseldorf, Cologne, Frankfurt and dozens of other inland ports; they crowd the twisting waterway, a nightmare hazard to captains bringing their ships into the docks. Deep-laden and with decks awash they are strange-looking creatures, narrow of beam to get through the locks and sometimes a hundred yards long. As often as not it's the old woman who manages the great horizontal wheel, steering the cumbersome, half-submerged monster through the steamer traffic, whilst the old man sits below with his meerschaum and his schnapps, and the children ride their bicycles over the hatches.

I last went up to Antwerp in the old *Dewsbury* from Harwich. It was a perfect morning, cloudless and bright, so that the haze lingering over the land gave it a mysterious, ethereal quality. Water, sandbanks, land, everything was flat—flat and still. The sky was a great uninterrupted sweep from horizon to horizon. I stood on the bridge with Captain Strange and watched the buoys slip past and the ship's head swing to the pilot's alterations of course. Astern an invisible sandbank marked by a pillar buoy caused our wake to break, a little flurry of white in a calm world that warned of danger to any ship straying from the marked channel.

Captain Strange bent to light his pipe. "Different in

winter," he murmured. "I've had ice up here so thick I've had to fill and back to break through it. Last year it swept all the buoys from their moorings—not a single mark in the whole river." I tried to picture the river in those conditions, my mind on Brueghel landscapes. "And fog," he added. "Come up here on radar and your screen's so cluttered up with barges you can't pick up the buoys." But it was a difficult picture to evoke just then, for Antwerp's square mile or so of oil refineries was glinting silver in the sunshine and the forest of cranes that marked the docks drooped against a blue sky.

Everything smiled that morning, even the Steen—that grim little castle crowded among the shipping at the quay. The Steen should be seen in cloud and rain, when the full menace of it hits you like a blow. Part legend, part history, it is father to the teeming city behind it; and its story is as grim as its appearance. A giant named Druon Antigon once held the river there, levying a toll of 50 per cent on the goods of all travellers passing up and down the water-way. Those who attempted to evade his demands had their right hands severed and tossed into the river. Then the Romans came and Salvius Brabo, nephew to Julius Cæsar by marriage is credited with the slaying of this monster, whose hand he amputated and threw into the Scheldt. The event is commemorated—as every historic event is in Bel-gium—by a statue. It stands in the Grand' Place, the nude figure of a youth in the act of throwing the hand, and from the severed wrist a gout of water gushes. There is nothing squeamish about Belgian art!

But though the Belgians love statues and crowd every open space in their cities with bronzes, they love giants even more. They have images of nearly four hundred of them now, with new ones appearing every year. Most of the old ones were burned or destroyed in the French occupation, or remain simply as heads shorn of their wickerwork bodies; but the sixteenth century figure of Antigon still exists, a carved and gilded colossus of wood seated in a car with his hand ready on his sword, his head worked by a hidden operator.

This raising of what was after all just a petty tyrant destroyed by the march of the Roman legions to the status of Giant, and the use of giant figures in religious spectacles, suggests a pre-Christian and deep-seated mythology. These people are descended from the Belgae, a Celtic race who impressed Cæsar with their magnificent courage. They spread northwards across the sea to Britain and in subsequent invasions were pushed westward; and in Cornwall a separate language existed until quite recently, together with such a mass of giant stories that even the rocks left on the hilltops by the Ice Age were thought to have been hurled there in battles between these legendary colossi.

These Cornish legends are almost forgotten now, but in Belgium the giants still walk the streets, nodding their great heads and peering in at second-storey windows. At Ath, where it all started, there is Ambiorix, Samson, the Bayard Horse with the four sons of Aymon as riders, and Goliath in a dual role, either fighting David or mock-seriously taking a wife. At Dendermonde the Bayard still scatters the soldiery who bar the exits from the market place. Some towns have a whole menagerie of beasts—lions, eagles, camels, and naturally a dragon or two, for the story of St. George is not peculiar to England.

Standing beneath the shadow of the Steen, looking along the quay that follows the curve of the river for almost four miles, one realises how consistently the centuries have shaped the city of Antwerp. That quay gave it its name, for once it was a little wooden wharf and the people spoke of going *aan 't werf*—to the wharf. The Romans built the first fortifications—Castrum Antverpsis; and after the Normans had conquered and gone, trade expanded and the town grew, was enclosed with fortress walls, spread out beyond those walls along the river bank until in the fifteenth and sixteenth century it had replaced Bruges as a centre of trade. It was then at the zenith of its power, a great cosmopolitan trading city full of merchants from Britain, Spain, Italy and Germany, even from Moscow, and galleys from as far afield as Venice crowded the *werf*. It became a centre of the arts, again supplanting Bruges—the Antwerp school, the French-Flemish school, the schools of Brueghel and Rubens all flourished there, backed by a bourgeois merchant aristocracy that was ahead of London and Amsterdam in establishing an international Exchange, the world's market for gold and silver.

Antwerp must have been a crowded, thriving, colourful port in those days with its fine old buildings of which the Vleeshuis (the Butcher's Hall) is the best surviving example. But fifty miles of river separates it from the sea, and the Dutch, struggling for independence, were lords of the Lower Scheldt. They closed the river and the port of Antwerp died. Not until 1863 did the Dutch finally relinquish the right to levy toll. A free port again, Antwerp's revival has been rapid, due partly to the business ability of its inhabitants, but more particularly to the site chosen by their ancestors. Its strategic position as an invasion port against England has been appreciated for centuries. The Duke of Parma filled it with ships to embark his army in support of the Spanish Armada. Napoleon did the same, calling it a pistol levelled at the heart of England; and Hitler, too. But in 1944-45 the barrel pointed the other way and Antwerp was the great terminal for ships supplying the Allied armies. Two world wars and over four thousand flying bombs have given only momentary checks to the resurgence of the port, and now all the natural energies of the people are directed towards making it the fastest turnround for shipping in the world.

Coming into Antwerp you are not conscious of having arrived in Belgium as you are when you enter Ostend. Antwerp is simply Antwerp, a proud, independent city, like all the cities of the flat north land that runs out into the sea with hardly a change in the landscape. Order a meal in French and the waiter will pretend not to understand.

He will speak only Flemish until you reveal your nationality, and then he will switch with evident pleasure to broken English. Ghent, Bruges, Malines—they're all the same. The people of these cities grow up in the shadow of history— history as told in carved stone, towering belfry and statue, or painted on the priceless canvases that fill to overflowing their churches and their city museums. The knowledge of their independence and past greatness is all about them, an overwhelming influence in their lives. To think of themselves as Belgians is something comparatively new. Belgium only became a nation in 1830 and her people live in a Venetian atmosphere, with the waterways that brought them greatness still running like silver threads through their lovely cities. They do not look south, but north, with their faces turned towards the sea.

I saw Bruges once at night, and not even Venice is more beautiful. Two pinnacles reach up above the city roofs to the sky—the delicate octagonal belfry and the great over-powering mass of the cathedral tower. These twin aspirations of a people living in a flat land greet you unexpectedly at every twist and turn of the narrow streets. But it is by the water that Bruges comes to life. Lit by the soft glow of orange floodlights, the quaint winding waterways by the Gruuthuse are as enchanting as Fairyland. The Quai du Miroir, the Quai Vert, the Quai de la Potterie . . . Place Van Eyck, Place Memling; everything in this city cries out to be painted.

But walk out to the old walls where great waterways stand, sullen and defensive, their bastion walls rising up out of the waters of the broad canal that still rings the city. The mood is different here, telling a story of a city's fears of attack upon its mercantile wealth and power. But the main attack when it came by-passed these defences. It was a political and economic attack that switched the bulk of Lowland trade to Antwerp. Bruges became a backwater, unscarred by the new buildings that followed in the wake of Antwerp's prosperity, so that what we see in Bruges to-day is a great medieval trading city almost as well preserved by its economic plight as Pompeii was by the ash of Vesuvius.

Ghent, on the other hand, managed to meet the competition of Antwerp, for its wealth was based on wool. As a result little but its great wool churches and the compact might of its Château des Comtes have survived the demands of a prosperity that is now causing the city to burst at the seams of its narrow streets. Here is a civic pride and a great love of everything English, for Ghent is a seafaring city. Even its own special dish—*Waterzooi de poulet à la Cantoise*—smacks of the sea, being an inland development of *moules marinière* in which the chicken of the rich Flanders farms has replaced the mussels of the coast. But despite the roaring activity of its docks, it likes to call itself the City of Flowers. It could equally be called the City of Paintings, for its museums are packed with the best of Flemish pictures and its cathedral of St. Bavon has one of the world's greatest masterpieces, the huge triptych of the Van Eyck brothers, known as the *Mystic Lamb*.

The story of the *Mystic Lamb* is as unbelievable as the beauty of its detail and colours. It is a complicated triptych, composed of a number of paintings, and at one period, when the city's finances were low, two of the upper wing portraits were sold to the Jews of Brussels, who in turn sold them to a Berlin museum. At the end of the First World War, Ghent recovered them as part of Belgium's reparations. Two further pictures were stolen by a disgruntled priest, who agreed to return them for an enormous sum of money. The money was paid and the city received a cloakroom ticket for their own railway station of St. Pierre; they only recovered one of the pictures. The other, which depicts a group of horsemen, is still missing, and it is the vital one, for in it the Van Eyck brothers signed their masterpiece with self-portraits. Somewhere in the world some rich hoarder of stolen works of art holds the Van Eyck signatures. The final disaster was the complete removal of the triptych by the Germans in the last war, and when the war was over no record of it could be found. Only after all hope of its recovery had been abandoned did it turn up amongst some of Goering's loot hidden in a disused salt mine in Germany.

Penetrating into Belgium southwards from the coast you are conscious of a gradual change. Wherever waterways reach inland to the towns you will find a friendly, cosmopolitan attitude—strangers are welcome for strangers are good business. But out beyond reach of the major waterways, the Brueghel character predominates. Malines, for instance. This city has for me a grimness that not even the raucous hurdy-gurdy line of the inevitable fair in the city centre could dispel. It is full of religious institutions, and it is Lowland to the core, with all the Lowland suspicion of the intruder that is the result of a turbulent history. This is the flat poplar country of so many Flemish landscapes, and all through the farmlands you see the Brueghel faces. The deeper you go, the more conscious you are of a backward countryside, until you stand in the beautiful old church of St. Leonard at Zootleeuw. It is a museum of the most exquisite primitive wood carvings. Invasions have passed it by. You are back in the fifteenth century and nothing seems to have changed.

But a little to the west the university city of Louvain stands on the route taken by the armies marching to the coast. There is Spanish influence here in some of the houses, but the most beautiful piece of architecture is the Hotel de Ville with its turrets so intricately carved in stone that they look like pieces from a Chinese chess set. In the last war the people of Louvain completely encased the building in sandbags. This saved it, though the buildings round it are badly scarred.

You have left the sea a long way behind now. Your gaze

is south and east, towards Germany, and you begin to feel the threat that has hung over these people for centuries.

Farther south still and you reach the industrial Meuse, a great inland waterway bustling with barge traffic and coasters, and beyond the valley's slag heaps lie the Ardennes. The country is no longer flat, but mountainous, and intense cultivation of arable land has given place to intense cultivation of forest land. The people have changed, too, for this is the Waloon country with a language of its own that is still spoken by the peasants and the people of the old quarters of the towns. This is in addition to the two official languages!

Street names, signposts, every public notice has to be given in both Flemish and French. Even the names of towns are different. Antwerp is also Anvers, Ghent—Gand, Brussels—Bruxelles, Bergen is the familiar Mons, and Luik —Liege. In Brussels the downward moving escalators are marked *montée interdite,* and underneath *verboden op te gaan.* For a Walloon peasant to understand this it would have to read *Vo n'polez nin monter!* Government publications are doubled in size at prodigious cost to the taxpayer by the political necessity of printing everything, even statistics, in two columns—one Flemish, one French. And just to add to the sense of living in Babel, I discovered there is yet a fourth language, *Bruxellois;* compounded of invasions and occupations, and including even words of Spanish, it is quite unintelligible to all but the old people of Brussels living around the Rue Haute.

It is not only a problem of the country being split linguistically. Everything—politics, labour relations, education, even social life—is be-devilled by religious dissension. Each trade, for instance, has a Catholic union and a Socialist union. But it is over education that the whole problem has come to the boil. The easterly province of Limbourg is the centre of this upheaval. Traditionally it is a Catholic stronghold. The sandy soil of the Campine has nurtured a sturdy peasant stock. But some fifty years ago coal was discovered there, and now many of its people are non-practising Catholics. They don't want their children brought up from infancy in religious schools. But the children have to be educated and more than ninety per cent of the schools are Catholic. The Government is now embarked on a long-term programme of providing State Schools as an alternative, where religious instruction will be voluntary; and this, of course, undermines the foundations of the Roman Catholic Church, so that the Church is now deeply involved in politics. A first-class political struggle is in progress for the minds of Belgium's youth in an era of social change.

If you go down the road from Haselt to Liege at night, you will see the evidence of that change. Blacked-out coaches roar past, bringing sleeping workers back from the steel plants and coal mines to their homes in Limbourg. The Catholic north has a prolific birth rate, with the result that wages are low and there is under-employment. But in the Walloon south, where the socialist worker mixes his religion with hard-headed realism, there is a shortage of labour and high wages. Migration is the inevitable and natural result.

At the hub of all this, and just about half an hour by train from any of the other cities of Belgium, lies Brussels. It is neither Flemish nor Walloon. It is a city apart. At first glance it is a little like Paris. It has the elegance and the gaiety, the restaurants, the night life, the tree-lined boulevards, and the *bois*. And when you have had time to notice the hills and the street vistas that end abruptly in sky, you are reminded of Rome. And later, after you have wandered through the narrow street around the Grand' Place, little alleys and sudden unexpected glimpses of old buildings make you think of London.

I rate Brussels one of the world's most exhausting cities. As in the rest of Belgium, you only need to have one friend and your life is full. The accident of their position at

Europe's cross-roads has made them cosmopolitans. They always speak several languages, and they enjoy meeting strangers. They are incredibly energetic, always in a hurry. Time is money to them, and to be busy is to live fully; and they fill every minute of their lives, unfailingly punctual, always working to a schedule. They have much in common with us—their parks, their love of flowers, their materialism, the hustle and bustle of their lives. They love money and dream of a house in the country. They live in suburbs and every day six hundred thousand of them pour into the city, two-thirds of them by tram. The trams wake you in the morning and sigh you to bed at night. And the shops are full of the most exquisite lace.

You cannot be long in Brussels without being introduced, so to speak, to the Belgian Congo. The Musée de Congo Belge, exhibitions of native arts and craft—they are intensely proud of this huge slice of Africa they administer. They have faith in it, too, and there is hardly a person you meet who has not got some of his savings locked up in Katangas or Union Miniére or Tanganyika Concessions. Their attitude to the colony is realistic, rather than idealistic, and they believe they still have twenty years and more of trouble-free administration ahead of them.

I asked my friend Georgette Ciselet how it was that, in a world where colonialism has run head-on into difficulties, the Belgian Congo remains an outstanding exception. Madame Ciselet is one of those incredible women thrown up once in a while by every country. She is a barrister and runs a flourishing law firm; she is also a Liberal senator, and when she isn't looking after women's rights or getting the divorce laws changed or pressing for action over the revolting traffic in worn-out Irish horses for human consumption, she is in New York representing Belgium's interests at the United Nations. She had just come back from an exhausting tour of the Belgian Congo that included the remotest jungle territory, and she gave me this explanation of the smooth-running of the colony: "Our policy is steadily to raise the level of education of the people, but all together, on a general level." Certainly it cannot be said that Belgium is holding the people back as a whole. Their ten-year education plan provides for the creation of nearly six thousand separate schools, ranging from kindergarten to primary and post-primary schools, together with apprenticeship workshop schools and nearly eight thousand classes for adults.

Fortunately for the Belgians, the Bantu is a backward race, and the Pygmies more so, for though Belgium could exist without the Congo, it could never sustain its high standad of living. This colonial creation of a great king—Leopold II not only employed Stanley in the original expedition, by which treaties were concluded with about a thousand different chiefs, but handled the subsequent political manœuvres so adroitly that, a year before his death, he saw the Congo finally established as the administrative responsibility of the Belgian people—is now the mainstay of the rich bourgeois life that centres on Brussels.

Culturally Brussels is overshadowed by Paris. The fact that it is a French-speaking city makes it difficult to support a talent of its own. Belgian magazines have to compete with the far bigger circulation French periodicals. The theatre is an international one, and Georges Sion, one of the best-known Belgian playwrights, admitted to me that he depended partly on Paris and partly on journalism. Even artists—and Belgium has always patronised its painters—find life difficult. Emil Langui, then *chef du cabinet* for the Ministry of Education, told me that there were more than five hundred Academy prize winners out of work. And he explained to me that at about thirty-five many artists took to teaching—to teach more artists to become eventually teachers. "It is a vicious circle."

When I was last in Brussels I visited two very unusual theatres. One was the Théâtre Flottant, composed of two barges moored in the canal; to starboard was the theatre, and to port the dressing-rooms, bar and dance hall. This theatre had toured as a complete self-contained unit as far afield as Paris. The other was the Théâtre du Toone VI. This was a puppet theatre like no other I have ever seen. In the sixteenth century Brussels had fifteen puppet theatres. Puppets were as popular as giants. Now there was only this one. Toone himself was sixth in the direct line of puppet masters. His repertoire consisted of almost five hundred plays, many of them dating from the Middle Ages. He had more than two hundred and seventy puppets, despite the fact that seventy-five of them were " killed " by a flying bomb. His theatre was a little cellar-like place off the Rue Haute holding ninety people, and when I went there to see *La Fille du Bourreau* (*The Executioner's Daughter*), there weren't more than thirty people on the rough wooden benches—not exactly profitable with the price of a seat about a shilling.

The miniature stage and scenery creates in one's mind the illusion that the puppets are life-size. But unlike most puppet theatres, there is no attempt to conceal the strings of their manipulators, and the giant hands of the operators give to the action a sense of the macabre, as though the players are in the hands of Destiny. It is all very medieval, and this sense of being transported back into a crueller age is increased by the constant massacres that are enacted. Sword in hand, the puppets stride on, duelling, declaiming, storming barricades and battlements, fighting shoulder-to-shoulder. Seven operators were needed for *The Executioners' Daughter*, and it was not too many, for the action was so fast and furious that puppets were roughtly slung aside as the dead piled up on the stage and more troops poured on.

Toone himself spoke all the parts—and except for a few French and Spanish phrases, it was impossible to understand a word of it, for it was all in the old *Bruxellois*. The play lasted for over two hours, and when I talked to Toone after the performance, he looked utterly exhausted, which was not surprising, for it was a *tour de force* and he had already done a day's work in a garage. How long he and his assistants will be able to continue, I do not know. They do it for love of the tradition that has been handed on to them. But they still have to earn their living.

The charm of Brussels is its dual personality—by day a down-to-earth, matter-of-fact business city; by night a jewel, brimful of gaiety. The Boulevard du Jardin Botanique loops like a string of lit pearls across the city to the canal bridge, the weeping willows drip fingers of green light to the lake waters, the statues stand out in white relief from their plinths around the Parc, and from the vantage point of that enormous hunk of masonry that dominates Brussels—the Palais de Justice—you look down upon the city's glow to the soft seclusion of the Grand' Place. Here all is peace, a golden ambience of gilt and stone, dominated by the towering Gothic spire of the Hotel de Ville, topped by St. Michael and the dragon. No picture has ever done justice to this square—so perfect, so comparatively small, so exquisite on all its four sides. By luck my wife found herself there when the lights went up at the end of the war—first the streets lights, then the floodlights, then the bells ringing out with joy and the people pouring in to jam the square from end to end. There is no more beautiful square in Europe, not even St. Mark's, and to see the lights come on there at the end of five years of darknes . . . she said it took her breath away it was so wonderful. The end of another war . . . and for Belgium there have been so many wars.

There was a sound of revelry by night. . . . Half an hour in a car from the Grand' Place and you are standing on the field of Waterloo. It is all very ostentatious, very, touristic with its artificial mound of grass-covered bricks, surmounted by a gigantic lion cast from Napoleon's captured cannon. And at the foot of the two hundred and twenty-five steps is a circular observatory-like building housing a complicated panorama of the battle. But your mood will have changed by the time you have seen the film and been conducted over the really excellent wax-works. Talk then to Norbert Brassine, who owns the Bivouac, the rustic-looking *auberge* next door. For him Napoleon is still *l'homme du destin* and it all happened only yesterday. He has a library of more than twelve hundred books on the Little Corporal and a collection of letters written by Napoleon's soldiers to their families, franked with the stamp of the *Grande Armée*. The day I was there he was bubbling over with excitement at the latest treasure he had acquired—Napoleon's camp chair, a folding arm-chair of wood with the initial N on the back. He had bought it at a local farm sale the evening before. " *C'est fantastique*," he kept saying. " *C'est unique*. I do not sell him for a million francs." My immediate reaction was one of scepticism. And then I wondered why he should bother to fake a chair when the old farmhouses around Waterloo probably contain many bits and pieces looted from the battlefield and handed on from father to son. Why shouldn't this chair have suddenly turned up in a sale? And his excitement was so patently genuine as he pointed to where the wood was worn below the N. " That is where the hat is rubbing as he turns his head."

Outside again, you look past the monument to Welling-ton's victory, out to the tilled fields beyond, and you re-member that in those three square miles some forty-five thousand men lay killed and wounded less than a century and a half ago. I have before me as I write a copy of *The Times* containing Wellington's despatch datelined *Waterloo, June* 19, 1815, and the leader opens with this fanfare : *Such is the great and glorious result of those masterly movements by which the Hero of Britain met and frustrated the audacious attempt of the Rebel Chief. . . .* And it goes on : *Buonaparte's reputation has been wrecked and his last grand stake has been lost in this tremendous conflict. TWO HUNDRED AND TEN PIECES OF CANNON captured in a single battle. . . .*

A hundred years later and fifty miles to the west, the story was very different, the slaughter immensely greater.

For anybody, like myself, born into the Great War and educated by men who had spent four years of their lives in the Flanders trenches, the journey to Ypres is a strange and moving experience. I went from Brussels by car on a morning of thick mist, through Oudenarde, Courtrai and Menin; and from Courtrai on, there wasn't a house that had stood for forty years. Rushed up in a hurry, they gave a newness to human habitation as though these people were intruders. Flanders horses ploughed the fields. The land was neat, orderly, intensely cultivated; the trees full grown. I wondered how they felt, these people, when their plough struck iron or turned up a broken bone. Did they remember how much it had cost to break the German hordes and give them back their country? This land belonged to other men and through the sodden, swirling mist, dim childhood memories fed imagination, until I saw it as it had been for my father's generation, and a line of Browning came into my mind : *Who were the strugglers, what war did they wage Whose savage trample thus could pad the dank Soil to a plash?*

Hell-Fire Corner is now a neat little level-crossing and the poplars stand tall and straight. There are signs out along the road—MUSEUM or TO THE TRENCHES or just the one word TUNNELS. I chose Hill 62, and drove down an avenue of maple, past the first of the Allied war graves, to an *estaminet,* which for ten francs admits you to some trenches. Rusty rifles, tin hats, mortars, breastplates, and the odd bone or two line a path that leads into a little copse. Here and there in the undergrowth are the remains of blasted trees. Trenches straggle round the hill, interconnected by a tunnel, which is electrically lit and shored with concrete. It had been a dry autumn, yet that tunnel was running with water. The trenches were just as they had been forty years ago, the sand all run out of the sandbags, the duckboards rotting. A cock pheasant strutted on the parapet. Back in the *estaminet,* rows of old-fashioned wooden box viewers yielded twenty-five pictures each for a franc—interminable pictures of mud, and shell holes full of slime, and dead and rotting bodies. It was a sad, unwholesome place.

But up in the Canadian cemetery, where the dead lay in a haze of autumn colouring, the atmosphere was quite different. From tht vantage point, the flatness was seen to have a slight undulation. The point where Bond Street joined Oxford Street had been obliterated by the plough, but, towards Ypres, Hill 60 showed as a little rise that must have seemed like a mountain to men who measured victory in a few hundred yards of mud regained. The mist had lifted now and the sun shone, so that I could look across to Paschendaele, and all the wretched flatness of Flanders stretched out, smiling, in front of me. I could see the great tower of the Cloth Hall in Ypres, too. Some forty years ago, almost a hundred thousand men had fallen there in one battle. Somewhere below me the first gas attack had been made. And away towards Paschendaele the Allied casualties had numbered a quarter of a million.

For half a lifetime, my generation has lived in the shadow of what happened here—a thing not experienced, but felt through all our formative years—and now that I had seen the place, I felt drained and a little exhausted. I went into Ypres, across the river and through the Menin Gate into the great square. Impossible to believe that the huge Cloth Hall was a replica, that the whole town, once the first great wool centre of the Low Countries, had been obliterated. But after forty years, they are still rebuilding at the back of the Cloth Hall, and out beyond the town, the Allied cemeteries, that mark the perimeter of the Salient, are a constant reminder of the way men were consumed at Ypres. And out on the road to the coast, relics of that First World War stay with you, until you reach Furnes and stand with relief in the shadow of old buildings once again.

Driving back that night along the newly-opened *auto-*

strada, I wondered how these people had ever managed to survive. In one day's drive through this little country, you can span two centuries of war—Bastogne, where the American paratrooper blocked Runstedt's Ardennes offensive, Waterloo, Oudenarde, Ypres. And for centuries before that, Austria, Spain and France had torn the country to shreds. There were the Normans, Charlemagne and his Franks, the Romans. Invasion and occupation; Belgium has never been free of either, for she stands at Europe's cross-roads, a stamping ground for every invading army since Cæsar conquered Gaul. Nobody can write her history, for it is not an individual history, but the sum of her neighbours' histories. And yet the people survive—not only survive, but prosper, for Belgium is a country of roaring factories, with almost the highest standard of living in Europe.

Drive along the Meuse, under the shadow of the giant steel plant of L'Ougrée-Marihaye-Cockerill that stretches for miles along its banks, and you will see what an indusrious people can do with a legacy of coal and iron ore. It is not pretty, but it is impressive; and you catch the Meuse at sunset, when the water is like steel and all the barges glitter, when the slag heaps are black pyramids etched against the sky; there is beauty in it then.

There is beauty in Liége, too, with its little alleys full of old houses, where people still speak nothing but Walloon. They mined coal here as early as the thirteenth century, and the independence of this metalworkers' city was always associated with its Prince Bishops. The monstrous sixteenth century palace, with its courtyard pillared by sixty fat columns, is symbolic of the fact that they were more prince than Bishop. Out near Tongres, they had a hunting lodge, and the Prince Bishop of the time of Louis XIII liked it so much that he enlarged it for his permanent residence, so that Château Hex is a little palace, with avenues almost two miles long. It passed to the d'Ansembourg family, and the present Comtesse, a charming old lady, showed me over it—room after room of the most finely carved and painted panelling, bedrooms with their original hangings and wall coverings, a Chinese room in brilliant, fantastic colours. The furniture was in keeping—Louis Treize, Louis Quatorze, Louis Quinze; there was an Empire room, too. It was a museum packed with original pieces. And yet, sitting in the Comtesse d'Ansembourg's sitting-room before a blazing log fire, cracking walnuts, I was conscious of the homely atmosphere of the château. Those bedrooms upstairs, with their four-posters, were not show bedrooms, they were where the guests slept. Later somebody said to me, a little enviously : " You see, Château Hex is tucked away, clear of the invasion routes."

Not so Château de Forêt, where my wife and I spent several nights as guest of the del Malmols on our way down into the Ardennes. There was a night in the autumn of 1944 when Forêt was the rallying point for a premature Belgian rising, and the Germans fired the château. " We were hiding," the Baronne told us, " in a little space between the rafters with our silver and our food reserves and two men of the Resistance. We only just got out. It was all so unnecessary," she added wistfully, " for the Germans were gone next day and the Americans arrived." Now they have rebuilt their home—and they have two secret hiding places, not one; a precaution that seems extraordinary to us, but is quite commonplace in Belgium.

All down through the Ardennes it was the same—stories of war, of the Resistance, of men hiding out in the forests. We had a friend, Paule de Hemptine, with us. This was her country and she had been there through the Occupation and the Ardennes offensive. *My sister had to take a gun to that house. . . . That was where the Germans came when we were hiding people, but they only wanted eggs. . . . We were given twenty-four hours to get out. . . . Suddenly found we were between the Germans and the Allies. . . . Shells going over, but the children thought it exciting. . . . That was where the American guns were;*

they cut all our lovely trees—they had to; it was desperately cold that winter. . . . We encouraged her in her reminiscences, for they were personal, domestic stories about bedding and food and children, and they underlined in our minds how different war can be for people whose accident of birth places them in the march of armies. For us, war is fighting. For the Belgians, it is being fought over.

We were in the Ardennes at the height of the autumn colouring—valleys dripping every shade of gold in the sunshine—and in château after château we were conscious of the forest, for this is a landed gentry whose roots are as firmly planted in the soil as the trees from which their wealth comes, and the talk is all of afforestation and *la chasse*. There are virtually no absentee landlords. They stay at home and manage their estates, and like everything the Belgians do, their forestry is intense, efficient and highly organised. Their money goes back into the land and into the châteaux which are their pride. Their recreation is *la chasse,* which can mean anything from pheasant shooting to wild boar hunting. Stag masks and boar tusks decorate their walls, boar hides strew the floors. It is a life very similar to the English country house life, but their families are much bigger and, because Belgium is small, they all seem inter-related, as can be seen from a glance at their *Debrett,* delightfully titled *Highlife de Belgique.*

In the thick stag forests of the Ardennes, the story of St. Hubert seems reasonable enough, though it happened more than thirteen hundred years ago. Hubert was out hunting and, close by the road that now runs from Laroche to the town of St. Hubert, he was confronted by a stag with a crucifix between its antlers. Converted to the Christian faith, he became the first Bishop of Liége. Even now the country can produce strange manifestations. This citation, for instance, from the Catholic Church : ". . . the Blessed Virgin Mary appeared eight times at Banneaux to Mariette Beco, a girl eleven years old, the eldest of a poor family of seven children." That was as recent as 1933. Now a million people the world over are pledged to pray every day to the Virgin of the Poor, and the village of Banneaux has become a sort of Lourdes, with a mass of ecclesiastical buildings, even hotels. And yet in the towns, people tell you—" Yes, but I am a non-practising Catholic," or " I do not believe in anything." They even admit to being agnostics.

What to make of this country? You return inevitably to the Grand' Place in Brussels, and you wonder. Religious and political dissension, language and racial difficulties, and wars—always wars. It defies all the rules of national existence. And you sip your drink in the heavily-timbered seclusion of Le Cerf, with its tooled leather walls, and look out on to the golden beauty of the square. So much of beauty has defied disaster . . . you feel the very stones of the ancient buildings have acquired the people's instinct for survival.

2. LAND BELOW THE SEA

Saturday evening, January 31, 1953—I remember listening to the radio with that sense of disaster that both fascinates and appalls. Gale warnings, tide warnings . . . all the coasts of the North Sea were threatened. It was a time of spring tides, when sun and moon combine to raise the level of the sea, and for days there had been strong northerlies, blocking the escape northwards of each ebbing tide. Now it was full gale right on top of one of the year's biggest tides. I thought of my boat lying in her mud berth, of the estuaries I knew so well on my own East Coast and in Holland and Belgium, of the buoys and lightships I sailed past every year; and those lines of Jean Ingelow's *The High Tide on the Coast of Lincolnshire* (1571) slid into my mind—

> *Men say it was a stolen tyde*
> *The Lord that sent it, He knows all;*

A stolen tide! It swept in over England's east coast, blotting out estuary, marsh and fen, and Holland stood in the direct path of the storm. Wind force close on a hundred knots, and almost one quarter of that country lay below sea level—five million people, half the population, with no protection against the elements but the dykes they themselves had erected over the centuries.

> *That flow strewed wrecks about the grass,*
> *That ebbe swept out the flocks to sea;*
> *A fatal ebbe and flow, alas!*

Fatal it was. In that first onslaught the sea did not breach the protecting dykes; it swept in over the top of them. In places a twelve-foot wall of water rampaged through farm and village. And in that and succeeding nights 1800 people lost their lives; 10,000 farms and houses were destroyed, a further 40,000 damaged. Three hundred miles of dyke were swamped, and the tides, attacking the dykes often from the rear, tore sixty-seven major breaches.

Almost a hundred years ago an American writer, Mary Mapes Dodge, wrote a book called *Hans Brinker, or The Silver Skates,* and since then everybody's view of the Dutch and their dykes has been coloured by her picture of the gallant little boy who saved Haarlem by sticking his finger into a leak in the sea dyke. It's a ludicrous story for anybody who has actually seen a dyke, but it captured the world's imagination as a symbol, and since 1950 a statue of the little lockkeeper's son has stood by Haarlem's Woerder Lock. But on the night of January 31, 1953, a group of men did in fact what the little boy did in fiction . . . all that night they lay shoulder to shoulder against their crumbling dyke at Kalijnsplaat, supporting it and holding back the waters by the sheer weight of their bodies.

They were not heroes. Or if they were heroes, then half Holland was heroic that night, for they were just one of many groups who did what they could in a desperate situation and fought the flood tide the way their fathers had fought it before them. Holland has had one hundred and forty recorded disasters!

On December 14, 1287, all the land between the old Zuider Zee and the River Ems was inundated and fifty thousand people drowned. In November, 1421, a great polder, reclaimed two centuries before, disappeared in the south with seventy-two villages and another fifty thousand inhabitants. And before that, in the north, the men of Fleve and Almere lakes had been digging their own graves for centuries, cutting the peat that kept their land above the sea and burning it in their homes. The day of reckoning was not recorded, but it was about the year 1300 . . the sea came roaring in through the protecting dune islands and the dykes, and in one cataclysmic flood created the Zuider Zee out of the old peat lands. It is said that eighty thousand people perished, and only now is Holland reclaiming those lost lands.

Jan Preger, who showed me round these new polders, talked of the Scheldt estuaries he had known as a boy. "You can find skulls and things at low water in the drowned lands of Saaftinge," he said.

"Now?" I asked.

"Yes, now you can."

I told him how the great port of Dunwich on the East Coast of England had disappeared two hundred years ago, leaving graveyard gones sticking out over the beach from a sandy bluff. "We have that, too, in Holland," he said. "At Westenschouwen in Zeeland. There, in 1458, the whole town disappeared in the night, and now you can walk out at low tide and find the town and the streets and the houses still there; maybe three or four times a year you can go when the tide is low."

Holland as a country is quite unique, and to anybody who knows the sea and its destructive power, utterly fascinating, for geologically it has no right to exist. Half the population is living in what should be water or swamp. As one Frenchman put it, "God created the world, all except Holland, which the Dutch created themselves."

I remember the first time I saw it, sailing into the Hook of Holland on a yacht. It was high tide and the break-waters of the Maas entrance were awash, and my impression was of a vast expanse of sea and sky with only the spire of a church or the sales of a windmill to show that we were coming in to land. We sailed up to Rotterdam, past oil refineries and cranes and miles of warehouses; it was hard to realise that this, the second greatest port in the world, was all built on piles in a quaking land of bog. And then down through the rivers and canals to Flushing—locks and bridges and barges everywhere, and from the deck no land visible except the dykes on either side, their green tops in silhouette against the cloud-spattered sky. But when I climbed the mast, then I could see all the rich land of Holland laid out below the level of the water on which we sailed—way, way below it, as much as twenty feet.

Holland is, of course, the delta of the Rhine. They have other names for this river—the Waal, the Lek, the Yssel. But it is all the Rhine. Combined with the Maas and the Scheldt from the south, it fans out into a great delta area of sand and silt and peat bog with tide-built dunes along the coast. And far inland are heights of sand—old sand banks left by the eroding Rhine waters. In a few cases they reach up to 300 feet above sea level, a truly mountainous height in a land where a standing field of corn looks high as a hill in the surrounding flatness.

A man who looked at this tidal delta in the ninth century—a Moorish merchant—described it as a *sebcha,* a plain of salt water and mud. How different it is to-day with its two thousand eight hundred polders, or reclaimed areas, each protected by its dyke; and beyond the polders lie the main sea defences—first, the Watcher or main dyke, then the Sleeper, and finally the Dreamer. A hard land to create, with the enemy of sea and river water ever at the gate. A hard land to hold. But the enemy at the gate provides nearly five thousand miles of waterways and floats the products of Germany's industrial Ruhr to every quarter of the globe. Go to Rotterdam and in the dust of rebuilding you can feel the thrusting industrial might of resurgent Germany.

The Dutch are afraid of that resurgence. They admit that quite frankly, particularly the Dutch of Rotterdam. They have reason. On May 14, 1940, German bombers tore the heart out of old Rotterdam, and all the centre of the city was laid flat in a holocaust of high explosive and incendiaries. I can still remember, after all this time, with what sense of shock we in England heard the news of this attack. It was brutal, cold-blooded obliteration of a city. Later the defeated Germans destroyed half the port of Rotterdam, but it is that first murderous *blitzkreig* that the Dutch remember . . . and so that future generations shall not forget, Zadkine's statue stands in the middle of the rebuilt city, a tortured, impressionist figure, with arms upraised to ward off the blow and all the heart torn out of the contorted people.

But the Dutch are a practical people, and the waters of the Rhine flow through Rotterdam to the sea. Go up to the top of one of their new buildings and look over the half-built city to the cranes and the silver thread of the Maas. The tideway is black with barges, black with trade flowing down the Rhine. "Already the port is too small," Anton Schutter told me. We were looking at it from the top of the partially-reconstructed Laurens Tower, and he pointed to an expanse of green meadowland on the outskirts of the city. "We are going to dredge all those fields and make a new haven. Then Rotterdam is the greatest port in the world."

Jacob Hardingsveld, whose life's work is the painstaking reconstruction of this blitzed cathedral, took my arm and drew me to the other side of the scaffolding, not to show me his own great work, but to point to a big modern building that had been erected before the war. "Next year we will demolish that," he said, " and drive a great new motorway through to the Moos. Then," he added, with the intensity of a man looking into the future, " then we are in contact with our existence."

Walk through the Lijnbaan, the new shopping centre which is largely completed. Everything is very modern—the design of the buildings, the manner of display. It is different, too. The Dutch are surely the only people, except the Italians, who have the feel for the straight-line patterns of concrete and brick and glass . . . perhaps because these are all materials that are made of sand, and the Dutch have plenty of sand. Moreover, for generations they have landscaped their country with trees and public buildings to overcome the monotony of its flatness. They have now an inherited sense of the look of things, particularly the look of their skyline, and this artistic sense is apparent in the new city that is rising like a phœnix from the ashes of the old.

There is a feel about Rotterdam that I have experienced in no other city in the world. The Dutch there are in a building mood with their eyes on the future, the way I imagine the monks were when they built for the glory of God. You can feel it when you go to St. Laurens and talk to the stone masons cutting and cutting with hammer and chisel to recreate, block by block, the great cathedral that the Germans destroyed. Jacob Hardingsveld will tell you that they wanted to work in the old original sandstone, though they knew their lungs would be damaged by silicosis. The same mood of self-dedication is apparent throughout the city. High up in a big new office block I talked to Johan Smits, secretary of town planning. Here is a small, intense man with the reins of the future in his hands. " Already we are planning to the year 2,000," he said as he took me through a great room stacked with models of Rotterdam as it will be—not just the city centre, but whole satellite towns and neighbourhood units, a hundred thousand houses in all.

In a spongy land, where the very roads sink as much as a

metre in a year and every building must be supported on sixty-foot concrete piles, it takes nerve and a lot of confidence to build for the future on such a scale.

Those who go to Rotterdam to look at a city of the future invariably make two pilgrimages into the past—one to Delft to see a medieval town as quaint as Bruges, to be soothed by the peace of its tree-lined canals and the sweetness of its carillon bells, and, of course, to buy the world-famous, blue-patterned Delftware; the other to Delfshaven, the little port from which the Pilgrim Fathers sailed. *A shining example of civil and religious liberty many of whose institutions . . . have given to the new world a distinctive character.* So reads the plaque that commemorates their stay in Amsterdam, the city to which they fled from England in 1607. They moved to Leyden and on July 22, 1620, they sailed from Delfshaven in the *Speedwell* for Plymouth where they trans-shipped to the larger *Mayflower*. You can still see the church where they gathered to pray for the last time before leaving the land that had been their asylum for twelve years, embarking for the unknown.

I also made two other excursions into the past—to Schiedam and to Kinderdijk. To Schiedam because I am fond of Holland's gin and this is where it is made. The waterway running down to the Maas has an atmosphere and an aroma all of its own—an aroma of juniper or geneva, which is the origin of our word gin. And the talk there is all of liquor, of wonderful, strange concoctions dreamed up over the centuries by men who have made their peat waters as famous as the Scots have made the waters of Glen Spey.

At de Kuypers I learned from Simon Steenbergen how it all started. Around 1600 the Dutch were short of wine due to the wars, and an enterprising Frenchman began distilling and shipping dehydrated wine to which water could be added on arrival. This attempt to economise in shipping space produced, not wine, but a most excellent new kind of brew that became rapidly popular on both sides of the

North Sea under the name of *brandewijn,* or burnt wine,
better known as brandy. With their business sense, the
Dutch were soon feverishly brewing their own corn distilla-
tions. By 1695 sailors putting into the Schiedamsdijk,
Rotterdam's old red light area, would first go along to the
coopers—the men who made the brandy casks in the
Kuipersgang or Cooper's Way—for a little of something
that does you good, but which was not as expensive as im-
ported brandy wine. The brothers John and Peter of the
coopers—de Kuypers—achieved something of a name for
themselves as distillers of geneva, and soon the factory of
de Kuypers was going full blast to keep Dutch sailors warm
at sea and happy ashore.

Holland's gin should, of course, be drunk neat. Nobody
but a barbarian would try to mix a dry Martini with it!
But from adding juniper to alcohol, the Dutch progressed to
other ingredients, and now they have a formidable array of
liqueurs—Parfait Amour, Fladderak, Pimpeltjeus, dozens of
them. In Amsterdam, at the sign of the naked Bacchus in
the Pijlsteeg, is a little seventeenth-century bar, the Wijnand
Fockink. It is the wine-tasting bar of the old Fockink dis-
tillery, and in this charming setting, with its racks of grand
old men of the bottlers' art, you bow down by custom to set
your lips to the brimful glass of that coffee-coloured elixir
known as Half-en-Halfje.

Pimpeltjeus has an amusing history. K.L.M., running
special flights to South Africa to celebrate the three
hundredth anniversary of Jan van Riebeck's landing at the
Cape, found that the period menu they wished to reproduce
included Pimpeltjeus as the liqueur. They asked Simon
Steenbergen whether he could produce it for them. He had
never heard of it. How was it made? And when K.L.M.
said they didn't know, he said, " Ah, that is different. Then
I know how to make it." And he dreamed up a new liqueur
for them that is not unlike Italian Strega, and now de
Kuypers sell it under the old name of Pimpeltjeus.

In a warm glow I left Schiedam for Kinderdijk—to look

at windmills. I have always loved windmills. At school I lived four years of my life in sight of the towering sails of one of the few still working in England, and perhaps because this was a corn mill, I always thought of windmills as corn-grinders. It wasn't until I had made several visits to Holland that I realised the Dutch used them mainly to solve their water problems. At one time they had over seven thousand of them, the wind in their swirling sails providing the power to lift the water, step by step, a metre at a time, from the polders to the canals.

At Kinderdijk, some ten miles east of Rotterdam, you can find the biggest cluster of the remaining twelve hundred; mill after mill, one behind the other, standing down there in the sunken polder lands with their big sails spread like dumb giants in perpetual conclave. They are still working, these mills, still lifting the water above the roofs of the little thatched houses snugged against the dyke. I introduced myself to one that was painted green with carved front board decorated red and white. It was pretty as a picture, standing, archaic and wonderful, in a field full of buttercups and Frisian cattle. Faded canvas sails were stretched across two of its four arms and it was turning to a moderate breeze with a zing, zing, zing of power.

" In winter I haf four sails up," the mill-keeper told me.

" Four sails?" I said. " But in winter the wind is stronger."

" *Ja*. But in winter more water, eh?"

Water, always water. Every single drop of rain to be laboriously lifted ten, fifteen, twenty feet. " Come. I show you inside." He was more like a seaman than a windmill-keeper with his black clothes and sailor's cap. We went through the wind-blown spray of the big iron wheel that was scooping the water up one step farther on its way to the sea. Clogs lay in a neat yellow row outside the door, the way you see them throughout all the country areas of Holland, and inside was a small cosy room full of women and children. The women were still and silent, only their fingers moving and they sewed, and the only sound was the rumble of the mill's great cog-wheels beyond the curve of the centre wall. The clogs, the crowded room, the straining, grinding noise of the mill's efforts—so had it been since the Dutch created the first polder.

There is a scheme now to preserve these old windmills by converting them to the production of electricity and so giving them the chance to earn their keep, for as water-lifters their days are numbered; in the new polders of the Zuider Zee two or three big diesel pumping stations suffice to keep the water level down in a hundred thousand acres.

To learn about these new polders, I went first to The Hague to see van Oosterhout. I found him in an office in the Binnenhof, that ancient brick pile whose cobbled court-yard has rung to the march of Lowland history since the thirteenth century, and I have seldom met a man who believed more fervently in what he was doing. Like Hardings-veld and Smits of Rotterdam, his mind was on the future—fifty, even a hundred years. The son of a docker, he was the mouthpiece of the Minister of Transport and Public Works—the Waterstaat; a short dynamic man, who talked of things he will never live to see completed.

"Every year," he told me, "there are sixty thousand more people in Holland. We must find work for them. We start new industries. But we are an agricultural people. We must have more land—much more land. Look! This is what we do now. . . ." Maps were spread, books, illustrations—all the future was flung at me in a rush of words. "First the Zuider Zee—we reclaim half a million acres there. That will take another ten years, maybe more.

"Meantime, we commence work on the Delta Plan. That is the second stage. It is essential. That was shown by the disaster of '53. Look! We make enclosing dams there and there and there." He drew swift pencil marks across all the main outlets of the Rhine north of Flushing. "It means giant sluices, secondary dams—and the tides are stronger in the south. Maybe it takes twenty-five years. I don't know. We have so much to do—all the reconstruction after the great flood, and we must raise the height of many of our dykes. All the time we are studying the problems in our water laboratories at Delft. And when the Delta Plan is finished, then all behind the dams is fresh water, for drinking in times of drought, for the crops—it will drive out the salt which is destroying the richness of our soil.

"And then, when it is finished"—he looked up at me quickly, intent on his dream—"then we will begin the third stage." More pencil marks, short lines linking the off-shore islands of the north—Texel, Vlieland, Terschelling, Ameland, Schiermonnikoog. "All the northern flats enclosed. Then we have reduced our coastline to three hundred miles. Then we are safe, even though we know the land is sinking by almost one foot every century. Or maybe it is the tides that are rising. Whatever it is, this threat must be met or there is no more Holland. And this is how we do it."

They were planning for the year 2,000, *and beyond*. I stared at him in amazement. "Where will you find the money?" I asked.

"The Dutch people," he said. "They will find it." They always had. They had this thing in common, this enemy at their gates. "Besides," he added, "it pays for itself—in land improvement and land reclamation. It is an investment.

"And then, of course," he added, "we have still another plan—Plan Four."

"Plan Four?" I was incredulous.

"Plan Four is when we throw a dam across the Straits of Dover and another between Harwich and the Hook and reclaim England for the Netherlands." He looked at me, his grey eyes twinkling. It was Dutch humour at its best, made wry with the sense of the past, for hadn't we taken their trade and made ourselves sovereign of the seas between us, and on the other side hadn't the presence of Dutch ships in the Thames rankled since the days of Pepys?

The sea is Holland's Enemy Number One, the constant protagonist against which the Dutch will always close their ranks. But it is also their friend. You have only to visit Amsterdam to see how much they owe to it. Here is a city of a milion people with a great history that is founded on the disaster of the Zuider Zee inundation. The Zuider Zee gave the people living on the Amstel River access to the North Sea and the Baltic, and as early as the thirteenth century they began to construct their dams and drive their house piles. Defensive ditches followed, and by the early 1600s they were building broad concentric canals of *grachten* and constructing a city more fantastic than Venice, a giant spider's web of water, with fifty canals and four hundred bridges that remain virtually intact to this day.

It is difficult to believe, as you stroll in the quiet of evening along the brick-paved streets that border the canals, that you are seeing it much as the rich Amsterdam merchant saw it three hundred years ago. The buildings, built largely of brick, look quite new as they stand shoulder to shoulder in solid ranks, their big windows looking out on to the canals. And then you notice that the upper windows are mostly smaller and that in the apex of each stone gable is a sturdy wooden gallows with a hook on it, and you realise that these were built as merchants' houses, the upper floors their warehouses and the gallows for tackle to hoist their wares. Here and there you can find a date inscribed in the stone. It always seems to be about 1670.

But there are some older buildings, too. The Oude Kerk, for instance, which dates from 1300 and is one of the few examples I have seen of a church that stands as it was built, with the houses crowding so close that they are an integral part of the whole. And nearby, at the bottom of the old Zeedijk, is a little tower called the " Tower of Tears," because it marked the end of Amsterdam and so many women stood there and wept as their men warped their vessels out into the haven at the beginning of a voyage to distant parts. One such voyage is commemorated in a bronze plaque erected by the Greenwich Historical Society of New York in 1927. It reads : *From this ancient "Tower of Tears" erected 1482 A.D. Henry Hudson set sail April 4th, 1609 A.D. on the vessel "Half Moon" on that voyage of discovery destined to bring him to the Harbor of New York and the Hudson River.* Did anyone weep, I wonder, for this Englishman who was obsessed with the idea of a North-West Passage and died a tragic death in search of it? He was in Dutch employ when he sailed from Amsterdam and twenty years later Dutch settlers followed the trail that he had blazed to the Hudson River and built New Amsterdam, later to be renamed New York after James, Duke of York, whom England's King Charles II had nominated "Lord Proprietor" of all that coast.

Wealth poured into the merchant houses you see along the *grachten*, until trade developed into banking, and the precious stones from the Indies and from Africa made Amsterdam the diamond centre of the world. Hitler lost them the marketing side of the business, for the Jews who fled to England returned to Antwerp because it was liberated long before Amsterdam. But the Dutch are still the world's cutters, and at the Moppes & Zoone factory Robert Streep, who handled the buying and selling told me that the loss in cutting from the rough stone was fifty per cent and that one-third of what you pay for a finished brilliant represents the labour of cutting it. With the middle man's profit as well, it doesn't seem to matter whether a method of manufacturing synthetic diamonds economically is discovered or not—the value of a stone is so largely in the work put into it.

There are fifty-eight facets to be cut in a brilliant, a lot of work. Going round the factory, handling diamonds like beads of glass, Peter van Rosendaal tried to explain to me how he was able to keep track of each individual stone, however small—and they have cut one brilliant as small as a pin's head. I never did discover how it was done, for in this one factory they have two hundred and thirty people all busily cutting and polishing. There are many other factories in Amsterdam, and in the south of Holland, particularly in Brabant, hundreds of farmers spend the long winter evenings cutting stones that they have bought themselves and will sell again when they have worked them into brilliants and baguettes and eight-cuts. The Dutch alone seem to have this art developed to the highest pitch. Maybe it is because their national characteristics include patience and industry—characteristics that are essential to convert a tidal estuary of mud flats into the market garden of Europe.

These characteristics, however, were not so noticeable in the sons of Amsterdam bankers two hundred years ago, and with the growth of a rentier class and the march of Napoleon and of the industrial revolution, the power of the city faded. It was not until her outlet into the Zuider Zee silted up that she was finally stirred out of her lethargy. Then, with sudden boldness, she cut through the coastal dunes in 1876 and brought the sea to her gates. The North Sea Canal was almost the capacity of the Panama, and with typical Dutch enthusiasm the largest of the Ijmuiden locks is big enough to take the *Queen Mary*.

It was whilst looking at this huge basin with Jan Preger of the Waterstaat that I first heard the phrase "water household." "Every time we open that lock we let in 3,000 tons of salt—not salt water, you understand, but salt. What to do with it, that is the question." And indeed it is a question. If it were allowed to remain, it would build up in the inland waters and percolate into the surrounding polder lands. That is what they mean by water household —to see each problem as a whole, from the point of view of the community as a whole. It made me understand what van Oosterhout had meant when talking of the benefits of the Delta Plan. "Already," he had said, "the salt water has reached Rotterdam." He had spoken of it the way a general speaks of a front overrun by the enemy.

The salt from the Ijmuiden locks necessitates the creation of huge fresh water lakes on the perimeter of the reclaimed

lands of the Zuider Zee. The height of these lakes will be
governed by the height of the 40-foot oak piles on which
Amsterdam is built, for if the level were allowed to drop
below the tops of the piles, they would rot in the air and all
Amsterdam would collapse. Nothing can be done in one
area of Holland without other areas being affected. Co-
operation is essential. And because this has been so since
the sunken lands first grey crops, the Dutch will always
make sacrifices for the good of their country. This is a
basic factor in their social and political life and is even
carried into their labour relations, which is why the word
" strike " is virtually unknown. The fact that the Communists are always in a separate union of their own, helps,
of course—no tail-wagging-dog and devil-take-the-rest-of-
the-people attitude in Holland!

There was work in progress a few miles inland of
Ijmuiden. A tunnel was being driven under the canal. I
say " driven under," but in typical Dutch fashion they
were shifting the canal about bodily and building the tunnel in open cuts. This seemed to me a somewhat laborious
method of construction, almost medieval, until I learned
what their problem had been. Water household again. The
bed of the canal was porous. Salt water would have per-
colated to the walls of the tunnel. So they were building it
in an open cut and then covering it with a layer of non-
porous clay.

We had come north from The Hague in search of what
a Waterstaat booklet aptly called " fresh fields and polders
new." We came by way of Bennebroek, Hillegom, Lisse and
Sassenheim, names all the world knows for their bulbs. The
season was over, the Keukenhof show just finished; but
here and there the fields showed splashes of brilliant colour
and everywhere men were working, kneeling, their hands
busy. Herons stood in silent sentinel watch for fish in the
ditches and the land lay flat under a Dutch painter's sky,
blue like the sea and dotted with cloud-galleons. Centuries
of community landscape gardening had broken up the

ruler straight edge of the horizon with tree clumps. Churches raised old spires and windmills their arms. It was a quiet country with the peace and repose of long occupation.

But after Alkmaar, that much-publicised town of cheeses, the landscape changed abruptly at the crossing of a dyke. We were in Wieringermeer then, first polder to be reclaimed from the Zuider Zee, and if the land looked flat before, it was now flat as a board. The trees were not yet full grown and the big barns attached to the farmhouses stood like mamoths against the flat skyline. And beyond that skyline was the Zuider Zee, or what the Dutch have left of it.

Nobody visiting the Wieringermeer now can readily appreciate the magnitude of the task of reclamation. It is just another piece of Holland, a little flatter perhaps and with a new-land feeling about the villages—the sort of feel you get in the development areas of western Canada. But go a few miles north to Den Oever, which is at the northeastern end of what was once the island of Wieringen, then the magnitude of it hits you in the face. You stand there by the great concrete blocks of the discharging sluices and ahead of you runs a ruler-straight road that disappears over the lip of the horizon as it follows the curve of the earth. To the left of it rises a green dyke top. Climb that dyke and you are looking out over the Wadden Sea to the dune islands and the North Sea beyond. All this is salt water, tidal water; this is the sea they conquered. And on the other side of the road? Water again—water all the way to the horizon with ships sailing on it. This is the old Zuider Zee, now called the Ysselmeer, for it is no longer a sea, but a fresh-water lake.

The story of this fantastic dam is worth repeating, for this is probably the biggest single project achieved by man since the building of the Great Wall of China. The idea of enclosing the Zuider Zee began to be considered about the middle of the 1800s, but it wasn't until the disaster of 1916, when large areas of North Holland were inundated, that the decision to go ahead was taken. Dr. Lely's plan was the one adopted, and in 1923, after four years of preparatory work, the first stage was begun, the building of a dyke from the mainland to Wieringen Island, with Lely himself as the Minister in charge. This was relatively easy and was completed in two years. Ahead of them then stretched twenty miles of open sea. They started from both ends, and at the same time created an artificial island in the middle, so that they had two more working points. And the incredible thing is that nobody, not even Lely himself, knew for certain that it could be done. All that work, all that colossal expenditure of energy, material and money, and they weren't sure that the sea wouldn't beat them in the end. How could they be? Such a thing had never been tried before.

The trouble, of course, was the tidal rise and fall in the North Sea, at this point anything up to eight feet. It meant a mean difference of levels between the waters inside the dyke construction and the waters outside of up to four feet, and as construction advanced the difference in water levels was bound to build up tremendous sluicing power as the tides ebbed and flowed through the narrowing gaps. Current-checking dams had to be built across all the main channels. This was done by first sinking huge woven mattresses of willow, weighted with stone, and then piling rocks above them until the dam had been raised to just below sea level, this causing the scouring currents to be confined to the surface waters.

But in the closing of the last two gaps, the power of the water became almost uncontrollable. It was scouring channels to a depth of a hundred feet and sweeping the dam material away almost as fast as it was brought to the site. The last gap but one was the worst. The checking dam itself was in danger of being swept away and, in addition, a south-westerly gale had already hit Holland. It was a race against time with the whole dyke threatened. The full

strength of the dyke-building fleet was shifted fifteen yards
to the inner side of the checking dam, and this shift of effort
won the day.

For those who like statistics, here they are. The dyke is
20-22 feet above mean sea level, anything up to 120 feet
above the bed of the sea. It is 300 feet wide at sea level,
600 feet wide at sea-bed base. More than 500 vessels were
employed in its construction and the total area enclosed
was over half a million acres. The method of building was
to dredge a channel along the dyke line where necessary,
flank with boulder clay dredged up from deposits in the
Zuider Zee and delivered to the site by hopper barge, and
to fill between with a core of sand blown in by giant suction
dredges, the whole made secure against tide and wave by
acres of willow mattress overlaid with stone. At the point
of final closure the Dutch have erected a simple tower from
the top of which the world can view the whole gigantic
project. *Here the dyke was closed*, 28th May, 1932, is
inscribed on one side. On the other : *A nation that lives,
builds for its future.*

But you do not enclose a great area like the Zuider Zee
without upsetting the lives of many people. " It was then
a question of the glass eel," Jan Preger told me as we stood
by the sluice gates. He took me into the Information
Room, and there, amongst the photographs and models of
the construction of the dam, was a diagram of the strange
journey of the young eel from the breeding grounds of the
Sargasso Sea to the Zuider Zee. And then he told me the
story of a deeply religious people's belief that the Wrath of
God had fallen upon Holland for disturbing the waters of
His creation. The fisher folk of the Zuider Zee are
dependent upon the eel, and in the year following the
closing of the gap the eel failed to come. Instead, there
was a plague of mosquitos. They rose up out of the
Ysselmeer so thick that houses and trees were coated, people
couldn't drive their cars and small boys played snowballs

with the cloying masses. It was a visitation of God, said the old fishermen, like the plagues of Egypt.

The answer, fortunately, was simple; it was to open the lock gates at night, for the eels were there all right, but sleeping in the mud during daylight hours. As soon as the authorities thought of opening the locks at night, the eels came in in their millions to feed on mosquito larvae and grow fat. Now there are no plagues, and the eel-fishing industry is more prosperous than ever.

Eel and the new herring—these are Holland's two delicacies. But the new herring has only a short season, about two weeks at the beginning of June. Then there are stalls selling them in every town, and all Holland, from labourers in clogs to business men with briefcases, can be seen standing in the street, their heads thrown back and the salted herring, held by its tail, disappearing whole down their throats. The eels, on the other hand, come in through the sluices from May till September, and if you miss the new herring you can always ask for *Gerookte Paling,* smoked eel. Maybe it is an acquired taste, but, eaten with a glass of Bokma, I for one find it delicious.

For anyone who knows Holland well, the crossing of the enclosing dam is a sad pilgrimage. The great dyke, so straight, so new, so much a product of our times, cuts right across the past. You drive your car where Hudson sailed, where the galleons sailed that made Amsterdam great—here beneath your wheels passed ships of war to fight the English for mastery of the seas. Fleets of up to five hundred ships came and went through the passage that no longer exists.

Even now, though their coast is doomed, the people of the Zuider Zee ports cling to the past, to their religion, to their customs, and to their national costumes. Marken, a Calvinistic island off the Amsterdam shore, was way back in the past when I last saw it—a little lost world that time and land reclamation was soon to overrun. Models of ships hung for God's blessing in the church, and men, women and children all wore their traditional dress. It was a little selfconscious perhaps, but Volendam, on the mainland just across the water was real enough. This is a Catholic fishing port with modern brick houses, and it is bustling with life. Go there on a Saturday when the fleet is in and the girls have finished work; then the men sit on the quay and the women are shopping in their little black witches' hats. The girls here are prettier than anywhere in Holland, and they all look like sisters, tall and sparkling and fresh in their gay aprons and little knitted scarves.

Among the less-known places of traditional dress are Spakenburg, where you can see the girls cycling back from work in a dress made gay with wide starched shoulders; Hierden and Urk, and, farther inland, Staphorst, where the women's headdress is a tight-fitting silver casque with sides reaching down across the cheeks. A strange place, Staphorst, with a strange dress and a strange custom. By tradition girls offer themselves by leaving their bedroom window open on certain fixed nights. If a child results, then marriage follows. No child, no marriage. And if any ungallant fellow should be unwilling to accept his responsibilities, the men of Staphorst call him to task in no uncertain manner. But surely that can't happen now, you say—not in modern times? I can't answer for it myself, but ask anybody in Holland, " Are the windows still open at Staphorst?" and they will answer, with a smile and a wink, " Yes, still open. You want to try it?" It is a joke to them. But I suspect it is no joke to the people of Staphorst, whose long, thatched farms, painted blue and white, straggle in ribbon-development across the main highway to the north. They are not friendly and their hard, uncompromising stares remind you that the custom exists and that it has in some degree alienated them from the outside world.

It is not only in North Holland and the coasts of the old Zuider Zee that tradition and national costume cling. At Scheveningen the older women still wear the cap with the

two deadly gold pins stuck out like horns above the eyes,
and this a shilling tram ride from The Hague. In the
south, too, in Beveland and Zeeland: I remember sailing
down through the canals one year and reaching Flushing
the night of the great fair. There was everything from
hurdy-gurdies to an appalling obstacle course of collapsing
staircases and swaying passages, a mile or more of booths
jammed around three huge dock basins, and all Walcheren
Island was out on the spree—boys and girls as well as the
old people in their costumes, and all as happy as could be
on Holland's gin. The women were a pretty sight in their
huge starched bonnets and little lace caps with gold springs
beside the eyes.

But modern clothes are now swamping the traditional
village costumes. It is a pity, because many of these costumes are vastly becoming. However, if you go to Arnhem's
open-air museum, you can still see them all, and the reason
for their passing becomes clear. Here, amongst the pine
woods of the Hooge Veluwe, the Dutch are gathering all
their past together, the way the Scandinavian countries
have done. Old farmhouses have been transported bodily,
each representative of their particular region, and each
furnished with original pieces. There are windmills, too, of
every type; and in a big new building, beautifully presented
in wax figure groups, are all the costumes of Holland—
some that you can still see in daily wear, but most of them
of a bygone age that you could otherwise see only by pry-
ing into the trunks of farmhouses up and down the land.

Becoming they may be, but look at those wedding groups
—all that needlework, all that elaborate embroidery, that
fine lace! With the jewellery, of course, it is different.
This is durable stuff, treasured heirlooms passed down
from mother to daughter. It is all there, ready to wear—the
deadly pins of Scheveningen, the coiled gold springs of
Zeeland, the gold and silver plates, and those little squares
of beaten gold worn over the eyes like twin mirrors, like
the wings of golden butterflies. But clothes have to be made,

and in a modern world the girls no longer have time on their hands. Like the windmills that had a sign language of their own, telling of birth and death and disaster—a language that was used by the Resistance in the last war— the costumes of the women, by colour, knot or headdress, announced to the world the age and condition of the wearer, her district and even her village. All this proud love of place has already vanished in the inland districts, lost amongst the neat little houses with their picture windows that line the modern motor highways. Soon it will vanish from the doomed coast of the Zuider Zee as farmers from the outside move into the new polders. And in the south—in Zeeland and Beveland—it will vanish, too, when the Delta Plan is completed and the estuaries sealed by dams.

At the far end of the great Zuider Zee dyke is Friesland. I remember once arriving in Dokkum, the place where they killed St. Boniface, and asking the way in English.

" Sorry—speak no English," was the reply. " I Friesland." So might a Welshman reply west of the border in Britain, for Friesland is as old as its artificial mound dwellings and it didn't become a part of Holland until 1804.

Great farms, house and barn all one and elaborately tiled in dark blue, shoulder their huge bulks against the sky, and the place names all seem to end in " um "—Dokkum, Hallum, Irnsum, Arum, Winsum, Tzum. Go north along the coast to Holwerd, out along the shell-encrusted causeway that stretches a dead-end arm into the sea to meet the Ameland Ferry, and all along the horizon you can see the apparently uninterrupted stretch of the dune islands, low and flat like Pacific atolls strangely transported to northern waters. All this vast expanse of water, all this sea will be land one day !

From this view of the Friesche Wad, its waters chopped by the wind the way Dutch artists paint their shallow seas, I drove south and west through the canal-encircled capital of Leeuwarden and the great barn country beyond, to the shores of the old Zuider Zee. Here, close under the age-old dyke, is one of the loveliest roads in Holland, one car wide, with the green dyke on the right and still water, mirroring grass and reeds, on the left, and every ten miles an ancient port : Makkum, where a master potter paints colours bluer than Delft; Workum, making its own individual pottery, with a great brick tower and a beautiful crest; Hindeloopen, a tight-packed huddle of ancient houses, a town in miniature, with miniature cobbled streets and a miniature hump-backed bridge lit with carriage lamps. And then eastward from Stavoren, on a little road running a causeway thread through a great mere, the road surface seemingly no higher than the surrounding water. And in the evening light—that wonderful translucent light of the wide Dutch skies—a little huddle of Frisians in every field, fat strained udders between the knees of the men milking, and all along the horizon the brick towers of the churches leaning their steep gables. Through Sneek, with its beautiful water gate, and so back to the Oostergoo at Grouw to drink a Bokma by the water's edge and watch the yachts come in, white sails scudding through fields of buttercups and sorrel.

All this is old country, but go south from here and cross the dyke at Lemmer, and suddenly it is different. You are in a flat pan then, the barns all new, the roads straight and the farms neat little rectangular holdings. This is the Noordoostpolder, Holland's dream-come-true. They drained it during the war with young men working, safe from the Germans, in a sea of mud. You would expect a rough bed here, for it is a raw, agricultural land. Instead, Emmeloord has a hotel that is one of the best in Holland, 't Voorhuys, or as they like to call it, " *Het hotel op de bodem van de zee* " — the hotel at the bottom of the sea. Only fifteen years ago the table at which you dine was sixteen feet below the windswept waters of the Zuider Zee.

Visitors pour into Emmeloord from all parts of the world, and it was nothing for Henk Wierenga, who was manager of 't Voorhuys, to serve lunch for five hundred guests. They come to see the work of Engineer Elizabeth van den Ban, who planned the town before the war, and they come to see the polder, for it is pure socialism, and socialism at its best. Everything is owned by the State—the fields, the farms, the workmen's cottages, the villages, even Emmeloord and it £100,000 hotel. And, stranger, the Dutch like it that way. They are co-operatives by nature. There were more than four hundred applicants for each holding, and a 75-acre farm, including reclamation, drainage, buildings, light, water and roads, stands the State in at 360,000 guilders. On present rentals, it will take one hundred years to pay off the initial cost. But what is a hundred years when you are reclaiming land for all time.

There is a museum at Schokland in the Noordoostpolder that is as fascinating as any in the world. No less than 156 wrecks were located in the reclamation of this one polder and the remnants of some of these can still be seen, together with examples of rigging and cargoes going back several centuries. And in the church, that is all that remains of a once-thriving island community, you can see everything of interest brought up by the dredgers from the wrecks and the drowned hamlets and the prehistoric sands of the Zuider Zee—pipes and silver tools and Stone Age axes and flint sickles and daggers.

From that extraordinary museum I went south through the old Hanseatic port of Kampen, down along the coast to Harderwijk and out along the sixteen miles of the Knardijk, to see land in the course of reclamation. Here an artificial island had been created in the very middle of the Zuider Zee. This island is now Lelystad, a growing town that is planned as the centre for the new lands. But when I saw it, the few houses were lost amidst a litter of willow stacks, stone heaps and floating machinery of all kinds. On every side was water. To the east, there were fishing boats under full sail, brown canvas dipping gently to the lift and fall of the waves. Within a year, I was told, all this would be a sea of mud, the water pumped out and-the first reeds growing. Now there will be crops and farms, and the ships I saw, with their brown sails, will never sail there again.

And what of the natural islands of the Zuider Zee? Schokland had been abandoned long before it became a part of the Noordoostpolder, but Urk was still a thriving island of fisherfolk when the dyke fingers of the engineers reached out to its harbour piers. Before that, the only bus ever to reach the island was driven into the port over the ice. I was told the story by the son of the man who drove it. They were out of liquid refreshment for both bus and humans by the time they arrived in Urk, and after skating back to the mainland for fresh supplies, they foundered their vehicle in a gallant attempt to sail it into Kampen harbour like a ship, too fuddled to realise that a shift of wind had freed the port of ice!

When the seas behind them were drained, how did they feel, these dark men of Urk in their baggy trousers? An island one minute, a part of the mainland the next . . . for an independent, God-fearing people, who had been the terror of the coastal towns whenever they stormed into port at the week-end, it must have come as a sad blow. And when the Zuider Zee is all land, then it will be the turn of the off-shore islands, and after that the fishermen of the Scheldt estuaries will have to start thinking of farming. So drastic a change, and all within the space of a few generations; the sea constantly being pushed back, the land taking a new shape. Will the people then change also? I hope not. But the Dutch character is water-fed. " Then " —Jacob Hardingsveld had said, pointing to the Maas— " then we are in contact with our existence." Those were the words of an artist who saw his country with clarity, saw it full of vigour and life only when it was in contact with the waters out of which it had been born.

V. CANADA

I. GO WEST YOUNG MAN

It was late afternoon, pale, translucent, dry as ice, as we came in to land on a dust-brown airfield that seemed to have no end, for the country ran out flat like the sea to the horizon's edge. I had been flying since early morning, and at each stage in the westward journey, the plane's shifting population had become more colourful, the city suits dwindling, the pale faces leaving, to be replaced by men in broader and broader hats, their skin browner, their bodies leaner and harder, their shirts brighter; until now, arrived in Edmonton, our human freight was mostly of the prairie lands, redolent of cattle, oil and corn.

Dazed with the long flight, I followed the others out towards the airport building, and the dryness of the air caught at my throat, the startling clarity of it dazzled my eyes. Slim-hipped men in blue jeans and cowboy hats lounged against the rail of the parking lot, their steeds behind them gleaming chromium in the sunshine. *Hi! Hi there! It sure is good to see you back.* Everybody seemed to know everybody else. A small town airfield, I thought, not realising that it was already on its way to becoming one of the busiest freight fields in the world.

But then it was my first visit to Canada, and though my contacts in the eastern cities had sketched a picture for me of a wild north land full of Dan McGrew types prospecting for minerals, few of them had seen it for themselves. The future was barely glimpsed in Ottawa, even then, and they had not bothered to tell me that all the North was supplied by plane out of Edmonton, with gold, uranium and furs piling in.

The Canadian West is a long way from the seat of Government, and standing there on Edmonton airfield, I felt suddenly overpowered by the vastness of the country. I was alone and very conscious of being a stranger, for it was different to anything I had ever experienced before, more foreign than a foreign country, the foreign-ness accentuated by the lack of language barrier; in fact, it had a sense of unreality about it, for it was a little like the film set of an American Western.

Standing there, alone and a stranger, I could not know that in the next three months I was to grow to love this country, to grow into it until I felt I belonged there. It was only later, on a subsequent visit, when I was no longer bewitched by the novelty of it, that I was to see the flaws.

But my first impression, which was one of rawness, has always remained. In Montreal and Ottawa and Toronto, I had felt reasonably at home; they were recognisable as something between European and American cities. I had had contacts, too, and everybody had been extraordinarily helpful, particularly my friends in Trans-Canada Airlines and the Canadian Pacific Railways. They alone had made it possible for me to cross Canada on a limited dollar allowance, for coast-to-coast travel is costly in a country broader than the Atlantic. And in Ottawa, the Department of Mines had gone to a lot of trouble to give me all the information they could about the new oilfields. For it was oil that had brought me west.

I had caught the first whiff of it back in London, at Canada House. In 1950, four years after the end of the war, people in Britain had no real inkling of Canada's fabulous future. There was no whisper then of the Canadian boom to come or the political stature that was to help pull the chestnut of our Suez debacle out of the fire, and the popular conception of Canada was still confined, as it had been for half a century, to the Mounties, the Hudson's Bay Company and the wild North of London, Service and Ballantyne.

But at Canada House, when I had pressed them for a new background, something with which to replace these outworn themes, they had, almost diffidently, proffered me oil as a possibility. A new field was opening up in Alberta, and with a sudden vision of the Rocky Mountains towering above a mass of derricks, I had armed myself with oil company introductions and had decided to head west as soon as I had made my contacts in the cities of the east.

"You Mr. Innes?" Two men in white nylon shirts and broad-brimmed hats stood facing me. "My name's Hume Cronyn. We're from Imperial Oil."

I was suddenly no longer a stranger, but somebody expected like all the rest of the plane's passengers. A visit to an office in Toronto nearly a fortnight ago had crystallised into instructions passed to Edmonton. The vastness of the country dwindled, became less overpowering. It was from that moment that I began to feel at home, and I think it is to Hume Cronyn, more than any other Canadian, that I owe that sense of longing that has never quite left me—the longing to be a young man in his twenties again and to head west into a new country just opening up.

He took me to the airport hotel, a sprawling pseudo-log-cabin affair, and in the clubroom of the petroleum executives, over Canadian rye whisky, he asked me where I wanted to go, what I wanted to see. That wasn't difficult. I'd had all day to think about it. "Leduc," I said. That was the new oilfield.

"Leduc's not very interesting now," he said. "Just Christmas trees."

I didn't know what he meant by that. "There's a complete new town there I was told I ought to see."

"Yeah, Devon. But it's just a tidy little bunch of houses. Nothing more, except it's got a night club, the only one in Alberta."

But I hadn't come five thousand miles to see a night club. "There are gas flares, aren't there?" I said a little desperately. "I was told I should see the gas flares there at night."

"Yeah, I guess you could see the gas flares." He

sounded uninterested. "The place I'd like to show you is Redwater. That's real interesting. A new field just starting up. But it's quite a way out," he added, as though that ruled it out. "What else did they tell you you oughter see?"

"Oh, an Albertan dawn," I answered lightly, because I felt I wasn't getting anywhere. "And the Rocky Mountains, of course."

"The Rocky Mountains? Geez! They're the best part of two hundred miles, and there's still snow up there."

I thought it best then to leave the subject of what I wanted to see and get what I could out of him in the way of information. We finished the bottle of rye whilst he showed me newspaper cuttings of outback farmers, broke to the wide, whose land had suddenly become worth a fortune. "That's unusual," he said. "Mostly farmers don't own the mineral rights." Apparently in most cases the rights didn't go with the land, but were retained by the provincial government or owned by the railways who had been granted the land bordering the tracks as an incentive in the race westward to the coast at the end of the nineteenth century. Alberta was desperately poor, he said. Almost two-thirds of the government's income went on servicing the provincial debt. "But at this rate, we reckon there won't be any debt in five years' time." And then he was talking about summer farming and how the land was becoming a dust bowl. "Just like it is down in the States," he said. "And for the same reason. The Government's trying to introduce legislation to make farmers look after their land, but it's difficult. The farmers don't like interference, and this is a farmers' province. They elect the government."

The bottle finished, we went into the pine-boarded dining-room and ate huge, rather tough, T-bone steaks off wooden platters as big as breadboards. And then he drove me into Edmonton, past rotting boards that numbered non-existent streets in hundreds. "There's optimism for you," he said. "This town was laid out by the old-timers of the

Turner Valley oilfield at the beginning of the century. The oil boom went to their heads and they laid it out as a city bigger than New York."

"Maybe they'll be proved right in the end?" I suggested. "I was told this was a boom town."

"Sure it's a boom town. You'll realise that at the Macdonald where you're staying. It's a boom town all right. But the people of Edmonton, they're sceptical. They got long memories here and they're gonna wait and see before they start investing in real estate again. Two thousand dollars per foot frontage, that's what real estate reached in the old boom, and in the end you couldn't give it away."

Certainly there was little sign of a boom. Edmonton remained what it always had been, little more than a shack town. Long streets running out into nothing, the prairie sea beyond, and the buildings all two-storey with the telegraph poles the most notable feature, standing gaunt against the evening sky. Even in the centre of the town, the impression that it was composed of shacks remained, many of the buildings built of wood and sadly in need of paint, so that they looked like the façade of some dilapidated film set, as unreal as the motley characters crowding the sidewalks or seated in the high chairs of the shoeshine establishments—men from the outback, bearded and bush-shirted, roughnecks from the oilfields with money to burn, cowboys with thin hips and high boots in from the ranches for a night on the town. Only the Macdonald Hotel seemed solid, a great block of masonry built by the railways like some border keep to hold the land conquered in the Company's advance westward.

"Okay," Hume said. "I'll call for you around nine."

It was the first I knew that he intended taking me somewhere. He drove off and I carried my bag into the craziest hotel I have ever stayed in. Edmonton was a boom town all right. You could smell it the instant you entered the Macdonald—the colour, the faces, the roar of voices. Drink and the devil, I thought. Canada was still in the grip of prohibition. The only public drinking places were the beer-parlours, sombre, practical saloons, where men and women drank in separate rooms, where there was no bar and every drink had to be drunk seated at a table. If you wanted hard liquor, you got it at the Government Liquor Store and drank it in the seclusion of your room. A heck of a lot of liquor was flowing through the rooms of the Macdonald that evening, and by the sound of it half Texas was in residence, lured there by the scent of new-found oil, for the Texans were driving the pipe that the Canadians had forgotten how to drive in the forty-year interval between one boom and the next.

At nine-fifteen I left my room and went down into the foyer. By nine-thirty I was back in my room again, my quiet English clothes having proved as conspicuous in that sartorial mad-house as they would have been at a Chelsea Arts Ball. I'd nothing to drink, nothing to read. At ten I began to turn in, wondering how much sleep I should get with the place full of the roar of voices, harsh music and drunken laughter. And then the phone rang and it was Hume down at the desk. "Say, why don't you c'm on down? We're waiting for you."

"Okay," I said. "I'll be right down, Hume."

Oh, yes, we were already on Christian-name terms. It takes about ten seconds flat to be on Christian-name terms with a man out West—anything longer produces an instant reaction, an exaggerated contempt of the stuffed-shirt manners of the Old Country. The remittance men have left a well-nigh indelible mark from the prairies right through the Rockies to the coast.

Hume had his fiancée with him, another couple, a spare girl, two spare "mickies" of Irish and the same number of spare wheels. I didn't know about the wheels, but they were to prove the most interesting of the whole cargo. We left in a hilarious hurry and went scooting south down a fine wide road, and then somewhere, I can't remember where, we left it for a track that jolted and bounced us

against the roof and that led towards the black edge of a
horizon picked out by a red, intermittent glare as menacing
as a battlefield.

" Leduc," Hume shouted to me.

The glow grew redder until it looked as though the
whole place was on fire. I remember a group of trees,
leaves picked out in glorious, lurid technicolour, and then
we had swung off the track and were bumping across the
tinder-dry grass towards the wood.

We could hear the roar of the gas flare before ever we
saw the flame of it, a roar that sank and wavered and then
throbbed out into full voice again. We got out and walked
through scrub to the edge of a bare earth pit, the shape of
a cricket pitch and more than twice as big. At the far end,
a blow-torch flame of fire flickered and nearly died, to
suddenly spring out, a dragon tongue of flame, billowing
and rolling down the pitch, swelling as it came until it
was big as a house and the furnace doors were wide open,
brow-singeing hot, and the noise was like a dozen trains
roaring through a tunnel. And then it dwindled again, as
though taking another breath, behaving so exactly the way
Vesuvius had behaved, when I'd looked down into the
crater shortly before the eruption in '44, that it was difficult to believe that this was man-made—man-made in the
sense only that it was a controlled flame, the gas waste of
well after well delivering oil to the storage tanks that were
all around us in the night.

But the flame itself, that was different. This was the
same sort of flame that had drawn the fire worshippers of
ancient times to Caucasian fields. And there, in the dark of
the night, rising and falling like the breath of some earth-
bound monster, I sensed the mystery, the awe that could
captivate man in his search for God.

We toured the field then. No derricks under the towering bastions of the Rockies. Just fields of corn with every
now and then a little wired-off square, in the centre of

The midnight sun

Above: In the Sahara; Dorothy on a mount of the Desert Camel Patrol

Left: Tea-time beyond the High Atlas

Below: Boy dancers in the Draa Valley

I reach Head of Steel on the Labrador Iron Ore Railway

A trestle bridge in construction as the railway pushes north

A Roman Catholic priest at Baker Lake

Southampton Island; an Eskimo girl helps with the unloading

Boat construction spanning four thousand years
Above: An Arab dhow being built now on Masira Island
Below: My new boat under construction in Holland

which stood the well-head, a short vertical length of pipe with valves and ducts; it looked like a Christmas-tree and was known as such. There were no "mechanical horses" nodding their power-driven heads to pump the oil to the surface. There was still plenty of pressure at Leduc. And then we had arrived at Devon, a town run up overnight and already sprouting gardens amongst the contractors' debris. In the centre, fronting what looked like a village green, stood the night club, gaudy as a cinema—it was just a dance hall, that was all, but still the only one of its kind in Alberta. It was run by a Chinese family, and the tables all had glove pockets, but not for gloves, for no liquor was sold, only soft drinks. The place was a roar of singing, faces sweating in the subdued light, eyes alcohol-bright. They were dancing square dances, singing cowboy songs. We stayed there through the sentimental stage and left before they got around to the hymns.

Breakfast in Edmonton, at three in the morning in a Chinese place that hung its sign on the film-set face of a side street. And before we were half-way through the huge meal, in came the owner and staff of the Devon night club. Chinese restaurants and Chinese laundries—and out of the towns only they and the Dutch really know how to cultivate the land. An irrepressible, energetic, businesslike people.

It was after four when we left, and dawn was breaking, a pale-grey light filtering in from the prairie seas along the east-facing streets. One by one we dropped our party in the dawn, each house a little clearer than the last, until finally Hume kissed his girl good night in broad daylight.

We turned back into town then. "Tired?" Hume asked.

"No," I said. "I was a little while back, but now for some reason I'm wide awake."

"Me, too." And then he added, "Not much point in going to bed, the sun'll be up in an hour. What do you say we go to Jasper?"

"Jasper?" I stared at him. Jasper was the gateway to the Rockies, the place where the old Grand Trunk engineers had found the low pass through. "Are you serious?"

"Sure. You said you wanted to see the Rockies. And an Albertan dawn, wasn't it? Well, here's the Albertan dawn, anyway. And there's gas in the tank and I got ground grips in the back. Okay?"

He drove back to the house where he had rooms and lugged the two big-tyred spares out of the boot. I changed the wheels whilst he got sandwiches and a half-bottle of Scotch to keep us awake. And then we left, driving down an arrow-straight road with the sun rising over the ruler-straight line of the prairie horizon behind us. Some distance outside Edmonton the macadam ceased; it was a dirt road then, a "black-top," oil-dressed and full of pot holes. A steady sixty allowed the car to ride them in reasonable comfort— any slower and it shook the car to pieces, any faster and the rear wheels began to sway beyond control.

We stopped about half-way, in a railway yard where the men had just come on duty, and drank a somnolent cup of coffee laced with Scotch. And later, much later, we stopped at the top of a long rise to watch some deer. We were in forest then and the gravel road was like a broad ride through it, with pines on either side, and ahead of us, straight over the bonnet, a line of jagged mountains thrust up from the end of the road, thrust straight up into the sky like the lower jaw of a gigantic whale, bone-white, cloud-capped and unbelievable.

We drove towards them for a long time, until we came to the grey-stone bed of the Athabasca, running milky with the water from the glaciers; and then we entered the national park—and after that we couldn't see the Rockies any more.

Jasper, when we came to it, sprawled dirty-white under a mantle of snow, the sheds and shacks beside the tracks all black and bitter cold, and the mountains close around it. I was tired by then and dazed with lack of sleep and constant travel, so that the rest is a confused memory, impressions no longer vivid, but blurred by fatigue. We stopped at a shop run by Harry Rowed, who had made a corner in photography in that area of the Rockies, co-opted his assistant as driver and rode out of Jasper, past men with skis over their shoulders, headed for Mount Edith Cavell.

The snow plough had been through ahead of us, but at almost 9,000 feet we were stopped by new snow just short of a rest house run by a friend of Hume's. There was nobody there and the place was shut. We stood a while and stared at the towering peak of Edith Cavell. "Well, I guess you seen the Rockies now," Hume said. And we turned the car and went back down the winding road, hairpin bend after hairpin bend, with all the world still in the grip of winter and beautiful to look at whenever a lurch of the car opened my eyes.

We passed through Jasper and out the other side, and the next I knew we had stopped at a little tent set in a clearing in some fir woods, and between the brown stems of the trees there was a glimpse of water, brilliant as an Italian lake in the sunshine. "Lake Edith," Hume said, and then he was introducing me to a woman who had appeared out of the tent. "Harry's down at the house," she said.

We walked slowly towards the lake, through woods that were clear of snow and already had the warm, resinous smell of summer. The pine needles were soft under our feet and there was a murmur of insects.

The house was something I will never forget. It was only half-completed, a log structure that took me straight back to my travels in Norway, for each log was notched to fit the one below, the ends dovetailed the way the Vikings built their stave churches. The pungent smell of barked wood and pine chippings stung my nostrils and brought me wide awake. The view across the lake was beautiful. It was a place of utter peace and the house would be beautiful, too, so that I was filled suddenly with the longing to change places with this unknown man, for he had done what I would like to have done—carved himself a nice little business out of the Rocky Mountain scenery and put down his roots on the shores of a lost lake. That house was like a dream house there on the lake shore on that sleepy June morning. "Is Harry a Norwegian?" I asked.

Hume shook his head. And at that moment Harry Rowed appeared out of the open gap where the front door would be a dark man full of vitality and enthusiasm. He could talk of nothing but the house that morning. He was full to the brim with what he was doing, as happy as a child with a dream come true. And as he showed us over it, I found I had been right after all—three brothers were building it, three Norwegians, the only men in all Alberta who could build a house in the old way, the way that the Norwegians themselves have almost forgotten.

We lunched squatting on our haunches in the tent and then went to sleep in the open with the baby crying and the dog sprawling over us. And in the early evening, as it began to rain, we started back to Edmonton with Harry Rowed driving and Hume and myself nodding in the back. The gravel road ran red with mud and passing trucks sprayed us so thick with it that the windscreen wipers, lubricated by a water jet fitment, barely cleared it before the driver was blinded.

Harry Rowed was going into town to get some pictures he needed for an American magazine, pictures which turned out to be of the gas flare at Leduc. And so, for the second night running, I found myself standing by the dragon's mouth, watching, fascinated, the great tongue of flame lick out with a roar and then gradually retreat, only to come flaming forth again in all its fury. Pictures of flame, of the tank farms lurid in the glare, of a Christmas tree gleaming redly. And then back to the Macdonald to sleep at last.

I was woken at nine by the telephone. It was Hume and he was already at his office. "I thought I'd show you the Redwater oilfield this morning," he said. "But it's raining and I got work to do. Pick you up at two. Okay?"

And he added, " There's a shack out there run by a Norwegian and his two daughters. They serve the only good steaks in Alberta. We might stop off on our way back."

I had a leisurely breakfast in my room, grapefruit on crushed ice, eggs and bacon in a heated cover, the whole so elaborately served on a trolley that it was hard to believe that I wasn't at one of the major hotels in London or New York. But down in the barber's saloon, where I went for a much-needed haircut the men were mostly in bush shirts and high boots and the talk was all of oil, of new wells spudded in, of mud schools and core samples, and of people who had made their fortune overnight. " See about this Irish family?" somebody said, rustling a paper. " Woke up to find themselves sitting on an anticline. Geez! Some people are lucky. Two hundred thousand dollars, and their farm no bigger than a hen run."

And out on the sidewalks there were men standing around—standing around and talking or just standing around savouring the feel and smell of a town. I went into a shoeshine place, and sat in a throne-like chair, staring at a newspaper that showed a picture of the happy Irish family that had sat on an oilfield for two generations without knowing it, and all around me were roughnecks and drillers and bearded men in from the North, even a Mounty looking smart as a new pin amongst all the riff-raff. And yet, rough though they were, they had the quietness, the gentlemanly manners of the frontier.

To see Edmonton at the start of that boom was to see a town like no other in this generation. It was as though I had been transported back in time to the great days of the American Middle West. But though there were Indians there and half-breeds and cowboys and the atmosphere was one of a new country opening up, there was none of the wildness—it lacked the guns and the liquor and the women. For this was Canada and the people of Edmonton were taking it all very quietly.

That afternoon Hume drove me north into gently rolling

country thick with spruce and fir. Some twenty miles or so from Edmonton we came upon the first derrick, a red slash on a scrub-covered slope, with the rig standing in a sea of mud. "Redwater's well named," he said, as he struggled to keep the car going on a road surface rutted by heavy traffic. And after that the country became more populated and the track deteriorated until it was a churned-up ribbon of red clay. We passed two heavy trucks, bogged down to the axles by their loads of drilling pipe, and every half-mile or so, bulldozers and tumble-bugs were butting into the woodland slopes, carving tracks and clearings to take the new rigs.

Redwater in the rain was a forlorn, incredible place of old clapboard stores and houses, a street of mud with raised wooden sidewalks, the sort of town Zane Grey described so often. But in place of horses, there were battered station wagons and huge transport trucks, all coated thickly with the red mud of the country. We had coffee and doughnuts in a big barn of a place that was full of the noise of juke boxes and crammed to the doors with men from the oilfield, men in khaki clothing and high boots caked with mud, men who were sweaty and grimed with the work of carving their way into new country.

In a wooden shack in the heart of the town, we found a young man and a girl getting out the local newspaper on a duplicating machine. The *Redwater Gazette,* I think it was called. I can't remember the editor's name, but he had come out there for his health, and looking out of the window at the dismal scene, the mud glistening with the rain that had only just stopped, I thought it was an odd place to come for your health. But his enthusiasm was infectious. He was going to build a real paper.

Everybody was the same in Redwater. There was an air of optimism about the place, a feeling of going places. Out from the hub of clapboard buildings that represented the old Redwater, there radiated whole streets of new construction, neat little houses rising out of the mud in all stages of construction, a Company town that would soon be as tidy and complete as Devon. And beyond the town were the rigs, with toolpushers from Texas driving teams of rough-necks in the scramble to push pipe down to oil.

"Redwater will soon be like Leduc," Hume said. "Already there's a new field opening up to the north. Imperial Oil drilled a hundred and fourteen dry wells before they brought in the discovery well at Leduc. Now look at this!"

It was certainly something to have seen. Not the rain nor the mud could obscure the thrill of it. Canada at the start of the big boom. Canada hadn't been invaded from across the border like this since the days of the Fraser River gold rush.

On the way back, we stopped at the Norwegian shack where the steaks were so good. But it was closed. One of the daughters, standing in the rain, her gumboots ankle-deep in mud, called to us that the Government hygiene inspector had ordered them to serve no more steaks until they had installed a refrigerator. "God-dammit!" Hume exploded. "That was the only place in Alberta where the steaks weren't carved from frozen meat. And this is a cattle country!"

Somehow that little incident stuck in my mind. Like the drinking laws, it was symbolic of Government inter-ference with individual liberty. And though the drinking laws have now been eased somewhat, the combination of Federal Government and Provincial Government makes the people as circumscribed by regulations as any bureau-cratic country.

From the oilfields, I went south to Pincher Creek, to live on a ranch and learn to wrangle horses, riding all day in a western saddle. Later, I joined a Government survey party operating in the mountains above Waterton Lakes, and learned how easy it would be to cross into the States, for we came down from a 10,000-foot peak of the Rockies to find the Canada-U.S. border no more than a solitary slash in the pine-clad slopes, with barbed wire running down the centre. And then across the Rockies, riding the foot-plate of one of the C.P.R. locomotives through the fantastic beauties of the fiords along the coast to the north. But in all those months of travel, I never quite recaptured the excitement of those two first days with Hume Cronyn. He crammed the new Canada down my throat in one wild rush and gave me the guts of a novel about the oil boom.

And when I came out West again six years later, the train showed me miles of tank farms beside the tracks, whole areas of "mechanical horses" nodding their heads as they pumped the oil from fields where the pressure had already fallen. It didn't seem the same then, and with Canada opening up at such a fantastic rate, there was no room for the pioneer. Everywhere big companies were piling millions of capital into the opening up of virgin country, everything so highly organised that the phrase "Go West young man," with its suggestion of a fortune there for the grasping, no longer held good. This conviction that there was little scope now for individual initiative, left me with a feeling of sadness, for I had seen it when, for a moment, the country had been wide open and the sky had seemed the limit.

2. THE IRON ORE RAILWAY

Jacques Cartier, who discovered the St. Lawrence River, called Labrador *the land God gave to Cain*. It is a barren place of incredible bleakness.

Picture a 2,000-foot high plateau just out of the grip of the Ice Age. There is water everywhere—lakes by the thousand, leaden-coloured under leaden skies. And between the lakes is bare rock and sodden muskeg, a wilderness of swamp land darkened by a stunted growth of jackpine. The climate, too, is unsurpassed for misery—bitter cold in winter and the short summers made hell by mosquito and blackfly, which breed in their countless millions in the steaming humidity of the caribou moss.

Thirty years ago, barely a dozen white people had set foot on that plateau, and most of those came out suffering from exhaustion and cold—one died. The Nascopie Indians once lived there, but they have disappeared, together with the great caribou herds on which they lived. Not the Sahara nor the deserts of Arabia are as terrible as this grim country, the most God-forsaken land I have ever travelled through.

But man is a tough creature and adaptable. When I went through the country there were over five thousand men ploughing there way into it, building a railway slap into the middle of nowhere. And only a few years before, all the land where the construction camps stood was just a blank on the map of Canada, uninhabited, unvisited even, except by Montagnais Indians and a handful of prospectors.

I remember a story I heard about a pilot who got lost and flew into the heart of Labrador by mistake. It was night and all his instruments had packed up. He had been flying on dead reckoning with his fuel getting shorter and shorter, and when the gauge touched zero, he reckoned he was still over the sea a long way north of Newfoundland. He sent his passenger aft to prepare the rubber dinghy for ditching and put the plane into a long glide.

It was his passenger who saw the light. It was some sort of a searchlight, shining up through the cloud away to starboard, maybe a ship. They banked towards it, diving steeply, and came out below the cloud base to find a lit runway stretched out below them.

It was unbelievable—a miracle. They thought for a moment it must be Goose Bay, but it was a gravel strip they landed on and the airport buildings were nothing but a scattering of wooden shacks. "Where in the world are we?" the pilot inquired of the airport radio operator.

"Menihek," was the reply.

"Menihek? Where's that?"

"In the middle of Labrador."

"Well, for heaven's sake!" Anyone who can visualise what Labrador is like will understand the pilot's shock of surprise. And it wasn't even an Air Force Field; it was nothing to do with defence. It was part of a civilian construction job. They were building a dam up there in the wilds, and the dam itself was just a part of the railway project that had airstrips strung out at intervals all the three hundred miles to the St. Lawrence.

That was what the radio operator told him. And he added, "You're darn lucky. That light you saw was our new cloud ceiling beacon. It only came in yesterday." He leaned over and flicked a switch. "I was just showing a friend of mine how it worked." A vertical beam blazed out for an instant at the runway end, and then vanished abruptly. The bulb had fused—and that was the only one they had!

That almost incredible story was told me by the engineer of a helicopter at Mile 290, and next day we flew up to Menihek, forty miles farther north. Where the ninety-mile long stretch of the Menihek Lakes flows out through the Hamilton River towards the Atlantic, a great concrete dam had been built—and every bag of cement, all the steel, had been flown in by air. I was seeing the opening up of the last great stronghold of the wild on the North American continent.

It was the float plane that brought Labrador within reach of civilisation. Thousands of miles of lake water made ideal landing, and prospectors and geologists flew in, drawn by stories of copper and gold told by the Montagnais Indians of Seven Islands, who are summer visitors to the plateau for the hunting and the quite fabulous fishing.

But it was neither gold nor copper that was responsible for the string of airstrips and the dam and the railway. It was iron ore; six hundred million tons of it with a 65 per cent ore content. At Knob Lake, bang in the heart of Labrador, you can shovel it out with a bulldozer by the

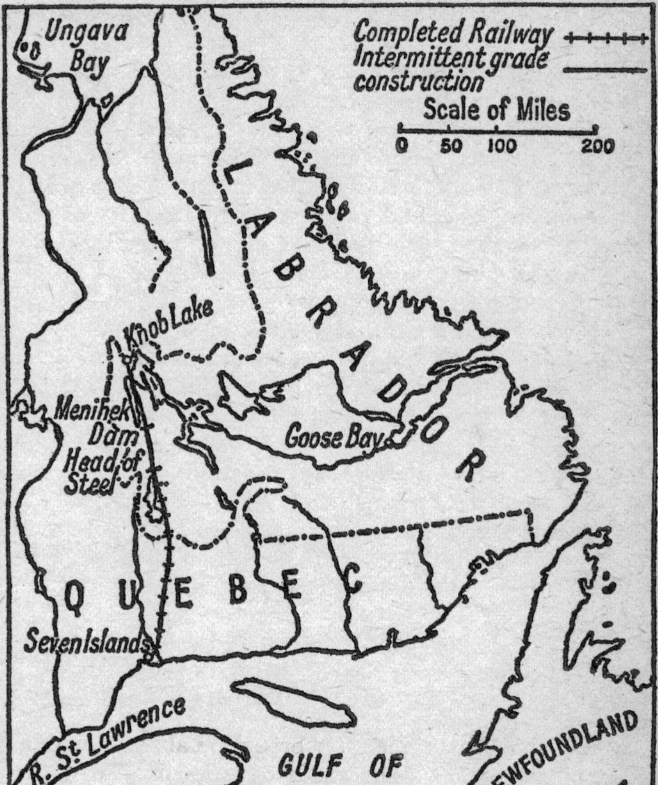

Completed Railway ┼┼┼┼
Intermittent grade
construction ───────

Scale of Miles

0   50   100   200

Ungava
Bay

L A B R A D O R

Knob Lake

Menihek
Dam
Head of
Steel

Goose Bay

Q U E B E C

Seven Islands

R. St Lawrence

GULF OF
ST LAWRENCE

NEWFOUNDLAND

truck load, by the train load—Bessemer, non-Bessemer, manganiferous, anti-moniferous, all kinds.

In 1947, an advance party was flown into Knob Lake. They cleared an airstrip for transport planes, and men and equipment were brought in—everything from food and fuel to bulldozers and churn drills. Among the twisted wreckage of an old forest fire, silvered with age, they built a permanent town and called it Burnt Creek. For four years they scraped and drilled until the whole field was proved. The iron ore was there—for anybody with the capital and the know-how to get it down to the St. Lawrence, four hundred miles to the south.

Canadians had found the ore, but it was the Americans who provided the capital to get it out. Hungry for ore, five of America's biggest steel companies put up 82 per cent of the capital. The plan was for a railway to connect Knob Lake with the St. Lawrence; Seven Islands was to become a great iron ore terminal with automatic graders and loaders and a deep-water wharf, and two dams were to be built to provide hydro-electric power, one at Mile 330 on Menihek Lakes, the other close to the terminal at Clark City.

I had heard about this project when I was in Canada in 1950. Three years later, when I flew into Seven Islands, it was already well under way and Head of Steel had reached Mile 235. The whole thing took me right back to the war days and the invasion of a hostile coast. First the beach-head at Seven Islands, and then the build-up, men and equipment pouring in, whilst an all-out effort was made to drive the steel up the Moisie River gorge, up to the top of the 2,000-foot escarpment. And whilst the main thrust followed the line of the river, float planes carried men and material far into the interior, airstrips were built and a fifteen-plane airlift got under way, a lift that was to carry supplies and fuel for the men who drove the grab cranes and bulldozers all the way from Mile 1, building the grade as they went; even the steel plates for conduits as big as twelve feet in diameter went in by airlift.

It is hard for me to believe that it is finished now, that the men and machines I saw toiling with such desperate energy have done their job and gone. Now you can travel up from the St. Lawrence by train all the way to Knob Lake and see the automatic loaders pouring ore into the railway wagons and see the great train loads leaving—a hundred and five wagons of a hundred tons each, drawn by four diesel electric locomotives; a total of 6,000 h.p. drawing a deadweight of some twelve thousand tons up to the height of land and then braking down the miles of twisting track beside the Moisie River, down through the tunnel that freezes solid with ice in winter, down off the escarpment to the empty ships waiting at the loading terminal at Seven Islands.

And far away across the Atlantic, in Britain, the little Welsh village of Angle faces an uncertain future because of that railway. I came to it by chance and the talk in the village inn was all of iron ore; a tunnel was to be drilled through the cliffs from Milford Haven so that ships could unload their cargo of red-brown ore and dump four million tons of it in the Welsh countryside behind the village, a reserve to supply the great steelworks around Swansea. It was three years since I had been in Labrador, but as I stood there in Wales, picturing the ore ships leaving Seven Islands for Milford Haven, it all came back to me . . . the siding I had helped to build, the trestle bridge I had travelled so far to photograph, and Burnt Creek with the brown acres of ore and the V.I.P. lodge where I had rested two days, a centrally-heated log house run by a Devonshire couple. Would they still be there! It was hard to visualise it as being different now, the airstrips all abandoned and the construction camps where I had lived.

I had come to it in October, when the battle was still only half-won and the big freeze-up expected any day. The

construction camps teemed with men then and the sixty
miles of uncompleted grade were littered with grab cranes.
Living with the engineers was like living with brigade H.Q.
Head of Steel was the battle front, and it was thrust,
thrust, thrust, with a target of thirty thousand tons of
gravel to be shifted daily and the steel being laid at the
fantastic rate of almost two miles a day; everything was on
the move, camps shifting, men being leap-frogged into the
forward areas and the planes flying over like a bus service
to keep men and machines going that were spread out all
along the line of march.

I can still remember the sense of loneliness I felt as I
embarked at Seven Islands in an old Dakota that carried
parachute jumping wires and looked as though it had done
its maiden flight in the early days of the war. It was
Indian summer weather down there on the St. Lawrence,
with all the country a blaze of autumn reds and the sunset
a fiery conflagration fading to deep purple; and as darkness fell a fabulous curtain of northern lights flung its
moving folds across the stars. My companions on that
flight were a strange mixture of races, from French-
Canadian and Italian to Negro and Chinese—many of
them bearded, and all equipped with cold-weather clothing.

In little more than an hour we had crossed the top of the
2,000-foot escarpment, a journey that only thirty or forty
years back would have taken an explorer six weeks by
canoe up the rapids of the Moisie river—six weeks, if he
was lucky, out of the short ten-week summer, which was
all the time he had if he was to get out alive. From a heat
wave we flew into a blizzard, landing on an airstrip of
glacial silt that was little more than a clearing in the grim
silence of the jackpine forest. A truck took me into the
camp, along a rutted track that was frozen hard as iron and
white with a drift of snow. The camp itself was just a little
huddle of huts in the stillness of the Arctic night, and the
only sound in the all-pervading silence was the putter of
the diesel engine that supplied the electricity. This was

Camp 134, a hundred and thirty-four miles up the railway from the St. Lawrence.

And then north again by speeder, one of those little open gas cars capable of travelling at thirty miles an hour along the completed section of the line, north through camp after camp, and every journey a bitter cold misery with hands and feet frozen and the sleet squalls coming up off the lakes with a sting in them that warned of the big freeze-up; mile after dismal mile, no change in the country —just the jackpine and the caribou moss and the lakes, the endless sombre lakes. One day I did a hundred miles—up over the height of land with the snow blowing in our faces, a husky dog sharing the tiny platform of the speeder with me. Every twenty miles or so we stopped at the cookhouse of a construction camp for scalding coffee to give us warmth, and in a lurid sunset we followed a ballast gang's rail cars to a section of double track and parked in the rear of a bunkhouse train.

It was my first construction train meal; a hundred men crammed along the benches, and steaks and pies and doughnuts and tinned fruit, mountains of food to be grabbed and wolfed and washed down with tea in a temperature that would have made a centrally-heated New York hotel seem like an ice house. And then on again through the blackness of the night, with the steel running out ahead like two silver threads in the speeder's headlight. I was with Gordon Racey then—a man of some fifty odd, who had come up there on a fishing trip and had stayed two and a half years as an engineer because he loved the wilds !

That was the first time I saw the siding that I was to regard as my own; a glimpse of great chunks of muskeg and caribou moss piled on the blade of a bulldozer as it struggled in the mud to make the cut that would be the switch. Every day after that, for almost a week, I would leave the litter of shacks and the din of aircraft that was Camp 224, and go down with Gordon Racey to that siding. We left at seven in the morning and most times the track

was so iced up that we had to use wire scrapers out ahead
of the speeder. Once, and once only, the sun shone!

In that first glimpse of the siding, I had seen a lone
bulldozer spearhead the attack on another stretch of
Labrador's virgin soil. Before I left, the siding was complete, the grade levelled, the track laid. And after that I
went on through Head of Steel, past the gangs labouring
to secure the ties, past the Burro crane swinging the
lengths of steel into position; plodding along on foot now
until there was no rail, just the brown gravel slash of the
newly-levelled grade. I travelled by truck and jeep then.
And later, when even the grade petered out and there was
nothing to show the line of the railway but the stakes
driven by the engineers through the trackless wild between
the lakes, I took to helicopter and finally float plane, living
all the time in camps that were either half-completed or
half-dismantled, in a whirl of men constantly moving forward.

There were five thousand of them up there in a land
where no white man had been before; men of every
nationality—French and British, Canadian, Italian,
Ukrainian, Polish. . . . I shared a hut one night with a
German, a Nova Scotian, a Jamaican and an Egyptian-
born Greek. They said if I had been there a few nights
before there would have been a Chinaman as well! At one
point there was an engineer from Abadan, still wearing silk
scarf and khaki over the bulk of his woollens.

And there was Heidlen.

Adolph Heidlen was Swiss. He was sixty-four years old
and he was responsible for five hundred grab cranes, bulldozers, tumble-bugs, "mules" and trucks strung out over
thirty miles of grade, responsible for that target of thirty
thousand tons a day. He was air-sick every time he went
up, yet he spent his days in the air, being flown around in
the helicopter by Hank Gates, trundling up and down the
length of the uncompleted grade, settling beside any

machine that wasn't in its right position, wasn't pulling its weight.

"Why don't you stay home?" Hank told him once. "All I got to do is fly this kite up and down the grade, and they'll all work like hell."

But even when the weather was too bad for flying, Heidlen would be rushing furiously up and down the *tote* road in his jeep. Drive, drive, drive; he had a bet that he'd get the grade through to Menihek Dam before the big freeze-up. I guess he did, too, for the "heat" was on from headquarters—this was the big push before the winter.

He worked for American contractors. All the top know-how was American. Canadian engineers shook their heads; they said the line was being rushed through so fast that whole stretches of it would sink into the muskeg and be swallowed up. Well, maybe—they know their Canada. But the railway has been built, and now the wealth of iron ore trundling down it to Seven Islands will keep it above the muskeg if it costs another million dollars a mile to do it.

And this is only the beginning of the development of Labrador. Not long before I was out there, one of the airlift planes got off course in thick cloud, flying down to Seven Islands. The pilot came down below the overcast to pick up a landmark and found his compass swinging crazily. Circling, he saw a patch of discoloured hilltop and marked its position on his map. Later, he and his flight engineer went into that territory on foot with a geologist. They found a hill of high-grade iron ore, roughly estimated at some four hundred million tons, and though it contained an admixture of titanium that made it much less suitable for exploitation than the Knob Lake deposits, they drew a nice little sum in option money.

But it isn't only iron ore. There's talk of copper in the north, of lead and zinc. Where a couple of pilots can find a fortune by chance, what may the prospector and geologist unearth by diligent search? The land God gave to Cain is a land of considerable wealth—for those who can stand the bitter cold, the mosquitos and the barren wildness of it without getting "bushed." To have been there when the first assault was being made on this Ice-Age fastness is something I shall remember into old age, a living proof that no country, however inhospitable, can remain indefinitely a blank on the map, unconquered by man.

3. THE BAY OF THE NORTH

That was what Radisson called it, the Bay of the North, and it drew him as it has since drawn three centuries of Scotsmen, myself included. Pierre Radisson was seventeen when he reached the little French settlement of Three Rivers as an emigré from France in the year 1652. He was from St. Malo, birthplace of Jacques Cartier, the man who first discovered Labrador, and this fact had given him some extravagant ideas about adventuring. "*If I die, I die valiant*," he cried as the Iroquois tortured him within months of his arrival in Canada.

He spent two years with the Iroquois, escaped finally and went trading for furs as a *voyageur*. In June, 1658, he left with his brother-in-law, Groseilliers, for the lands beyond the Great Lakes in a desperate attempt to save the fur trade on which the French colony depended. Abandoned by their more timorous companions, they were away two years and given up for dead; and then in the summer of 1660, they came paddling down the St. Lawrence, accompined by five hundred Indians and a great wealth of furs, and the bells in old Quebec gave them a heroes' welcome.

It was an incredible story they had to tell, for those two lone men had travelled far. They had seen the Mississippi and the Missouri, had journeyed so far south that they had heard Indian tales of the Spanish in California; they had lived with the Sioux and knew about the Rocky Mountains;

they had roamed through half of what are now the northern
states of the American Middle West, and had then gone
north to live with the Crees. All that at a time when no
white man had ever before penetrated beyond the Great
Lakes.

It was the Crees who told them about the Bay of the
North and the yearly hunting trek to its shores; and from
that moment it was the Bay of the North—Hudson's Bay
—that was to draw the two of them like a magnet.

Success brought envy, and envy drove them into the
wilds again. They went west and north, a journey of three
winters, back to the friendly Crees in time for the yearly
trek to the Bay—and then north and north and north in a
last desperate attempt to achieve their goal, with Radisson
ill and almost frozen to death. They crossed the height of
land and went down the swollen rivers in new-built canoes
to the Bay. Or so Radisson claims in the journal he wrote
many years later. *We passed the summer quietly coasting
the seaside.*

Whether they really reached the Bay or not is unimp-
ortant. What is important is that it had now become an
obsession with them. And when an ungrateful Government
confiscated half their furs by way of taxes, they chartered
a ship to try and emulate Hudson and force their way into
the Bay by sea. Their attempt failed, their ship was
wrecked, and faced with an action for damages in the
courts, they escaped to England, where the were fêted at
Court and granted audience by King Charles II. The story
of their travels was so fabulous that it caught the fancy of
the merchant adventurers of the City of London, and on
June 3, 1668, they left Gravesend in two small ships, the
Eaglet and the *Nonsuch,* bound for the great Bay of the
North by way of the Atlantic, the route that Hudson had
taken more than forty years before.

The *Eaglet* was forced back by gales. But Groseilliers in
the *Nonsuch* passed through Hudson's Straits into the Bay,
and after wintering there, returned on October 9, 1669,

bringing into the Thames a superb cargo of furs. With Groseilliers' return, the Bay ceased to be a fortune hunter's gamble. The first trading post, Charles Fort, had been established; the claims of the two Frenchmen had been proved. A company was formed with the magnificent title of The Company of Adventurers of England Trading into Hudson's Bay, and Charles was persuaded to sign one of the most fantastic charters ever granted to a merchant trading organisation. It gave to the Company "*the whole trade of all those seas, streights and bays, rivers, lakes, creeks and sounds . . . within the streights commonly called Hudson's Streights*"—a concession that proved ultimately to encompass almost a million and a half square miles of land

So was born the great Hudson's Bay Company. But you will not find the names of Radisson and Groseilliers in English encyclopædias or listed among the great explorers of history. They died forgotten men, their names buried by greed and the fact that they had been forced by circumstances to become renegades to both sides. I do not intend to recount the full story of their expeditions here, but I must add this : ignored and poorly rewarded by the Company who owed its existence to them, they sailed again on their own account in two leaky little vessels of fifty tons, and in one short season swept England's full-rigged ships from the Bay. Radisson, in particular, played the devil with the Company, and in the end, though they hated him, they were forced to take him back. It was the start of a long struggle for supremacy in those ice-bound waters between the English and the French, a struggle that was to culminate in full-scale naval battles and sieges undertaken against almost impregnable forts.

It was a fantastic period up there in the Bay—intrigue, war, murder, starvation, frost-bite and Indians . . . and striding across the scene those two remarkable Frenchmen. I first heard their story when I visited Canada in 1950 and it has remained in my mind ever since. In my view, at

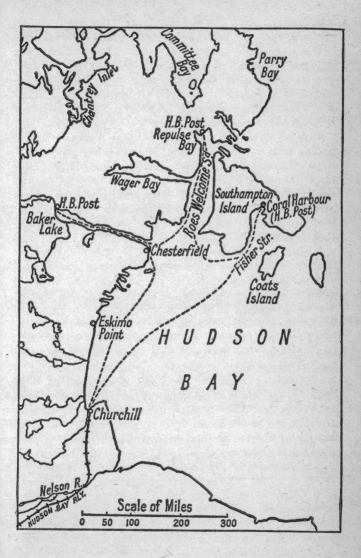

Committee Bay

Parry Bay

Chantrey Inlet

H.B. Post
Repulse
Bay

Wager Bay

Roes Welcome Sd.

Southampton
Island

Coral Harbour
(H.B. Post)

H.B. Post

Baker
Lake

Chesterfield

Fisher Str.

Coats
Island

Eskimo
Point

HUDSON

BAY

Churchill

Nelson R.

HUDSON BAY RLY.

Scale of Miles

0   50   100   200   300

any rate, they are probably the greatest of all explorers, for they adventured farther and with more success than any man before them, except possibly Drake; and yet their story is a tragedy, for their temperaments were incapable of consolidating success. It is a sad commentary on our history books that only Canada, and very belatedly, has seen fit to accord them their due.

Because of the way I work, I knew that one day I should have to go north into Hudson's Bay to see for myself the country in which Radisson had achieved so much against such impossible odds. A man who, almost single-handed, could capture a large and heavily-garrisoned fort and sail out of the Bay in a captured " pirate " ship, leaving another large ship wrecked, was a man worth writing about.

In 1956, a film company asked me to go out to Canada again to write a story for them. I agreed—provided I could include Hudson's Bay in my journey. And so, on a hot day at the very beginning of September of that year, I flew into Winnipeg. I had come five thousand miles and I was on the last leg of my journey to link up with a Hudson's Bay Company ship, the *Rupertsland,* due to sail from Fort Churchill, in the south-west corner of the Bay, on Tuesday, September 4. A short seven-hundred-mile flight and I should be in the Bay I had read so much about. The flight left on the Monday morning, and half-way to the airport my taxi driver was stopped. Through the hole in his throat left by a successful cancer operation, he informed me that the flight was cancelled. Fort Churchill was blotted out by a blizzard.

All my careful planning was suddenly tumbled to ruins, and as he drove me back to my hotel, I sat numbed and silent. To come so far and then to miss the ship because of the weather . . . and all the time the sun beat down out of a clear blue sky. The Bay assumed something of the menace it had for those early explorers, its Arctic weather suddenly very real to me.

It was Labour Day in Winnipeg, everybody on holiday and all the offices closed. The next flight wasn't until Wednesday, and the train that left that afternoon took two days to get to Churchill. There seemed no way of reaching the *Rupertsland* before she sailed.

Desperate, I tracked down a contact in Canadian National Railways. In Canada it is essential to have contacts in the transport world. There followed a three-hour wait with no news. And then suddenly everything was all right. He came into my hotel to tell me that he had contacted Churchill, the *Rupertsland* had been delayed by the bad weather. More, he had had an extra coach put on the train to accommodate the passengers of the cancelled flight.

I have discovered that when things go wrong in travelling, it is often for the best in the end. He accompanied me to the station, and having seen me to my coach, abruptly left me. He was gone a long time and only returned just as the train was about to pull out. "Quick," he said. "Come with me. The Chief Engineer, Major Charles, has his business car tacked on to the end. He'd be glad to have you travel with him. You'll be much more comfortable."

I abandoned my baggage, my camera, everything, and just as the train pulled out, I climbed up into the last coach to be greeted by the man who, as a youngster, had surveyed the route we were going to travel. The coach was a luxurious one. A saloon with deep armchairs gave an uninterrupted view back down the line. There was a dining-room with a steward who served us excellent meals, several small bedrooms, even a shower. And as we sat over drinks, watching the steel reel out behind us, Major Charles told me the story of the early days of the " Muskeg Railway " and how a whole section of line, with a train on it was swallowed up by the muskeg, near Armstrong Lake, because the engineers had been fooled by a false bottom and had specified trestle piles that were too short.

He knew every bend, every alteration of grade along the

track; he knew all the section gang foremen who waved to us from their isolated huts set at ten-mile intervals. He was the line.

And it was a fantastic line. Known as the Hudson's Bay Railway, it began late that night at Hudson's Bay Junction and ran north-east, straight as a die, the only variations the slight changes in gradient, and the country streaming away behind us was an unchanging view of pine forests, with here and there a homestead or the pewter gleam of a lake. And the following morning, the talk, as we trundled north at a snail's pace, was all of surveys and spur lines and problems of construction, for Major Charles had with him a young engineer who was taking a survey party into Mystery Lake and Moak Lake to plan the route for a new thirty-mile stretch of line. International Nickel were opening a mine at Moak Lake, and this might well solve the problem of grain wagons coming back from Churchill, empty and uneconomic.

At The Pas, where we stopped for an hour or so, I got my first whiff of the north. In the little church, beside the Saskatchewan River, was a plaque commemorating the fact that the ill-fated Franklin had passed that way and had given a sundial of all things to the community. There was a monument, too, to Henry Kelsey, first Hudson's Bay man to venture into the interior. The sky was grey, the air bitterly cold after the heat of Winnipeg, and The Pas itself was full of Indians, leaning listlessly and somehow tragic against the clapboard buildings. What the settlement lived on, God knows. Incredibly, men retired to this place to end their days, for wherever Charles went, he was greeted by old-timers of the railway.

North of The Pas, the country was all swamp spruce, jackpine and larch, with some alder and willow, and the birches turning to gold, the trees getting smaller as the Bay came nearer. And in the evening we came to Thicket Portage, in a country ledged with limestone outcrops, and I said good-bye to the luxury of Major Charles's business car, wishing them luck as they unloaded canoes, tents and cold-weather equipment from the baggage car. And next morning, I breakfasted in the Land of the Little Sticks.

The country was as sombre as Labrador then, the jack-pine so stunted they were little more than the height of a man, and the huge expanse of sky gave the impression of land without end. There was muskeg everywhere, spreading and encroaching on the stunted trees until there was nothing else, and then patches of water appeared, reflecting leaden skies. It began to snow.

Shortly afterwards the train stopped. We had reached Churchill. A bearded doctor, accompanied by two nurses, assured me that the *Rupertsland* had not sailed. "The Captain can't sail without me," he said, and disappeared in an Air Force car for the comforts of the Service Mess, leaving me standing alone amongst my bags, staring at the strangest town I had ever seen.

It was a frontier town, and it lay under a cold sky with the permafrost only two feet below the surface of the glacial silt on which it rested. Leaden water lay along two sides of a promontory, and the town itself was a straggling, unplanned conglomoration of clapboard buildings and broken-down shacks, the place full of dirt and refuse of a community labouring in a bitter climate. Humanity there was a shapeless bundle of clothing, whites, Indians and Eskimos all mingled together. It had two hotels, and these were always full, the large beer parlours always open. There was a fine new Hudson's Bay store, a Mounted Police barracks housing the largest force in the north, all six feet tall, but still barely capable of dealing with the Scots who came in in the grain ships. There was a church, too, and a fine little Eskimo museum run by Roman Catholic fathers, primitive art in walrus ivory, chunky and powerful. And on the waterfront, dominating the whole scene, the huge grain elevator.

Wheat pours into Churchill from the prairie lands of central Canada, for the port is no farther from Liverpool than Montreal; and in the short ice-free season, from July to early October, more than fifty ships clear for the east with their golden cargoes. A 10,000-ton freighter can be loaded in a matter of nine hours, and it was under the shadow of this elevator that I found the *Rupertsland,* looking little larger than a tug.

Held up by ice on her journey through the Hudson's Straits, she had only just begun to load her cargo, and for the whole of the rest of that day, I watched, fascinated, as she took on drums of petrol and fuel oil, sacks of coal and flour, packages of Pablum biscuits, spring mattresses, sewing machines, water tanks, stoves and stove piping, marine engines in crates, outboard motors, sheets of glass and building materials, paint, varnish and putty, whisky, beer and Christmas fare, even a pram. It brought home to me the simple needs of those who winter in the Arctic; and next day, when the hatches were battened down, the decks were piled with huge timbers for a new mission building, two motor launches, half a dozen canoes and a heap of heavy sled runners.

That morning Dr. Wood and his two nurses joined ship, and Captain Lloyd gave us the use of one of the two small motor barge tenders, so that we could visit Fort Prince of Wales. It was blowing hard and sleeting as we crashed from wavetop to wavetop down the estuary in a flurry of ice-cold spray. The fort stood on the northern shore, commanding the entrance to the anchorage, and we went up to it from a little beach through grass and wortleberry; and when I saw it I could scarcely believe my eyes. More solidly constructed than any border stronghold along the Welsh marshes, it was quite the most astonishing fortress I had ever seen. Built in the form of a star, its walls were thirty feet thick, the stone masonry perfect and all the guns still in their embrasures, their wooden carriages and wheels as sound as when they were made, for neither rot nor termite can survive in such bitter cold.

The building of this white elephant of a fort, begun in

1731, took thirty years, and as I wandered round the ramparts that look out to Hudson's Bay and dominate the estuary and all the country round, I thought of Radisson and the French and how frightened the Hudson's Bay governors must have been to feel the need of such monumental protection.

Down in the small central part were the remains of the great mess hall where the half-breed governor, Moses Norton, had presided over night-long carousels, the smoking torches and the roaring fires glowing red on his gaudy buckskin clothing, his lank black Indian hair falling over his flushed face, and his innocent daughter, Marie, standing in the shadows, watching him wide-eyed and adoring.

Norton had been a little king in this isolated, frozen world—a king with a court composed of hard-bitten sea captains bent on "privacy" (the Company word for pocket-lining), old fur traders and a scattering of wretchedly paid clerks out to make their fortunes by fiddling the accounts. And in the fort, and all around it, sailors from ships, soldiers, Indian chiefs and a whole host of hangers-on—cast-off squaws, half-breed brats, scavengers of the refuse bin. It was common in those days for Bay traders to take Indian wives and mistresses, but Norton had been in a class by himself. Insanely jealous, rapacious, sadistic, and a moraliser, he had ruled the fort with the whip, supporting the Indians in most of their disputes with the whites, but not above using his powers—and even a little arsenic or some laudanum upon occasion—to get the use of their daughters. He was supposed to have a whole harem of wives and to have murdered two of them.

Standing there, with the cold wind driving in from the Bay, I could imagine what the place must have been like for those men, with no grain elevator dominating the scene, nothing but that dismal country stretching out north into the barrens and south into the limitless jackpine forests, and their homes three thousand miles away across an ice-jammed sea. No wonder they clung in fear to the fort and the shore, terrified of the Indians, terrified of the solitude, seeking refuge in the bottle.

One man, and one man alone, had had the nerve to adventure out into the country—Samuel Hearne. Looking at the forty-two cannon standing guard as they had done since the fort was built, I could see the smoke hanging white in the air as they fired their salute to the lonely sailor starting north. He didn't get far, of course, that first time, and when he set out again a few months later, after recovering from exhaustion, exposure and frostbite, there had been no salute. But Hearne, pursuing the sailor's pipe-dream of a north-west passage, had reached the Copper-mine River and walked on the shores of the Polar Sea. And then, after such a display of fearless exploration, he had surrendered the fort to the French without firing a shot, when he in turn had become its governor. It was unbelievable, and now that I had seen the thickness of the walls, the size of the cannon, the mystery seemed greater than ever.

There is also a modern " fort " at Churchill, part of the defence system of the north, and I saw it that night, driving to it in the Hudson's Bay factor's car down a dirt road with the glint of water, frosty and pale in the starlight. A military checkpoint, and then buildings looming up, black shapes above the scoured and bulldozed silt of the old river bed, and as we penetrated deeper, the place became a blaze of lights, and the buildings, illuminated, looked raw and insubstantial. Impermanent, unwilling tenants of this hostile country, they were strangely deserted; not a soul about. It was science fiction come to life—an earth-born settlement on the moon, with all human life extinguished.

We parked by a bulldozer that was scraping out the foundations for yet another barrack block, and after some searching in the dark, found a door. The buildings were strangely short of doors. An interminable corridor, suddenly and miraculously full of people, and then we were in the foyer of a cinema. It was a big theatre and there must have been a thousand people there, many of them children, some in thick Norwegian-patterned sweaters, others in singlets or sports shirts, for the central heating had the temperature up in the eighties.

And after the cinema, half a mile of crowded corridors, electrically lit and centrally heated, brought us to the Officers' Mess. Everywhere you went in this extraordinary camp it was the same—corridors leading to married quarters, to canteen, to offices, to barrack blocks, garages and airfield. The place was built to hold several thousand, and no person need ever go out in the teeth of the elements.

I remember much later that night a dish of beautifully cooked prawns eaten in the clean, gay kitchen of the factor's house. They and the drink were too much for me, and I returned to the *Rupertsland* desperately sick. It was the first warning of an illness that was to dog me for two years, legacy of the war and my travels through the Sahara and Arabia.

We sailed next day in brilliant sunshine, following a small boat out down the estuary. It belonged to a French-Canadian, and only a few days before, I had watched him installing a new engine in the flimsy shell of the hull. It was not much more than thirty feet long, far smaller than the boat I had left behind me in England, and he was sailing it up to Eskimo Point, where he would spend the winter alone with his trap lines. And in the spring, he'd bring the furs back to Churchill in his boat, threading his way through the ice, sailing single-handed and hunting seal as he sailed.

Fur and seal and walrus, that was all anybody seemed to think about up there— the real people of the country, that is. And the spring . . . how they must long for the spring! The factor had told me that when the spring did come, late in May or early June, he and his wife would sail out into the Bay, and the sun would be hot off the ice, and the sea quiet, sheltered by the debris of the winter freeze.

But now the winter was looming. By October 15, all

ships had to be out of Churchill. Just over a month to go, a month in which to see that all those Posts in the far north were victualled and provided for. Churchill is the supply point. It is also the limit for the casual visitor—yes, there are actually tourists who visit the place. But north from Churchill it is strictly business—traders, missionaries, doctors, radio operators, prospectors, and of course the men of the DEW Line, the distant early warning screen of radar stations that are the outer ring of American defence. And for all but the military, the way in to the north is by boat, or for those with money, the small float and ski planes of that intrepid band of men, the bush pilots.

On the *Rupertsland*, besides the doctor and his two nurses, we had a team of construction men going out to build a hangar, and Father Danielo. Father Danielo, like so many Roman Catholics who have given their lives to the North, was from Brittany, a small, dark man, very quiet and reserved. He had only been home once in twenty years, and all that time he had spent in the north of Baffin Island. He had converted, he said, one family of Eskimos. So little to show for twenty years of toil and hardship in an alien land, and yet he was neither bitter nor depressed. He was upheld by his faith, and like all the Roman Catholics I met up there, he seemed content and at peace with himself, sure in the knowledge that his life had been spent in the service of God and his fellow creatures.

Next morning, with the sun still shining out of a clear sky and the sea as blue as the Mediterranean, I was helping the Mate put extra lashings on the deck cargo of canoes, when Captain Lloyd called me. He had a cable form in his hand. " I'm afraid I have some bad news for you," he said. It was from my wife, to tell me that my mother had died, suddenly and unexpectedly, following an operation. There was no means of getting back, nothing I could do— and the sea so sparkling and blue.

Thirty-six hours later, when we anchored off Chesterfield, the sky was leaden, the wind twenty knots plus and the temperature had fallen to six degrees below freezing.

It was night then, the decks alive with small dark men in parkas, chattering their guttural Eskimo tongue, and out beyond the stern, the ghostly gleam of a big Peterhead police boat. The Mounty came aboard. Even here he wore his scarlet-sashed breeches, and the yellow of his peaked cap showed beneath his fur-trimmed parka hood. Our hatches were open, the winches clattering away, and over the bows a line of lights marked the land, lonely in the surrounding darkness.

I went ashore with the Hudson's Bay Post manager and the two nurses and Dr. Wood, a wild wet trip through hissing waves and biting wind, with the friendly lights of the *Rupertsland* dwindling in the night. A wooden jetty, the flicker of torches, and then a priest was leading us over rock and gravel to the only hospital in north-western Canada.

Here was sudden peace and warmth, a friendly scrubbed and starched world of Grey Nuns, French women who are wedded to God and the North. The forty-bed hospital was almost full of influenza and measles cases, all Eskimo. We handed the resident nurse a case of haemoglobulin bottles, for injections against measles, and trudged on to the Roman Catholic school.

Seventy Eskimo boys and girls were resident here, children from seven to fourteen whose parents had been evacuated south because of serious illness, mainly T.B. They were lying in their beds in two great dormitories and Dr. Wood had just an hour in which to inoculate them. "Measles," the doctor said, "is a deadly disease for these people—that and T.B. and pneumonia. They're all white men's diseases. Even the common cold was unknown up here till we came."

The girls came first, rows of little Mongol faces with

black hair cropped pudding-basin fashion, passive, unafraid, shyly smiling as one by one they bent over, a sister discreetly baring one buttock to the jab of the needle.

The boys followed, more excitable, more individual in face and behaviour—comical little gnomes in their old-fashioned woollen combinations. And in charge of them was the only really beautiful Eskimo girl I saw in the North, the first of her people to become a nun.

" Come and look at this," the doctor called to me. He had bared one boy's backside and was pointing to a faint purplish tincture of the skin just above the tail. " There's proof that they came from Asia. All the Mongols have that mark."

A priest came in to warn us that the wind was rising, the tide dangerously low. We went out by canoe through the waves breaking on the bar, and it took us half an hour to reach the ship. " Too much wind, eh?" an Eskimo yelled in my ear, his face streaming water, and then the boat crashed against the ship's side and we jumped.

In the grey light of an ugly dawn, Captain Lloyd took the *Rupertsland* to sea in a hurry. The wind had swung through 180° and the ship was dragging her anchor on to a lee shore. It was the only time I heard him swear. " Always the same in this damned place. Worst weather in the whole Bay." It was blowing full gale. In years of sailing I have never seen an uglier sea. It was all white, the waves short and steep because of the short fetch, and all the broken water merged and half-obscured in sheets of white spume driven flat across the surface of the sea. It was snowing.

All the rest of the voyage, I was to hear stories of this gale which blew hurricane force. Arthur Mansfield, a young English student of marine mammals, working out of Coral Harbour tagging walrus for the Department of Fisheries, nearly lost his life, caught on a lee shore in a small native craft. " I didn't mind," he told me with an

air of bravado. " I could swim. But the Eskimos couldn't."
As if that made any difference in those icy seas.

Father Trinel, who had come all the way from Halifax
through the Straits in a Peterhead police boat with four
Mounties, was more matter-of-fact. They, too, had been
caught on a lee shore, at Seashore Point off the eastern
tip of Southampton Island, the ice piling in and forcing
them on to the reefs. Only a sudden shift of wind had
saved them.

But the *Rupertsland* didn't have to face this gale in the
open sea. We were headed inland, 166 miles, to Baker Lake
to meet the People of the Deer. Naitok, a small, squat
Eskimo with a wizened face and slit eyes, piloted us up the
112 miles of Chesterfield Inlet. He did it only once a year,
yet his hunter's brain, unclouded with the complications of
our civilisation, remembered every inch of the rock-strewn
fiord.

And as bare, glacier-scarred rock gave place to the low,
rounded hills of the tundra, green with summer's stunted
vegetation, he searched the land indefatigably through the
ship's glasses. We, too, were searching. " Do you see any
caribou, Naitok?" He shook his head, grinning. " Naa-a.
N'khar-boo. Aa-ugh." The last a guttural, animal-sounding
laugh, as though the absence of caribou were a huge joke.

But it was no joke to the Eskimos of Baker Lake. Caribou
to them meant food for the winter, clothing, boots, harness
for the dogs, trade goods—and there was only one small
herd two day's march away.

Sandy Loonan, the Baker Lake Post manager, could
remember when all to the west the land was black with
caribou, a herd almost half a million strong. But the im-
provident Eskimo, armed with the rifle, has now almost
obliterated the basis of his precarious existence.

As always when the boat is due, most of the Eskimo
were in from the " land " and gathered about the Post,
living in tents and makeshift huts, their sled dogs tethered

in lines and half-starved on a miserable diet of dried fish. The impression, as our two motorised barges trundled the year's supplies ashore, was of a small beachhead, but there was more excitement, for this was the highlight of their year, with everyone, young and old, laughing and cracking jokes, and even the smallest children staggering up to the Post under loads of Pablum biscuits, the staple diet that is the Government's attempt to make good the loss of the caribou herds.

Sandy Loonan, sixty-two years old and twenty-seven years in the North, regretted the scarcity of caribou as much as the Eskimo. "Och, ye never get tired of it—it's a wonderful meat." Particularly the tongue, which is a delicacy. Unfortunately, there was no caribou meat at the Post, only hides, which were shipped out to the *Rupertsland* in great bundles, payment by the Eskimo for their winter stores.

Close by the Post was Canon James's house. He had lived there twenty-six years, and as I sat over a cup of tea with him in the spartan simplicity of his home, two things worried him—rheumatism that was affecting his hands and an insufficiency of coal. The Anglican Missions seemed to be far less well organised than the Roman Catholic; they operated on a shoe-string. Close by was the little church that he and the Eskimos had built themselves, a neat clapboard structure, beautifully appointed inside and spotlessly clean. I shall always remember that church, for it was the first place of worship since I had received that cable, and kneeling there on the edge of the Arctic, the boards so lovingly polished, I remembered my youth and the fun we'd had together, the long years of childhood and the security of being loved, and was thankful that we had had so much. And in the evening, I followed the lonely sound of the single bell through the dark and stood in the lamp-lit interior, now crowded with men and women and children, all Eskimo, and sang with them psalms and hymns that had been carefully translated into their own language.

They sang beautifully and with that wonderful ebullience that characterises everything they do.

Farther along the curve of the shore was a new settlement erected at great cost with taxpayers' money, part of Canada's contribution to the Geophysical Year. Here trained technicians of the Department of Transport studied the ionosphere and other phenomena, living relatively in the lap of luxury. Some even had their wives with them in centrally-heated married quarters that were newly furnished and bright with colour. Newcomers to the North and flush with Government money, they paid the Eskimo more for any job than the Hudson's Bay Company rate, employed the most intelligent of them about the camp, regardless of the fact that they were always the best hunters and that the future of the families that depended on them would be bleak indeed when the Government closed the camp, for the art of the hunter requires constant practice and is a habit soon lost. In their comfortable quarters, in the construction men's hut and in their powerful launch, the conversation was all of how the Hudson's Bay Company was exploiting the natives and how they themselves were paying them better, treating them better. But it was they who called the Eskimos "natives" not the Company men. They did two years in the North, whilst the Company men spent their lives there. They stayed in the isolated security of their warm camps, and never lived with the Eskimo as the Company men did. They were critical, too, of the Mission, and of the R.C.M.P., completely incapable of understanding the problems of the isolated people these men had spent a lifetime serving.

The R.C.M.P. was represented by Corporal Wilson, a tough, fair-haired young man, whose territory ran north to the Polar Sea and covered more than 125,000 square miles. As though to hold the balance between the newcomers and the old-timers, his Post was half-way between the new camp and the old. He had been five years in the North, and his wife, who was with him, acted as postmistress when he was away on his lonely journeys, by sled in winter and canoe in summer. It was he who paid the Eskimo the $5 a month family allowance, marking the store slip with the commodities in which it should be paid, so that it should not be wasted on tobacco or other luxuries. He kept the census, registered births and deaths, marked on his map the location of every family when they were out on the "land," so that none should die of starvation in the depths of winter if the hunting were bad. It was he who ensured that the Eskimo obeyed the white man's law and not their own natural laws. "It's coming," he said, "so I guess they better learn."

He was tough with them, agreed—and greatly feared. But how else could he run such a huge territory? It was he who had to order them out on to the "land" for hunting. "Otherwise they would just hang around the Post till they starved." Of their absence of any sexual morals, he said, "They are given in marriage as children— the man hunts, the woman sees to the clothes and the house. If a man wants a girl or the woman a boy-friend, then that is a private matter and nothing to do with their families." He had to watch for prostitution, even incest. I asked him about venereal disease, but he said this was not a problem. The men coming into the North now were a much better type than in the old days; they came because they had a feeling for it and liked the life. "But I still got to watch them," he said. "If a girl found she could sell herself to the whites, then she wouldn't regard that as wrong—she'd just think she was sitting on a gold mine!"

As soon as the *Rupertsland* sailed, he would be off up the Thelon River to the game sanctuary, where he was trying to preserve the musk ox, now threatened with extinction. The journey would be by canoe, which, with its powerful outboard motor, was capable of a speed of almost 20 knots. And then, with the first snows of winter, he would be away overland by sled whilst there was still some daylight.

Apart from the people, he had to keep a census of the caribou population, a count of all those killed—a tally of the foxes trapped, too, and the number of wolves poisoned. There is a price on the head of the wolves, for they, too, live on the caribou . . . they jump them in the first hundred yards dash; if they don't kill then, the caribou is into its loping stride and can outrun any wolf and keep going a whole day without pause.

We were three days at Baker Lake, and all that time Naitok was confined on board ship, haunting the rail, slit eyes gazing longingly at the shore out of his gnome-like face, for he had a friend there who would lend him a gun, a wife, anything he wanted. But, poor fellow, the delights of the trip were not permitted him, for he had been in contact with the whites and was considered medically "unclean." Even the common cold is a deadly problem amongst people who have never known it before. I remember Sandy Loonan shaking his head as we said good-bye. Dr. Wood and his nurses had inoculated the whole population against measles, but even so he was convinced there'd be an epidemic as soon as we left. "Always is after the boat's been," he said.

And when Naitok had piloted us back to Chesterfield, I began to understand how terrible can be the visitation of "civilisation" to as isolated people—the hospital was full to overflowing, three to a bed and patients lying in the cold corridors. A hundred and ten cases in all—the common cold, measles, pneumonia; one death already. In the largest settlement in that part of the Bay, there were only eight fit Eskimos to help off-load the winter's stores. And in the R.C. Mission dining-room—so full of company after Canon James's lonely little house—I talked with Father Trinel. Neat in his habit, shaved and well groomed, it was hard to believe that that same evening he had come ashore from the big R.C.M.P. Peterhead that was lying out by the *Rupertsland,* had come ashore after a four-month

sail from Halifax by way of the Hudson's Straits, by the
same means and by the same route that Hudson himself
and later Radisson and Groseilliers had come.

We weighed anchor in the early hours, steaming north
for Repulse Bay, and by morning the ship was plunging
wildly in a bitter grey world of tumbled, broken water. All
day we battered our way north up Roes Welcome Sound
in the teeth of an Arctic gale, making little more than $3\frac{1}{2}$
knots headway in poor visibility that dropped to nil in
squalls that came at us full of snow. And all the time we
had news of other ships, their positions, their gossip. It's a
small world, the North, now that everybody is linked by
radio. "I don't see you yet," said a disgruntled American
voice. And another voice answered him : "I can see you
quite clearly one point on my starb'd bow, four miles. I'll
be passing you two miles to starb'd." One of the DEW
Line supply ships passing a grain ship bound for Churchill.

Captain Lloyd, peering anxiously into the gathering dusk,
smiled wryly. Our own radar had been out of action for
hours. "Always is when you most need it." We were then
in the narrowest part of the Sound with only ten miles
between Southampton Island and the mainland coast; no
radar, the compass out by anything up to 10°, for we were
close now to the magnetic pole, and the chart a sketchy
piece of work, mostly blank, with a few islands marked and
only a single track of soundings.

Dead reckoning put us right in amongst a group of
islands. Tidal information was as sketchy as the chart.
The echo-sounder clicked at a steady forty fathoms. Except
for the echo-sounder and our engines, we were no better
off than the ships that had come north in the early days.
We shared the same doubts and anxieties as night fell and
a glimmer of moonlight showed a black waste of heaving
water.

The coastline would be low here, almost invisible till we
struck—and if we did, it would be a wicked shore of
naked, ice-glazed rock, laced with outlying reefs, a shore

that would steal up on us unawares with no hope of rescue for many hours. The Mate, a humorist, chose that moment to tell the story of a ship he'd served in that had run slap into a vertical granite cliff. And then suddenly the echo-sounder was shoaling. Thirty fathoms, twenty-five, twenty . . . the engine room telegraph rang for Stop and the Mate disappeared in a hurry to be followed by the clatter of the anchor chain. We let out ninety fathoms of chain and then kept watch through the night, drinking coffee on the bridge and listening to the snatch and grind of the chain as the ship dragged it over a rocky bottom.

The strain showed then on Captain Lloyd's face, the kindly features lined a little deeper, the eyes puffy with lack of sleep. It was a face that had experienced many such moments, for the ships of the Hudson's Bay Company's fleet enter coves and inlets in conditions that would send deep-sea skippers round the bend in a week. The day I joined the ship, they'd had a diver down, checking the hull for damage, because she had been blown broadside on to a rock in Rankin Inlet, a place where there was hardly room to swing a cat, let alone a 364-ton ship.

It is hard for men like Lloyd when the passage between Posts is bad—particularly perhaps for the Mate of these ships—for it is on those passages that they are expected to make up their arrears of sleep. The instant the anchor is down, it is cargo, all day and into the night, with the crew working without respite until everything for that Post is off-loaded and trundled ashore in the lighters and the ship sails again with whatever in the way of skins the Post has to export.

Morning came and with it the sun, and we steamed into Repulse Bay where one lonely ice floe glimmered white as a winter goose. The Post stood in a little rock-bound cove, the clapboard gleaming white in the sun, the red shingle roofs sparkling bright, and behind it were a huddle of tents and shacks on a headland marked by graveyard crosses. A small R.C. Mission, and that was all. A little community on the edge of nowhere—isolated and forlorn looking in a land that was naked rock right to the Polar wastes of perpetual ice. And as we went into the beach, a Norseman float plane went past us, trailing a white wake, took off and disappeared in the direction of Southampton Island.

Almost every year the Company's Arctic Manager makes a tour of the Highlands of Scotland, a recruiting drive that has continued down the centuries. And here, as elsewhere, the Post Manager, Don Mathieson, was a Scot, for the Company knows that the wild north of the British Islands breeds the men who can best stand the tough, wild solitude of life in the North. He was a raw-boned, black-haired youngster with parka thrown open and peaked cap on the back of his head, and he gave me the first news I had had of my friend David Walker, an author who has taken up residence in Canada and was then on a sled journey somewhere to the north of me with the Mounties. Mathieson was just down from Holman Island and David had passed through his post. He produced pictures. Strange how close these scattered communities seem, yet the distances so vast, the going so hard. Like the desert, everybody is accounted for, known about, discussed.

We hadn't been at the Post an hour before the Norseman was back and I was being introduced to Rocky Parsons and his crew man, both long, rangy types, with eyes running into lines at the corners and a two-weeks' growth of beard. "All *crud* right down to the ground," Rocky said. "Couldn't find a hole anywhere, so we had to turn back." And when I asked what would have happened if the fog had closed in on Repulse as well, he just shrugged his shoulders and said, " Be too bad, I guess." He left it at that and put a tin of beans and one of sausages on the stove to cook.

That just about sums up bush flying in the North. They shrug off danger, hoping for the best. Sometimes they buy it. Other times they cling to life by their eyebrows and come out of it to fly the same routes again and again. Sooner or later the luck runs out.

We took on a passenger at Repulse—a young husky pup that yowled like a wolf at the dismal prospect of sea all around him. Bought for breeding, he had already travelled down by plane from Iglulik, and now he was going by ship to Churchill and then by train to The Pas and by car to Cumberland House—a dog's life! We turned about and went back down Roes Welcome Sound, for all to the north the ice was solid according to the pilot's report. One more call—Coral Harbour, a Post no different from Repulse and just as desolate—and then the temperature was back above freezing as we headed south for the bottom of the Bay.

We, we are Cæsars, Radisson had written. He had been king of these frozen wastelands, lord of the Bay, a cunning, reckless daredevil of a man, his skull disfigured by the tomahawk of a drunken brave. I wondered what he would have said if he could have seen Fort Churchill as I saw it on the morning we returned, the grain elevator visible twenty miles away and no less than nine ships entering or leaving the estuary or tied up at the loading quay. All this and the Posts I had visited far to the north was his work— his and Groseilliers'. Without those two Frenchmen there would have been no Hudson's Bay Company and paradoxically Canada would have remained French. Having seen the bitter cruel land in which they fought and explored and intrigued, I salute them down the centuries for the great adventurers they were.

VI. THE ELEMENTS

FOG

Consider for a moment the words that come so easily to us when we speak of the elements—words like rain and hail, snow, thunder and lightning. These must have been among the earliest words produced in our language, for the weather was a basic factor in the lives of all when man first learned to communicate with man. Each of these words is exactly expressive of the elements it names. They are onomatopœic. And so is the word FOG. It drips misery. It is a cry of sheer terror. From the soft *f* to the closure of the throat on that hard *g,* those three letters describe exactly this creeping thing, this miasma that so abruptly isolates, rendering man helpless and sightless in a wierd void that takes him back to his primitive beginnings.

Unlike the words for other elements, this one is not traceable to eastern and northern invaders of Britain; probably because they were not accustomed to fogs of any real density, other than at sea, until they reached our coasts. There is an old Welsh word, *ffyg,* meaning moss or rank grass that has not been grazed—in other words a damp growth—and this may well have been the origin.

Whatever its derivation, no one who has experienced a real fog can fail to appreciate the aptness of the word or the claustrophopic effect of the thing itself. It has the stillness, the heaviness of death. It lies cold on the eyeballs and thick in the throat, an intangible blanket that makes a void of the familiar street, a shoreless waste of every open space. " Fear death?" Browning wrote, "—to feel the fog in my throat, the mist on my face. . . ."

Born and brought up in England, I find it hard to realise that there are people who have never seen a real fog. A sea fog—the scientifically-minded call them advection fogs

—yes. They occur in many waters where warm, moisture-laden air passes over the colder water surface and is cooled to dew point. But there are not so many places in the world where the inland or radiation fog is common.

For this type of fog to form, minute particles must be present in the atmosphere to provide a nuclei for the water droplets. Certain other conditions are necessary. The wind must not exceed more than ten miles per hour, or the fog will be dispersed. Again, if the wind is less than two miles per hour, the moisture will not remain in suspension in the atmosphere, but will be deposited on the ground as dew. And the basic cause of the fog is, of course, the same as for sea fog—a lowering of the temperature of a humid atmosphere to dew point.

The minute particles, that form the nuclei to which the water droplets cling, can be salt from sea spray. This is often responsible for the white fogs of coastal districts, usually called mists. Inland, the dust particles, always present in the atmosphere close to the ground, will provide the nuclei. But there is nothing these droplets love more than the tiny particles produced by smoke—particularly coal smoke; which is why the thickest and most unpleasant fogs occur in industrial districts or over large cities.

But whether it is what the Londoner calls a "pea-souper" or the grey fog of the open country, it is still a strange, eerie and somewhat frightening phenomenon, quite unpredictable. Seen from a car at night, it is a grey, impenetrable wall, each minute droplet of water reflecting the gleam of the fog lamps so that the straining eyes of the driver can see nothing, not even the edge of the road. Then the "cat's eyes" are the only guide and I have driven sixty miles at a steady thirty miles an hour and never seen a thing except those cat's eyes coming up in a steady stream beyond the bonnet.

These fogs usually occur in the autumn, particularly November, for then the sun is still warm enough to draw moisture up into the atmosphere, and the nights are cold and clear, producing the necessary drop in temperature. One October, I remember taking five hours to drive the thirty miles to the coast. This was at night, on a road that had no cat's eyes, and I drove completely blind, my wife leaning out of the side window and reporting the distance from the edge of the road every few seconds for mile after weary mile. The strain of that drive was so great that I spent the remainder of the night fighting the wheel in my sleep as imaginary cars came at me out of the fog.

But it is not only at night; in broad daylight I have been forced to turn back, unable to penetrate for more than half a mile through the fog—and that was not in an industrial district, but trying to get out of my own village, where I knew every twist and turn of the road. Other times, I have progressed in jerks, the fog suddenly lifting and then as suddenly clamping down again.

But when the fog lies thin in layers, then it is at its weirdest. Then sometimes you drive just below it, as though a canopy had been stretched above the road.

Once, when I owned a little, low-slung sports car and was groping my way through thick fog, a coach went roaring past. The driver could see the hedges on either side, his head just above the fog layer. It sounds absurd, but a little farther on, in a slight dip, I passed him, driving with my head just under the fog, whilst he in his turn was driving blind.

These are commonplace experiences, shared by most people who live on the North Atlantic seaboard, but they may help to give some idea of the nature of inland fogs to those in other parts of the world who are not accustomed to them.

Fog is not, of course, peculiar to Britain alone, as some people seem to think. I have seen it very thick in Labrador and much farther south in the valley of the Shenandoah, and under the bastard name of " smog " it is not unknown in sunny California ! In Europe, it is largely confined to the northern coastal areas, but nevertheless I

have had it clamp down on me in the Po valley in winter;
and, in fact, records show that all of Europe is liable to fog.
A description of the great fog of 1783 even includes North
Africa : " It extended from the north of Africa to Sweden.
It rose above the loftiest mountains." This, of course, is
quite unusual—most radiation fogs are shallow, 500 to
1,000 feet at the most.

Nor is fog the prerogative of London. What with smoke
abatement and smokeless zones and the conversion of many
office blocks to oil-fired heating, the accolade for prime
thick fog is rapidly passing to the northern industrial belts.
In fact, with the exception of the extraordinary "smog"
of 1952, which persisted for four days and is supposed to
have caused the death of 4,000 people, I cannot remember
anything in London since the war approacing the pro-
verbial " pea-souper."

However, the delusion that fog is special to London still
persists, nourished by half a century of literature. Like the
Hollyood idea of the London taxi-cab, it is an association
that dies hard . . . and like all associations it is founded on
the reality of the past. London fogs *were* exceptional.
They were the yellowest, filthiest, most choking in the
world.

This was particularly true at the turn of the century. By
then the "Great Wen" had sprawled for miles over the
countryside and several million open coal fires were pouring
their filth into the atmosphere. The result : "a London
particular," as Dickens called it in *Bleak House.*

Who coined the word "pea-souper"? I do not know.
But it is apt.

My father still vividly remembers the fogs at Kew when
he was a boy: "They came up from the river, seldom
more than twenty feet in depth, but like a thick soup, so
dense that there was not a carriage or cart on the road, and
at night I have stood right under a street lamp and only
seen the faintest glimmer of the gas mantles."

The "soup" was doubtless thinner when I first came to

London in the early thirties, but it was still of that consistency and thick enough to stop the traffic dead; flares would be out along the kerbs at Hyde Park Corner then and men would walk ahead of the buses with flaming torches.

"The yellow fog that rubs its back against the window-pane." That description of T. S. Eliot recalls it exactly. It still had that sort of solidity and there was always a menacing quality about it . . . very different from the autumnal mists that cloak London evenings with an unbelievable magic, a magic more sadly romantic to me than either Paris or Amsterdam, both cities of great charm in such conditions.

But a city literally blacked out by fog is a dead, unlovely place, peopled by ghosts that grope and feel their way along the brick fronts of the houses or call to each other in lost, disembodied voices. Then the footfall behind you assumes a menace strangely personal. . . .

> *Like one that on a lonesome road*
> *Doth walk in fear and dread,*
> *And having once turn'd round, walks on,*
> *And turns no more his head;*
> *Because he knows a frightful fiend*
> *Doth close behind him tread.*

Those lines from Coleridge's *Ancient Mariner*, how they leapt to mind as I groped my way home alone through London streets; and thoughts of murder. How many murders has the fog cloaked . . . the hands of Mr. Ottermole reaching out from the pages of Thomas Burke. . . .

. . . . and on an evening of fog, when London was a world of groping phantoms, a small girl, in the bravery of best Sunday frock and shoes, shining face and new-washed hair, set out from Logan Passage for St. Michael's Parish Hall. She never got there . . . through the fog somebody's large white hands reached after her, and in fifteen minutes they were about her . . . with the speed of ill news came the crowd, pale and perturbed; and on the story that the unknown monster had appeared again, and this time to a child, their faces streaked the fog with spots of hate and horror.

Limehouse. And farther west, as every devotee of Conan Doyle knows, you can hear the clip-clop of the horse's hooves and see the vague shape of the hansom loom through the fog, as it brings another of those mysterious clients to Holmes's door. The literature of the period is steeped in fog. Not because it was new in London. Evelyn records in his Diary for 15th December, 1670: "The thickest and darkest fogg on the Thames that ever was known." And earlier still, Shakespeare has a dozen references to it. But the city had grown so big in the Victorian Age and coal fires had given such a foul solidity to the fog that it made an indelible impression on all writers who lived in London.

I suppose the nearest approach to these conditions that anybody has experienced in modern times is the suffocating artificial black-outs produced by smoke-screens in the Second World War. It is an indication of the obliterating effect of fog that man should have turned to it as a weapon of war. The seaman, living much closer to the elements, was the first to use it, as a means of escaping from a more powerful adversary; but in 1940, canisters of oil were snuffing out whole cities in Britain, and four years later I groped my way through the panic-stricken streets of Naples in a nostril-clogging man-made fog as thick as anything London has ever experienced.

But now let us leave the dirt of city fogs and go back to the open country—to the hills where up-slope fog is the traveller's nightmare and carries with it the threat of death through exposure. It has the same uncanny quality, but, being unpeopled, the menace is impersonal. No groping phantoms here, only the dim-seen shape of a rock or the gaunt arms of a wind-racked tree to make you start and catch your breath.

Seen from a distance as it coils up the valley, it is a white, writhing, ectoplasmic substance, weird as a witch. Enveloped in it, the world is suddenly grey—a moisture-laden void. These up-slope fogs or mists are to be found in hill country in many parts of the world; but because of personal association I would speak particularly of two places in the British Isles—Dartmoor and the Highlands.

Both have been written about extensively; Dartmoor in particular. Out of the sleepy Devonshire countryside, this grim moor, blackened by *swaling*—the yearly burning of gorse and heather to encourage the grass—rises less than 2,000 feet; but so abruptly and to such strange outcrops of rock, or tors, as to astonish the visitor. Its area is less than four hundred square miles, yet the impression of its personality is indelible. Anybody who has stumbled across it step by step in the company of Holmes and Dr. Watson, listening to the baying of that ghastly hound, will understand what I mean.

Right in the centre of it stands the " Moor," a bleak starfish of granite prison blocks. I have seen prisoners clearing snow from the road with visibility down to thirty yards, watched over by a single warder, and have expected, at any moment, that one of them would make a break for it. Many have tried—mostly in these conditions—but ten miles of bog-filled moor, the mist and the bitter cold defeat most of them at the outset. And when the great bell tolls, then the work parties are recalled, the prison gates are shut and the tracker dogs are loosed.

Maybe it is this association with countless escapes that makes the moor such a grim, terrible place in mist. It is difficult to rid places of their association and I have never walked Dartmoor without the thought of those mists nagging at my mind; the worst I have experienced was a light mist, and then the hounds were in full cry after a fox and the eeriness of that sound was appalling.

But in the Highlands it is the emptiness. There, in the

extreme north of Scotland, it is a world almost remote and unpeopled as the north of Canada, a world of bog and loch and granite mountain with the sea thrusting long fingers into it. To see it you must walk, and to walk—even in summer—is to take your life in your hands. Nobody but a fool goes out, even on the fairest day, without extra clothing, food and compass, for, if the mist comes down there is nothing for it but to stay put and sit it out.

Mist in high country can, on the other hand, be wonderfully rewarding. I have climbed all morning with nothing visible but a ten-yard stretch of mountainside around me, and then suddenly a puff of wind has torn the veil from my eyes and given me a fragmentary view of valley and lake basking far below in clear sunlight—a breathless glimpse of another world.

One more picture of mountain mist : We were high up on the great Jostedals glacier of Central Norway. The blue of glacier ice, the white of snow shone brilliant all about us in the hot sun. But at a containing edge of the glacier, where bare rock outcropped from the ice and dropped 5,000 feet to the fiord below us, all was dark and obscured, a swirling greyness that recalled Milton's description of Hades. Into this witch's cauldron of unstill vapour we tumbled large rocks and from the depth below rising air currents brought the sulphur smell of rock-struck sparks to our nostrils. It was strangely exciting, like playing with the Devil himself, for at the back of our minds was the knowledge that we had to go down through the mist. But the Devil was kind that day.

From the mountains to the marshes, to the " fen-sucked fogs, drawn by the powerful sun to fall and blast her pride." Over estuary and river valley it lies like a wraith, not dangerous in itself, but only when man persists in travelling through it. Nerve-racking to the driver on the road, and even to the passenger in the train as it moves in short rushes through the void, reacting with a shudder of brakes to the explosion of each fog signal along the line. But to the pilot in his aircraft, a pure hell of nervous strain as airfield after airfield blacks out.

But these are land fogs. There is another type of fog, infinitely more dangerous to those whose business forces them to face it. It is to be found in most parts of the globe, but particularly in the North Atlantic, in a great sweep from the Grand Banks off Newfoundland via Greenland and Iceland to the British Isles and Norway. I have no experience myself of what it is like along the northern shores of Siberia, but from all accounts the conditions in those icy waters are just as productive of sea fog.

All these fogs are of the advection type. That is to say, they are caused by the temperature of a warm airstream being lowered by contact with the cooler water surface. When this lowering of temperature reaches dew-point, the moisture in the atmosphere condenses into minute droplets that remain in suspension.

A peculiarity of this type of fog is that it will persist in quite strong winds. I can recall my astonishment the first time I experienced this. I was headed down-Channel off the coast of France, and though it closed down on us so thick we couldn't see more than fifty yards, the wind held and we were making over six knots under sail in a steep, short sea. We ran with a large school of porpoise and their wild leaps seemed to indicate that they were enjoying it more than I was, for there are few places in the world where these sea fogs are more dangerous than in the crowded shipping lanes of the English Channel and the North Sea.

I have experienced many of them, sailing my own boat in and out of the ports of Europe, and I can say that with each experience my dread of them has increased rather than diminished. One of the first I encountered was in the North Sea, coming back from Belgium. We were closing the Galloper banks, and all ahead was a brown smudge, as sharply defined as the horizon itself.

There was no moment when we could say : " This is the edge of it, we're going into it now. The sharpness of vision gradually vanished and the world became grey and cold. And then suddenly we were sailing in a vacuum—a claustrophobic void, divorced from all reality, and as strictly confined as a room with a salt-water floor and tenuous walls of vapour. Moisture gathered on the mainsail and dripped from the boom, and as we sailed on, we took our little patch of _lebensraum_ with us, an apparently unchanging area of the sea's surface, and strain our eyes though we might, we could not see beyond those tenuous walls, nor could we sail up to them.

Somewhere close ahead, the Galloper light vessel boomed its warning to shipping. And then, with the sound of it almost on top of us, there was a darkening of the fog ahead and a shape slid by, so vague and indistinct, so abruptly swallowed up again, that it was difficult to believe that it had been a vessel—except that the sound of the fog horn was astern of us now.

Ahead of us then lay the Sunk light vessel, the Eros of a Piccadilly of traffic where the steamer lanes that lead between the Thames banks converge on one focal point. The tension mounted as we picked up the distant sound of a dozen sirens bellowing like cattle in a Highland mist. I had just decided that there was nothing for it but to put about and lie-to until the fog cleared, when there was an abrupt cessation of all sound as though the ships ahead had been suddenly struck dumb, and a moment later the fog was swept aside and there was the Sunk light vessel and the ships steaming on their courses and everything looking so normal that it seemed impossible we had not seen them before and that we had been scared to go on.

That is the nature of fog at sea; sudden, unpredictable—and dangerous.

It is not a thing to fool with, and I have only fooled with it once. I was closing Alderney, the most northerly of the Channel Islands, where the tide runs seven knots through the Race and the narrower gap of the Swinge. It is a deadly area of rocks, but I had twenty minutes of slack water and the wind was free; I stood on for the harbour, navigating by ear alone, the lighthouse fog siren my sole guide.

Suddenly the grey void ahead darkened and solidified, becoming in the instant a fortress of towering rock.

I put about in a hurry and tried again, and this time I had one of my crew up in the bows. Again the fog darkened and became a solid black rock—incredibly the same rock. I kept going this time, hoping against hope that it would prove to be part of the huge breakwater built to hold the British Fleet in the Napoleonic wars. But then I saw the seas breaking through gaps and I turned about in a hurry.

For the third attempt I came in with the sound of the fog siren right over the bows. The fog seemed thinner now and brighter. We could feel the warmth of the sun through it. And then a shout of warning from the bows. " There it is. Up there on the cliffs." And, suddenly, there was the lighthouse, a white blob against the vague blur of the eastern ramparts of the island. The tide had started to make and had carried us right down on to it.

We hugged the coast, hoping that there were no rocks, saw the leading marks, and then we were inside the harbour. There was reaction then from the danger and tension and we felt utterly drained. And then, as though to make the point that we had risked our lives unnecessarily, the sun came through, and in an instant the fog had vanished and the coast of France, ten miles away, was visible under a clear blue sky.

But at night a fog at sea is different. It can creep up on you unawares. I remember lying-to one night off Cherbourg, waiting for dawn in order to get into the little fishing port of Omonville-la-Rogue. It was around two in the morning. It was dark and cold, not much wind and a lumpy sea. I was at the helm when suddenly my companion gripped my arm. " What's that?" he cried, pointing astern. I looked over my shoulder and all behind us was a green translucence as though some phosphorous-coated monster were emerging from the depths.

And then it seemed to gather itself together, hardening abruptly into a pin point of light, and I yelled to him to get the signalling lamp. It was the starboard navigation light of a steamer seen through thick fog, and it was very close. I put the boat about, and when I looked again, there was a big passenger ship lying stopped, with all her lights blazing, not a hundred yards astern of us. The sequel proved more satisfactory than the experience, for the fact that I had so nearly been run down gave me the opening for a book about the sea that I had been wanting to write for a long time.

In the open cockpit of a small yacht, one is in very close contact with the elements, and I have tried in these three personal experiences to convey something of the strain of fog at sea. The danger of being run down is the thing that haunts one, and the invention of radar has increased rather than diminished that danger. Big ships now maintain their speed, even in crowded waters, relying on the seeing eye of this instrument—though every master knows full well that small boats, fishermen, even barges are often invisible in the pattern the waves set up on the screen. Only last year a friend of mine nearly lost his boat. . . . " She was suddenly there, a 10,000-tonner going past us like a cliff and only her bow wave saved us. I could have leaned out and touched her plates."

Even for the big ships, radar has not solved the problem entirely, as the collision between the *Andrea Doria* and the *Stockholm* proved. In any case, this is but the latest of a long series of gadgets invented by man to reduce the dangers—from the bell-metal Chinese fog gong to the weird cow-like fog blast of our modern light vessels, a sound that has been a part of my memory since early childhood. And how often have I lain at sea off a dangerous shoal listening to the dismal clang of clapper on metal? " 'Tis a fog bell on a rock-bound coast."

But the dangers faced by Longfellow's *Hesperus* are nothing compared with that Arctic manifestation of fog— black ice. Fishermen on the Newfoundland Banks know it well, so did the men sailing the convoys to Murmansk during the war. And only a few years back two British trawlers, the *Lorella* and the *Roderigo,* abruptly ceased radio contact with the words : "Listing badly . . . going over on side." Like the invisible ice surface so deadly on roads, it appears out of nowhere on rigging, masts and deck, increasing with the rapidity of a fungus growth. Shackleton nearly lost his life through it in that incredible journey he and his companions made in an open boat from Elephant Island to South Georgia, and there is that strange story—fiction, but near to fact—of a Newfoundland fishing boat transformed into a half-submerged block of ice with all her crew trapped alive below decks.

I will let Shakespeare have the last word :

> *The starry welkin cover thou anon*
> *With drooping fog as black as Acheron.*

VII. THE SEA

1. BEAT TO WINDWARD

It was ten o'clock in the morning and we were off the north coast of France, beating across the bay of the Somme towards the little fishing port of Le Treport. Cayeux lighthouse stood like a needle straight over the bows and already we could make out the v-shaped gap in the chalk cliffs that marked the entrance to Le Treport. It was only nine miles away and it never occurred to me that we shouldn't make it before the lock gates of the inner basin closed around midday, for though the sea was fairly calm, we had plenty of wind and were sailing at six knots under the big yankee jib, staysail and full mainsail.

In the broad entrance to the Somme, we went about, sheeting the sails in flat, driving the boat hard into the wind, urged on by the knowledge that there was a gale blowing up and Le Treport our only immediate shelter. This was my first cruise in a boat of my own.

My original intention had been to get a boat in which my wife and I could poke our noses out of our east coast estuary and make short passages along the English coast. But as is the way with boats, imagination had outrun both pocket and caution. I fell in love with a well-known ocean racer. Her name was *Triune of Troy,* ten tons and thirty-eight feet long with some six hundred square feet of canvas to handle. She lay at Blyth in Northumberland, and I brought her two hundred and fifty miles down the coast with a scratch crew, a book-learned knowledge of navigation and so little sailing experience that I'd no right to be outside of an estuary at all.

Now on the north coast of France my luck ran out on me. Beating past the Cayeaux light we struck a freak patch. We were close inshore and the wind fell away and our

speed with it. We lowered the yankee and hoisted the
genoa, our largest sail. But it was an old sail and we could
not point so close to the wind. Winching it in flat, so that
it reached back almost to the cockpit, the sheet rope broke.
More time lost while we rove a new rope. The wind fell
lighter. The tide turned against us.

It was twelve-thirty when we sailed between the concrete
piers of Le Treport. With a sinking heart I saw the wet
slime marks indicating that the tide had already started to
fall. " *Le bassin?*" I shouted to the harbour official. " *C'est
ouvert?*"

" *Non, non monsieur,*" he called back. " *C'est fermé.*"
Shut! My mouth felt dry. We weren't a strong crew,
only three of us, and we were tired after two days and
nights at sea—tired and wet and hungry. And we couldn't
stay in the outer port of Le Treport, for it dries ten feet or
more at low tide.

Le Treport, with its quaint shops huddled round the
waterfront and the gaily-coloured fishing boats doing a
roaring trade in Paris trippers, smiled at us mockingly in
the sunshine. If we had been fifteen minutes earlier!
"Down mainsail," I ordered. We could stay just one hour
—no longer if we were to get safely across the bar at the
entrance.

The mainsail dropped two feet, then jammed. I motored
round and round the harbour, the crowds staring at us, as
the crew struggled to get the sail down. The slides that run
in a track on the mast were sticky with stale grease and
salt. Then minutes struggling and at last it was down on
the deck. We regreased the track with margarine from the
galley, and then we moored and had some food.

The shipping forecast spoke of gales in the Atlantic and
a depression moving north-east across Ireland. But for the
Channel it was still *winds fresh to strong, south westerly.*
Donald and I looked at each other.

" It's fifteen miles to Dieppe," he said. A young yacht
designer who now lives at Fiji, he had a good deal more

experience than I had at that time and I knew he was thinking that it would be a dead beat westward against wind and tide, and we'd all of us had enough of beating to windward for the time being.

"We could go to Boulogne," he suggested.

It would probably have been the sensible thing to do. But it was sixty miles away and though it was down-wind of us, it would mean another night at sea, possibly in a gale. I looked at John, the third member of the crew. He was a youngster who had sailed nothing but dinghies before and was just completing his National Service. Sleep had already overcome him.

"No," I said. "We'll stand off and on outside Le Treport until the basin opens again."

It was the first big decision I ever made in command of my own boat. It meant ten hours out there being tossed about by the seas breaking over the shallow banks. But the charm of Le Treport had cast its spell—that and the thought of sleep in a secure harbour. I glanced at the barometer and I didn't like it. It was falling fast. We cleared the table, woke John and went on deck. Already the top of the harbour wall was level with our lower cross trees, fifteen feet above our deck. Our mooring lines had tightened. The tide, which is a big one here, was going out fast.

A crowd of Paris trippers watched us hoist sail and helped let go our mooring lines. "You go out now?" a *douanier* from the Customs House asked me. I nodded. "I think it is bad out there. Very bad." He shook his head.

We went out under engine with no reefs in our mainsail and the No. 1 jib and staysail set. The last of the fishing boats loaded with trippers was just putting out. We followed its course exactly. Stoutly built though she was, she probably drew less than our sixty feet. I prayed that we hadn't left it too late to cross the bar in safety.

There was a vicious tide-rip off the entrance. *Triune* bucked and reared, the boom of the mainsail jerking violently, tugging at the mast. In the troughs I held my breath, waiting for the bump as we touched the sand bar. But it was all right and soon *Triune* was sailing, heeling over and riding the overfalls of the waves with an easier motion. I cut the engine and eased the mainsheet out to take the weight of the wind out of the sail. Spray was bursting from the bows as our speed rose to six knots. The fishing boat, butting into the seas under engine alone, was a smother of foam, its load of trippers cowering under the bulwarks.

It turned back.

The sun vanished. It began to rain. We headed north-west into a grey murk of toppling seas slashed with white caps. The spray was wet and salt on my lips, my mouth dry. The sea had got up quite a bit since we had entered Le Treport. The wind had risen, too; it was about Force 5, which is fresh, almost twenty knots.

A mile out we dropped the mainsail, lashed it to the boom with canvas tie-ers, and then lowered the jib and handed it below. We were now under staysail alone, jogging along at about one knot, almost broadside on to the waves.

I had purchased *Triune* only three months before and I had no idea how she would behave hove-to under staysail. This sail was set just for'ard of the mast. It was quite small and the foot was rigged to a boom for ease of handling. I lashed the helm, experimenting with the length of lashing until I got it right. Then I lit a pipe and sat there for a while, smoking and watching the behaviour of the boat. The motion was fairly easy now and only occa-sionally a breaking wave hit the deck. Our course varied hardly at all. Behind us Le Treport was just a blur in a gap in the hills. All to the south-west of us was a line of chalk cliffs, grimly grey, an interminable, rather frighten-ing battlement veiled in a mist of rain.

I went below, took off my oilskins and climbed into my berth.

It was a weird sensation, lying there with the hatch

closed and the boat sailing herself through a wild,breaking
sea. The interior of a ten-ton ocean racer is pretty small.
The six-runged ladder leading to the deck was just by my
right hand. By sitting upright, leaning outwards from the
deck beams, I could push open the hatch doors and look
out to the blue ensign ripped out stiffly from its staff by the
wind. Across from me, within reach, was the galley. Behind
me was the saloon—six feet of sleeping space on two
berths with the table jammed between, held in place by
the base of the mast. For'ard of the mast was the foc's'tle
and the sail locker, a black cavity because the deck lights
were blanketed by the dinghy lashed on deck.

Noises in such a small place are magnified. The thud of
a wave breaking against the side sounded like a mountain
of water hitting the boat, the slap of the staysail boom was
the thud of a steam hammer; and the boat talked through
her timbers— *Watch out! Watch out!* a voice kept saying,
and then lost itself in a confused jumble of orders. And all
the time I was conscious of the gurgling sound of water
close against my ear as it seethed and foamed along the thin
skin of the hull.

We slept fitfully, periodically peering out; twice we went
on deck to put about and check our position in relation to
Le Treport.

At nine-thirty Donald woke me with hot soup and stewed
steak in a mug. At ten we went on deck. It was dusk now
and the lights at the entrance to Le Treport showed green
and red. The wind had got up further, bearing out the
forecast which had been for strong to gale force winds in
the Channel. The waves were steep and breaking. " Time
we got moving," Donald said. I took a bearing of the
harbour entrance with the hand compass and nodded. The
basin opened at midnight and we were three miles off.

And then trouble crowded in on us.

Le Treport lay just about dead into the wind's eye. It
was the engine or nothing—and the engine wouldn't start.
I sweated at the starting handle. I used the self-starter till

the battery ran flat. And then, stripped to the waist, I slaved at the starting handle again. Not a kick; and precious time passing.

"There's a fishing boat bearing down on us," John's startled voice came from the cockpit.

"Then flash the signalling lamp on the sails," I shouted back. I had the engine cover off and was removing the sparking plugs.

The lights of the lamp flashed with eerie brightness. "He's coming right at us . . . he's coming alongside." I dived up the ladder. It was black night now and out of the seething white of the waves emerged the stubby, heavy-timbered shape of a fisherman. We shouted for it to stand clear of us, scared he'd smash our flimsy hull; but he came right on, rolling hugely, a great black barrel of a ship, handled superbly. One of the crew was shouting to us, holding the bite of a rope out over the bulwarks. "He thinks we're in trouble."

"We shall be if he doesn't sheer off," I said.

"He's offering us a tow." There was a note of eagerness in John's voice. But the last thing I wanted was a tow. In these seas it would strain the bows, maybe tear the boat apart. I waved my arms in refusal, shouting frantically.

The fisherman passed across our bows, turned and circled, coming back and lying so close alongside us that his rolling mast almost touched our cross-trees. "Non, non. Okay!" I screamed at him. "Okay?" The blue-clad Frenchman dropped the rope. The engines thudded and the black shape waddled clear of us, heading in for Le Treport, the light at his masthead swinging drunkenly. Donald grinned at me. "He thinks the crazy Anglais like it out here."

I turned and flung myself below. We had lost twenty precious minutes. One by one I dried the wet plugs, replaced them and after that the engine started like a bird. We began the long plug into the wind. But the vicious seas stopped us dead. We were on one of the banks with probably less than three fathoms of water under us. The prop thrashed in the troughs. God knows when the engine had last been de-coked, there seemed no real power in it. I was at the helm, with nothing on but a light windbreaker. Yet I was sweating.

We had to make it in time!

But when I checked the bearing of Le Treport, I found we were doing no more than holding our own, maybe creeping a little inshore. The tide had turned now. Tide and wind were against us, and the waves were breaking over the foredeck, their tops smoking with spindrift. We hadn't a hope.

And then a gust of wind on my right cheek. I twisted my head round, glancing up at the ensign. The wind had freed a little. There was just a chance. " Hoist mainsail ! Hoist No. 1 jib !" The sails went up with a run. The boat heeled over—thirty, thirty-five degrees. Water creamed to the edge of the cockpit coaming. We were sailing. The wind freed further, gusting off that long line of chalk cliffs. *Triune* gathered up her skirts, swooped over the waves, thrust back their breaking tops in a smother of foam. Water poured green across the deck. Spray swept over us, higher than than the upper cross-trees.

It was a mad, fantastic sail under engine and over 600 square feet of canvas in near gale-force gusts and big, breaking seas. But we barely noticed the water we were taking inboard. The light of Le Treport were coming visibly nearer every minute and we were keyed up to a pitch of exhilaration. The seas decreased as we neared the cliff line. A mile off I told Donald to flash P on the signalling lamp—P was the local sign for " gates open." We were going to be late, but there was just a chance they'd hold them for us.

We must have been a fine sight from the pierhead— almost flattened by the wind, smothered in spray and sailing at nearly eight knots.

Right in the entrance, I rounded-to into the wind. The

mainsail came down with a run, thanks to the margarine in the slides; God knows what would have happened if it had jammed then! I swung *Triune* in through the steep swirl of water off the entrance. And then suddenly it was calm and quiet and a voice was shouting—"*Vite, vite, monsieur. Le bassin est ouvert.*"

I never wish to hear a more welcoming voice.

Tied up in the basin, listening to the roar of the wind overhead and drinking hot tea laced with rum, we read the instructions for Le Treport in the Admiralty Pilot: *During bad weather from the south-west this coast is unapproachable . . . sailing vessels should avoid approaching the cliffs where they are liable to experience dangerous squalls.*

Well, well! How blissful one is in one's ignorance.

2. BISCAY-BOUND

We hoisted sail at dawn on June 23 and slipped out of our east coast estuary, bound for the Bay of Biscay. Across our course lay the long, buoyed streamers of the Thames banks, and once through the Straits of Dover and into the English Channel, the prevailing wind would be against us and we should face four hundred miles of some of the world's most treacherous sailing.

Three major obstacles stood between us and our goal— the Channel Islands with a near forty-foot rise and fall of tide sweeping over miles of reef, Ushant with its fog and foul weather, and the Chaussée de Sein, the final gateway to the Bay. Each of these obstacles has an inside route, involving a passage through dangerous tidal races, and all the last part of our voyage would be along the Brittany coast of France, where a dragon's teeth litter of rocks runs far to seaward.

There were four of us on board *Triune* and we sailed in glittering sunshine following a day of storm and rain. The

sea was calm and the sun shone bright on the red hulls of
the light vessels as we reeled them off like milestones on
our course—the Cork, the Sunk, the Kentish Knock, the
North Goodwin. By nightfall we had passed inside the
Goodwins, those dread sands that a bare thousand years
ago were an island protected by dykes and which are now
fringed with the masts of sunken wrecks.

We were in the straits then, and Dover and the white
cliffs of England faded away astern. The ghostly glimmer
of *Triune's* canvas stood aslant the stars as she tramped
the midnight waters of the Channel underfoot in a steady
splurge of sound. We went into a night watch routine that
wouldn't be varied until we were in the Bay—one man alone
at the helm, the other three asleep below.

Red and green the lights of ships came up in a steady
stream, an endless thread of seaborne traffic converging on
Dover Straits. All to the west of us their masthead lights
shone like twin stars low in the sky. They came up over the
horizon's edge and went thumping past us in a blaze of
cabin lights, to drop behind us as a single, solitary light.

How was it ever possible for man to think the earth was
flat?

And there were others, coming up astern of us out of the
east, already beginning to sort themselves out into their
separate lanes—the coasters hugging England close, whilst
the deep-sea tramps and tankers headed for the Bishop
Rock Light, last contact on the North Atlantic run, or
farther south for the Casquets and Ushant, *en route* for
South America, the Cape or Suez.

A small-scale map shows the English Channel so choked
with these steamer lanes that you'd think a sailing vessel
in imminent peril of being run down. And if you should
pass through the Channel in a passenger ship, this impression will be confirmed, for the ship would keep to the
steamer lanes, and these are narrow and about as full of
traffic as Oxford Street in the rush hour. But even half-way
down the Channel there is as much as fifty miles between

one steamer lane and the next— and in a small boat you can feel as lonely there as you can in mid-Atlantic—particularly when a sou'westerly gale is blowing and the seas are steep, and breaking with a vicious curl and thrust of white water that fills the cockpit.

As we headed across the Channel, the steamer lanes dropped astern of us one by one, each lane a line of light as bright as a coastal town; until finally the last of them disappeared below the horizon. We were alone then, with nothing but the compass light to keep the helmsman company on his solitary watch. And though the night was not as perfect as one a year before when I had glided my boat down the moon's path with the white cliffs of the Seven Sisters standing like seven silent ghosts over our stern, it was still a night to dream about, the wind free and *Triune* trailing a luminous wake of phosphorus, heading at a steady seven knots for a coast of brandy and wine.

Twenty-four hours and a hundred and thirty sea miles later, we entered Cherbourg, slipping into the Grande Rade by the eastern entrance, our salt-tired eyes confused by the mass of lights reflected in the black mirror of water.

The open sea is a matter of routine, and sometimes of endurance. Bar an occasional ship, there are no obstructions. But coming into port is another matter. It is always a strain, particularly at night, when the navigation lights of vessels, the leading lights and lights of buoys and on piers and harbour walls, all have to be picked out from the welter of shore lights, identified by colour or periods of flash, and checked against chart and Pilot Book—and if the wind is fresh, it is surprising how quickly you come down on them.

One always hopes, of course, to make one's landfall just before dawn. Then one can use the flash period of lighthouses to fix one's position, and yet make the actual port in daylight. But it seldom happens that way, and all we saw of the eastern entrance of Cherbourg was the shadowed bulk of those twin fortresses, Ile Pelée and Fort de l'Est; and then suddenly the black line of the *digue* masked the shore lights, and a moment later we were in the shelter of this massive, two-mile breakwater erected by the Napoleons to provide a fortified base for the French Navy.

We lay that night near where the Cunarders berth on their way to and from the States, and as we put the boat to bed, the fat red funnels of the *Queen Mary* were brilliant in the loading lights. And at eight in the morning we hoisted the blue ensigns of the Royal Ocean Racing Club, raised our courtesy tricolour flag to the cross-trees and motored into the yacht harbour.

There are few things in this world that produce a greater sense of satisfaction than to sail your own boat across the sea and into a foreign port. She may be only ten tons, but you have most of the rights—as well as the responsibilities—inherent in captaining the largest ship afloat, including (bureaucracy be praised!) the right to taken on tobacco and liquor " out of bond," in other words free of Customs Duty. To visit Monsieur Henri Ryst's ship-chandling office and see hard liquor, like Scotch and gin, listed at less than a quarter of the price ashore, cognac at a third, cigarettes at a fifth—it is enough to raise the morale of even the tiredest Scotsman; and then to have Monsieur Ryst apologise for not delivering until after 5 p.m.—because he has to victual the *Queen Mary*! And finally the moment comes when all those beautiful bottles are collected in the dinghy and taken back to the ship to be stored lovingly away against the day they will be drunk, the crew all lending a willing hand amongst a litter of paper and straw.

It is for this that one puts in to Cherbourg. . . . Why else, when close-by are such attractive little ports as Omonville-la-Rogue?

We took on enough liquor and cigarettes to last us six weeks and left the following morning in time to catch the west-going tide. Catching the tide on this coast is as im-

portant as the train is to the commuter for it runs 5 knots
inshore. Indeed, just to get out of Cherbourg is something
of an achievement in June, for at that time of the year the
place is bedevilled by fogs, and twenty miles to the westward lies the outer bastions of the Channel Islands. The
Alderney Race, the Swinge, the Ortac Channel—any one
of these can suck you into a maze of reefs and granite
rocks. Stand a while on Alderney Island and watch the
Swinge turn white as the tide starts to run and listen to the
mounting roar of the overfalls—you'd never go near the
place in a fog after that. And to head seaward is to run slap
into one of the busiest steamer lanes. Scylla and Chary-
bdis! I've tried it once like that, out of Cherbourg in a
fog, and made the port of Alderney by the skin of my
teeth; but never again.

On this particular morning, however, the sky was blue,
the seas calm, and by midday we were off the entrance to
the Alderney Race, sailing close-hauled with Alderney and
the Sasquets straight over the bows. A slight shift of wind
enabled us to take the inside route, and still headed for the
rocks of Alderney, we were swept broadside into the Race,
the rush of tidal water sucking at the hull of the boat, so
that one moment she lay dead with no feel to the tiller and
the next she had gone into a wild canter, for the rocky
bottom does odd things to these big tides.

In the sleepy haze of later afternoon, we hove-to close
off the rocks of Guernsey Island to wait for the tide, whilst
James produced from the small gas-fired galley stove our
first French meal afloat—*Artichaut en vapeur* with Gevrey
Chambertin, *Entrecôte de Veau avec pommes frittes* with
Pouilly Fuissé, *pêches naturelles*, followed by *Nescafé* with
French Gauloises cigarettes.

It is surprising what you can do in the way of food, even
on a small ship, and afterwards the luxury of brief relaxa-
tion and talk of other voyages—the landfalls made (the
errors, too), moments of fear and near disaster, and the odd
experiences . . . that line of breakers that appeared for no

apparent reason in the middle of the North Sea, the way
the sea suddenly changed colour in Dover Straits . . .
moments of humour, too, like the occasion in Concarneau
when the laughing French fisherman shook his fist at us
as we rowed ashore in our yachting caps and shouted:
"*Toujours le bloody Navy.*"

That night it was cold and damp, with a heavy dew.
From my bunk I could look up through the open hatch and
see the face of the man on watch, pale and disembodied in
the compass light. His hand was on the tiller, his eyes on
the sails, or searching the dark horizon for the lights whose
flash periods he had memorised before going on watch. He
was a still and lonely figure—and yet not lonely, for below
him was the warmth of the lit saloon, with its galley stove
and his three companions asleep in their bunks.

It may be cold and wet up there in the cockpit, it may
be blowing a gale, but the helmsman has only to call out
and the rest of the crew will join him at once; and always
there is the knowledge that, at the end of four hours, he
will be tucked up in his own warm bunk.

It is a complete world in itself, just yourself and the
boat and the sea—a way of life almost, for you are on
your own, entirely self-sufficient.

Why do people do it? It's not just to get to the other
side, the way the mountaineer thinks of getting to the top.
And this sort of day and night sailing in dangerous
waters is far removed from just "messing about in boats."
My own feeling is that it is a combination of many things
—the challenge, the exhilaration of using, and sometimes
fighting the elements, the sense of achievement when you
have made your landfall and brought your boat safe into
a foreign port; above all, the peace of being away out of
reach and on your own in a world that has become too
crowded.

To lie in your bunk, smoking a cigarette and listening
to the radio—a symphony concert, maybe—and in the
background all the time is the sound of the wind in the

rigging, the plunging roar of water being thrown back from the boys, the hiss of it along the outer skin of the boat, close beside your ear . . . sounds of travel, a concert of movement that fills you with that ineffable joy of going somewhere, independent of any mechanical aid.

And around you your few chosen companions; tired maybe, but content, making light of the little nuisances—the drip that has developed from the deck roof, the pump in the heads (the lavatory) that has jammed and must be cleared—reverting to a boyhood level of humour because they are relaxed and at peace with the world.

There is David, ex-Navy and a well-known author, who is for ever rudely commenting on the sail bags with which he has to bed down in the forepeak; James, ex-publisher turned literary agent, now turned cook; and his son, Hamish, a somewhat untidy character who will stay happily at the helm for hours at a stretch and is always willing to be hauled to the top of the mast to see to the rigging or to stay under water for long minutes clearing a mooring line that has fouled the prop.

And most important of all, there is the ship herself. Her wooden hull is like a violin, magnifying every sound—and she talks as she ploughs through the waves. There is a little gremlin lives in a working beam above my bunk, and in heavy weather I have heard it whispering to me in a creaking voice, " Too much sail—too much sail." And in quieter conditions it chatters gaily. " Getting along fine now, getting along fine." Other voices whisper in other parts of the ship, and at anchor the chain cable talks, giving warning when the ship is beginning to drag her anchor.

But perhaps the most salutory thing about crossing the seas in a small ship is that, whoever you are, the elements cut you down to size. There is no room in a crew of four for the man who doesn't fit or doesn't pull his weight. The character of a man is revealed absolutely, and it always astonishes me how tough and wonderfully reliable my wife is—though she loathes the sea and only likes the excitement of getting somewhere. In moments of stress, when the going is bad, when you and the people with you are face to face with nature, the way your prehistoric ancestors were when they first ventured out in their coracles.

And there are other moments—moments of sheer beauty, when you feel God made the world and made it wonderfully, and that you are close to Creation.

One such moment I remember off the Tregoiz Plateau and the Seven Isles; dawn broke on a sea of molten lead patched with weed torn from the bottom by a recent gale, and as *Triune* slid quietly through the water, there was such serenity, such a strange, absolute quiet that the heart ached to see the world so still and beautiful. The sun came up in a red ball, flared into brilliant warmth, and immediately the leaden mirror of the sea was turned to gold—burnished bright and dancing with light.

And there were puffins about—those queer little sea birds with the parrot beaks that you find west of Cherbourg. They had just breakfasted and were sitting on the water in huddles of three or four, discussing plans for the day in their small, croaking voices. I amused myself in the quiet of that dawn watch by trying to creep up on them unobserved. But always they broke off their discussion when the bows were a few yards from them, and then they would look at me with a little squawk of annoyance and try to fly away. But they were so gorged with fish that they couldn't lift their fat little bodies off the water, and with another sidelong glance, as much as to say, " You really are a bore," they would duck their parrot beaks into the sea and dive.

Now once again I was off Les Sept Isles at dawn, but this time there were no puffins and the air was humid with mist. It gathered on the mainsail and dripped from the boom on to my face, cool and fresh, washing the salt from my lips. And instead of absolute peace, there was that constant, rhythmic surge of the boat travelling through the

water, for we had a fair wind and were plunging westward
under the white and blue striped spread of our nylon spin-
naker.

For the first time in a dozen voyages to France I was
running the whole length of the Channel with the wind
behind me. The sun burst through the mist, and up
through the hatch came the smell of bacon and eggs.

We were steadily closing the Brittany coast and in the
afternoon we hauled a balloon on board, marked with the
name of the Cunard Line. With it came a vivid picture
of the bright-lit dance floor of a big liner, and we formally
presented it to Hamish, for it was his twenty-first birthday.

The light tower of the Ile de Batz appeared as a slender
column seen through a heat haze, and as dusk fell I began
to think of Ushant. It was looming close now and we had
sailed hard for over four hundred miles. We intended to
try one of the inshore channels, where the tide runs furiously
through narrow gaps in the reefs, and because we were all
a little tired, I decided to put into L'Aberwrac'h, for a brief
rest.

To be honest, I was a little scared of Ushant. I had
rounded it twice before, and each time had run into a murk
of low cloud, with poor visibility and filthy, breaking seas.
And Ushant is not to be taken lightly by even the most experienced mariner, certainly not by me. Bank upon bank
of half-submerged reefs run twenty miles out into the
Atlantic, to culminate in the Ile d'Ouessant (the French
name for Ushant), and the tides set in on to the rocks,
boiling at a rate of knots through the innumerable gaps,
so that from earliest times sailors have been wary of the
place. Rocks and tides apart, it has a weather all its own,
for it is the meeting place of the Atlantic and Continental
systems, and when it isn't blotted out by fog, or the smoke
of burning seaweed from the kelp-gatherers' fires, it is
blowing half a gale with a wrack of cloud hanging close
over the island and all the waters round about.

And so we ran in towards the coast, steering for the

five-second flash of the Ile Vierge light. And by the time
we had picked up Ile Wrac'h, with its occulting red light,
the night glasses were showing us the rocks as miles of
black fangs against the swirling white beam of Ile Vierge.

Paralleling the coast, just clear of the rocks, I stood in
the bows, well away from the distractions of compass and
navigation lights, and searched the dark shore through the
glasses, waiting for the moment when the leading lights of
L'Aberwrac'h, five miles in amongst the rocks, would reveal
themselves. But when they finally appeared, they were
widely separated, and we ran on westward for more than
half an hour, uncertain how far off the reefs we were, until
at last the lights came into line and we put the helm over
and turned in towards them, running through a welter of
white water, where the tide was pouring over the Libenter
reef.

It's a strange thing to run blindly through the night up a
narrow, rock-strewn passage, with nothing to guide you but
the keeping of one light over another. You feel in God's
hands then, for suppose you have failed to identify them
correctly, and that frail upper light is the window of a
house?

The wind increased, as it often does in the channels leading to an estuary, and we were going very fast, much
faster than I should have liked. But with the channel
narrowing any moment to little more than a hundred
yards, it was no time to think of shortening sail. And then,
from my position in the bows, the glasses showed me the
vague shape of a buoy sliding quickly past; other shapes,
dimly-remembered from a previous visit, emerged out of
the night and quickly disappeared—the outline of a rock
on one side, the shape of a small pillar buoy on the other,
and then at last the Petit Pot de Beurre. The great black
pile of masonry slid away into the night, and a moment
later we had reached the dog leg and I could see the leading
lights of the port itself.

The strain was over, and as we let go the anchor, close

by a line of fishermen, dawn was beginning to give a grey
opaqueness to the night.

We would get some sleep, fill up with fresh water, buy
some *essence* out of bond for our small auxiliary engine,
maybe have a drink ashore, and sail in time to catch the
tide through the Chenal du Four. That was the plan. But
when we woke, it was to the moan of fog signals and a
cold, grey, clammy world, with the stone harbour of the
little port barely visible.

Ushant weather! I stood and stared through the fog, an
oilskin jacket over my pyjamas, wondering whether it
would be as bad outside. But there was no way to find out,
for the channel through the rocks was utterly obscured, and
I went back to my bunk.

We slept and read the afternoon through, and in the
evening we went ashore to feed on cockles, which the
Bretons call *palourdes,* and oysters, fresh crab and lobster,
and to phone our families on the other side of the Channel.

It is surprising how quickly the morale of a crew
deteriorates when the ship is at rest and there is no longer
the business of sailing to keep them occupied. One day in
port and they were bored stiff, the ship no longer a
machine with which to defeat the elements, but a hull in
which we were cribbed, cabined and confined at too close
quarters; and the fog was still there the next day.

In desperation we climbed through humid air to the
inland village of Landeda and drank Muscadet with a
fisherman who had escaped from the Vichy Navy during
the war and been picked up in the Caribbean by an
American submarine. And then we returned to L'Aberwrac'h for more oysters, more crab, lots of cognac, and to
stare out across the harbour at fog that seemed as though
it would never lift.

Back on board, in a wine-glow of optimism I got the
anchor up and the sails hoisted, confusing a slight thinning
of the fog with a promise of clearer weather. We could
have made it out to sea that afternoon, hopping from

dimly-remembered rock to the vague shape of a buoy. But what to do when we got outside, with the rocks on one side and the steamer lane on the other, and Ushant ahead and night coming on? Dutch courage ebbed and we turned about, beating back into L'Aberwrac'h to drop our hook in the self-same spot.

Two days fogbound, and the Bay seemed already a distant dream, with Ushant standing there between us and our goal and growing more formidable with every tide we missed. Sunday dawned, and we watched the fog gradually thin again until by midday we could just make out the beginnings of the channel, narrowed now by the fallen tide, with all its black, weed-grown rocks exposed.

It was the day of the *Fête Nautique* and in the afternoon, out of pure *joie de vie,* the French launched the lifeboat. Our ensign streaming in the clammy breeze, we groped our way after it, down to the Petit Pot de Beurre, and there it abruptly turned about and left us, all gay and with flags and laughing French fisher girls, who waved us *bon voyage* and so dazzled Hamish that we were out beyond the Libenter reef before the big yankee foresail was up.

Clear of the solid mass of the coastal rocks, we turned west. The fog had suddenly gone, but the sky remained chill and grey, and ahead of us Ushant lay under a yellow murk that looked thick as smog. But this was it—the tide under us and just time to slip through the inside passage of the Chenal du Four before dark. And if it was fog that lay so thick over Ushant, then we would cut across the steamer lane and go round Ushant, relying for our positional fixes on our direction-finding radio—a wretched, nerve-racking prospect for myself as navigator and skipper, and little comfort to be got from the knowledge that a mere fifty years ago Bristol pilots would lie off this same treacherous area a week or more at a time, in cutters not much bigger than *Triune,* waiting to board a grain ship or a steamer from the Plate.

Visibility gradually lessened. We cut inside the Porsal

buoy, fighting our way through a broken area of sea, where the waves jumped up at us from all directions as the tide roared over reefs, that had only just sufficient depth of water to carry us through. The Four light tower came up out of the murk, a great, grey *donjon* of a place with waves breaking white against its base. The wind had risen as it always does around Ushant. We dropped our fores'ls and turned into the Four Channel under mains'l alone.

There was no turning back now as we roared down on the huge pillar buoy of La Valbelle. It towered above us as we swept through the narrow gap into the channel proper, and the mournful note of its whistle was with us long after we had lost sight of it. To the west of us now was nothing but rocks to the limit of visibility, the submerged reefs marked by innumerable buoys and beacons. Every short cut that the fishermen use was marked, a whole reef-strewn area so liberally signposted as to be utterly confusing to the stranger.

But one by one the buoys at two-mile intervals came up out of the murk, and in less than an hour we were being thrown about right at the base of the huge red octagonal beacon of the Grande Vinotiere. This was the exit, the final tide-rip; dusk was falling and we were through. Ushant was behind us.

I breathed a sigh of relief until the helmsman called to me to inquire which side of the next beacon he should steer. I had been so intent upon the Chenal du Four that I hadn't given much thought to what came next, and when I pushed past James, who was busy cooking up some sort of a hot meal, and popped my head out of the hatch, I was astonished to see a sixty-foot beacon, menacingly painted in diagonal black and white stripes, close to our bows. It was blowing almost gale now and we were going very fast with the tide under us.

That wretched beacon seemed to leap at us out of the gathering darkness.

It was La Parquette, and beyond that was the coast, flashing a multitude of warning lights and buoys marking more reefs to the westward—and ahead, only a few miles away, the Raz de Sein.

I ate my meal, poring over the chart and the Pilot Book, working with a torch because the electric light had fused, and shouting my instructions up through the hatch to the helmsman. A decision had to be reached, and reached quickly. To go through the Raz de Sein on this tide, or not? It was dark and blowing a gale now, and I'd never been through this tidal race before. I decided to turn in to the shelter of Douarnenez Bay. I felt I'd had enough excitement for one day.

It was just as well, for Douarnenez is the first of the sardine ports, and Monsieur René Beziers was expecting us. We lay the night close under a small lighthouse, in the shelter of sombre cliffs, and the next day sailed across the bay in brilliant sunshine to where the sardine fishers and the tunny-men lie tight-packed along the fish quays of Douarnenez.

Ashore for breakfast in the morning, the sky-blue nets of Finisterre hung drying in the sun from the masts of the sardiners, and fishermen in blue canvas smocks and black berets walked the water front with the slow, slack roll of men convinced the roadway has the motion of the sea, crowding into the cafés for the first absinthe of the day; and above them, the rich little town, built on fish, rose steeply, a series of terraced streets.

This is one of the original sardine ports, but though it still has a big financial stake in the industry, it is no longer a main packing station. Year by year, this epicure's dream of a fish, this lovely flash of silver, moves farther south; and the packing stations have moved with the shoals, south to Morocco, where I have seen them like solid walls of white below Casablanca. And now they are farther south still, reaching down to the edge of the Sahara sands.

I asked René Beziers why this southward drift of the shoals, as we drank champagne, looking across his walled garden with the peaches to the narrow estuary of the Pouldavid. But he only shrugged his shoulders. Nobody seems to know.

The true sardine is the young of the pilchard, and like the herring, to whom it is related, it follows the movement of plankton, on which it feeds. In the course of a month on the Biscay coast we were only to eat fresh sardine twice —a sad disappointment, for it was one of the reasons we had sailed there. Straight out of the sea, and fried in butter with a squeeze of lemon—or just plain grilled—its delicate piquant flavour is something to make the mouth water. However, we left Chez Beziers with the next best thing— tins of Beziers-packed sardines, matured over three years in the best olive oil. The tins are constantly turned to keep the sardines moist, and as a result their flavour is exquisite.

We sailed out of Douarnenez in the wake of a gay little sardine fisher with the name of a saint, headed for our last major hazard, the Raz de Sein. The wind was light, the air clammy, and the shores of this most beautiful of all French bays were withdrawn and sombre. Black clouds hung like a pall over the entrance of the bay, hiding the Sein rocks and the headland that marked the Race.

Behind us, Douarnenez stood for a moment, stark and white against a jet backcloth, and was suddenly engulfed and blotted out by rain; thunder rolled in a drum beat of sound along the cliffs, lightning crackled, darting long fangs at the hills as it struck. The wind died and the rain came in a cloudburst of heavy drops.

In those conditions the Raz de Sein looked grim in-deed when we finally saw it. It is the worst of all tidal races on the French coast. For almost fifteen miles the Chauséeé de Sein runs seaward, a great natural breakwater of rock, and the tides, sweeping north and south along the coast, build up against it, pouring in a tempestuous flood through the one real gap, which lies close under the mainland cliffs of Pointe de Raz. There are violent eddies and confused seas, and when the wind is against the tide and it is blowing hard, then even a big ship would rather go outside.

But now the rain had flattened the sea and we swept through on the first of the south-going tide, David using his sextant to obtain distances-off, myself taking bearings with a hand compass. As David said, we navigated " according to the book," and when we were through and this last hazard was behind us, we looked at each other and roared with laughter, wondering what in the world we had been so worried about.

It was the relief of nervous strain. Now we were in the Bay of Biscay, and we lay that night behind the stone breakwater of Audierne, whilst electric storm after electric storm crackled and banged the night through in flurries of tempestuous wind and rain, secure in the knowledge that the really hard sailing was behind us.

Biscay must be visited from the sea to be fully appreciated, for its people, its whole life is of the sea. Go up the Aven estuary or brave the roaring, white-water, tide-ripped entrance to the inland sea of the Morbihan and take the dinghy up to Auray or Vannes—it is oyster beds all the way, with charming châteaux tucked away in the trees and unexpectedly beautiful stone towns at the end of each trip.

And seaward lie the islands. . . . Ile de Groix, Belle Ile, Ile d'Houat out beyond Presqu' Ile de Quiberon. These are the fishing islands; Ile de Groix in particular. All along the inner harbour the old sailing tunny men lean to their props, their gear all gone, their spars rotting, gay paint flaking from the wooden walls of their hulls—the place is sad as a graveyard, for in their heyday they were a magnificent sight, their long whips trailing the fish lines as they drove forward under a press of canvas.

You can still see a few of them afloat, and though the tunny-men that sail out of the great fish port of Concarneau are steel-built, diesel-powered monsters as big as a deep-sea trawler, they are still building the old wooden hulls. Up the Aven River, at Kerdruc, I anchored below the newly-cut oak ribs of one such boat, and just below it lay the weed-rotten skeleton of another that was quietly passing, with each tide to its ancestors.

And though sardines are scarce now, the fleets are still big, for the Bay is rich in all sorts of fish. Once, on a previous voyage, I roared into Ile de Groix's Port Tudy and made fast to a big iron buoy in the midle of the empty harbour, and within the time it took to cook our meals, the whole sardine fleet had poured in after us and we were lying squeezed between a dozen of these big wooden boats. They left again at three in the morning, the night made hideous with the roar of powerful diesels and frantic French cries, the boats charging each other in their haste to get to sea; it was as nerve-racking as if we had been parked, say, in the madhouse of L'Etoile in Paris.

But to see the fleet at sea, that is really something—the colours so gay, and lone men puttering about in dories, hand-fishing for mackerel. We came up on the fleet this time between Iles aux Moutons and the headland of Trevignon, the sea calm and oily, the sun shining. There were fifty or more vessels, so massed together that they looked like a huge pier running out from the mainland, their hulls clear of the water in the mirage-effect of brilliant sunshine. And then, as we neared them, they separated out and became ships—and there were men walking to and fro between them—walking on the water.

It was a mirage, of course, but still puzzling—and the puzzle not solved until we were right on top of them. Then they were no longer apparently walking on the surface of the sea, but were men standing up in their small motor dories, pulling in mackerel, hand-over-hand, for all they were worth.

These are the same sort of quiet, obstinate, independent people who sailed out of La Rochelle to a New World, free of persecution, who fought the Algonquin and the Iroquois on the St. Lawrence and founded Canada, almost three hundred years ago. And on Ile d'Houat they still live in much the same primitive simplicity, in charming little gabled dolls' houses, all newly whitewashed, with shutters painted gay as their fishing boats. Here they still speak the Breton tongue and their names are Charles le Fur or Georges le Gurun, as though you were in that other Celtic land of Wales, where the village people talk of Taffy the Post and Dafydd the Milk. They buy their groceries, and almost anything else they may want, from a shop run by nuns, and their church is hung with models of ships the way the churches are in Holland. The sea and the rocks and the barren windswept land—that is their living and their way of life. So it has been since men came to these islands, and so it is to this day. A hard life and a simple one, but one that is free from the fear of the Bomb and Space, and nearer to God than ever man will be in his cities and factories.

We had a month down in the Bay, a different port every day. And moments I particularly remember : the oysters at Kerdruc, straight from the *parc*, and served with such unexpected charm at the primitive little *Auberge* of Tal Moor; Monsieur du Four's exhibition of paintings at Aven, the Breton mood of boats and water so vividly captured; being ferried across a raging flood of tidal water from the Ile Berder by a Breton Charon in an old rowing boat; a meal of *langoustines*, which is French for Dublin Bay prawns, bought straight from the fish quay of the little port of Loctudy and eaten on board in blazing heat; puttering our lonely way up the long estuaries of the Morbihan in the dinghy, to the towns of Auray and Vannes, the one grim and medieval, the other, with its Venetian approach and beautiful formal gardens laid out in what must once have been a huge city moat, a place of infiinite charm; children letting off fireworks in the dusk outside a *pension* on Ile d'Houat to celebrate *le Quatorze Juillet,* the Fall of the Bastille; and two exhilarating sails—beating out through the narrow entrance of the Morbihan sea through white water that had the slope and roar of river rapids, and a thrash to windward, heavily over-canvassed, through the rocks of the Glennan Isles to Concarneau.

And then we were homeward bound against a nor'-wester. We ducked through the Raz de Sein in a brief moment when the white fog that shrouded it was torn asunder by the wind. And because it was now familiar, we took the Chenal du Four in our stride, though darkness had fallen and a bank of fog had laid a ruler-straight line across the sunset. We were barely through the narrows, marked by the big pillar-buoy of La Valbelle, when it closed in so thick we could barely see the compass.

Three hundred and twenty-one miles in fifty-six hours of continuous sailing, with the wind rising to gale behind us. It was a wonderful sail. And as we roared up-Channel, there was sea all round us to the circling rim of the horizon, nothing but sea—and just ourselves and the boat and the wind in the sails. After two thousand miles, we felt as though we belonged in this watery world and were a part of it; and at the same time, because we were homeward bound, we had the snug feeling of something achieved, another hurdle crossed in the long battle for experience, the long battle to prove whatever it is that each of us has to prove to live life to the full.

3. MAIDEN VOYAGE

All that I have written in this book so far is of the past—journeys I have already made. But now my eyes are on the future for I am writing this only a few days after bringing the empty hull of my new boat across from Holland to the east coast of England. There she lies in the estuary, only half complete, but already she has a shape and a name, something of a personality, and the form of her holds the promise of long voyages to come . . . a dream beginning to come true.

At first I had nothing but the name clear in my mind. The original *Mary Deare* was a Bristol brigantine that sailed into history in 1821 as a pirate ship with the Cocos Island treasure on board. I used her name as the title for a novel about the sea. It brought me no ill-fortune—quite the reverse, for it proved the most successful of my books to date. And so I had no hesitation in using it again, and it pleased my wife, for her second name is Mary.

But to know the name of the boat is a long way from knowing the boat herself. It is rather like having the title before you have written the book; and like a book, so much of oneself and one's experience, so much of thought and dreaming and effort goes into the final result.

I think I started to build the *Mary Deare* in my mind from the moment I first began sailing. It was a natural, almost subconscious process—a shape that constanly grew, constantly changed, a mental picture as insubstantial as a ghost, but one that added to itself bit by bit as knowledge grew with experience. I was perhaps fortunate in that, though I took to sailing very late, I took to it under the ensign of the Royal Ocean Racing Club, for ocean racing, like car racing, is the testing ground of design and materials; and one's ideas are inevitably influenced by the boats one knows and the men with whom one sails.

After seven years I said good-bye to my beloved *Triune*. She was a little too tender, a little too wet, and she had no self-draining cockpit, which scared the life out of me whenever there was a gale forecast, for pumping water out of a boat is killing work and men are tired and battered by wind and wave. On the other hand, she was as pretty a boat as I have ever seen, sea kindly and responsive to the lightest touch on the helm. She taught me most of all I know about sailing, for I bought her when I barely knew how to reef, let alone how to navigate.

She was, above all, a lucky boat—the sort of boat you knew instinctively would never kill you.

Would the new boat have the same quality?

I am not particularly superstitious, but I always remember my east coast builder assuring me that he could tell a boat's nature by the way she came together in the yard. Some, he said, were good from the word go—others were pigs. Whether this is in the design, or in the owner, or just a matter of luck, I do not know. But I do know this . . . if a boat went wrong from the start, I would drop the whole project, for to go to sea in what you are convinced is an unlucky ship is to court disaster.

Mary Deare, I am glad to say, got off to a good start. I was fortunate in that I caught Robert Clark, a designer well known for his ocean racing boats, just at the right moment, when he had finished work on a 480-ton schooner, the largest sailing yacht to be built for over thirty years. My requirements were not quite so ambitious—a mere 16 tons. But size is not the factor governing the amount of thought and work that goes into a design and my requirements cannot have been easy to meet. What I wanted was a stiff, weatherly boat that would handle with ease and the minimum of crew, a boat that would take me to the Ægean Isles or the Caribbean just as happily as to the Brittany coast or Danish waters. I wanted a boat that would be as easy on the helm, and as beautiful to look at as *Triune* had been. At the same time, she had to rate well and sail fast enough to compete without ignominy in ocean races, and yet be able to sail herself or stay hove-to in a gale in reasonable comfort, and still be able to explore the shallower estuaries. And if she were to have an engine, then it was to be an engine that would really earn the space allocated to it.

In other words, like every other owner building the boat

of his dreams, I wanted the earth—and the trouble with designers is that they are only human! However, the result looked good on paper. And so we came to the point of transforming a drawing into reality.

Triune had been an old boat and so I had learned that wood planking eventually begins to weep at the seams and the paint to crack along the seams as the boat works in a seaway. I toyed with fibre glass, eventually decided on steel. This, I realised, meant building the hull at any rate in Holland and I was fortunate in finding a new yard who were very anxious to build her. But I wanted her completed in England, at my east coast builder's yard. Should we ship the steel hull across? Apart from the transportation cost, there was the heavy charge for building a cradle, and she would still have to be towed to the yard. Finally we decided to deck her, instal the engine and motor her across the North Sea under her own power.

This then would be the test so far as I was concerned. The contract called for completion of the hull by mid-January and if she could cross the North Sea in winter under engine power alone, then that would be the end of any lingering doubts about the name. Oh, yes, I had doubts about it. It was one thing to use *The Mary Deare* as a title for a novel, another to call a boat by that name. Not only had the original *Mary Deare* been a pirate ship—forty Jesuit priests had been made to walk the plank and all the crew, except the master and the mate, had been strung up to the yard arm—but the ship of my novel had broken up on those infamous Channel Island reefs called The Minkies. Two unlucky ships . . . I needed to be reassured. "All right," I told Robert, "provided you come with me (it was his idea after all) and we have an engineer on board." I'd never been to sea in a boat of my own without sails before, and the engine, though reasonably powerful, was still only an auxiliary.

I went over to Holland to see her for the first time early in January. She stood in an ice-cold shed on the banks of the Noordzee Canal just below Amsterdam, a bare steel hull resounding to the deafening onslaught of men pounding at her plates with heavy hammers. It was clear to me then that she would not be completed by the contract date.

But at least I had seen the drawn lines of her hull miraculously transformed into a solid reality of steel, and to that extent I was content. She had the powerful look of a boat capable of shouldering her way through heavy seas.

The weeks passed, with promise after promise. I went over again in March. The engine was in, the decks and coach roof on, and the hull, shot-blasted and hot-zinc sprayed, was now painted. But she was still not in the water. Easter, they said.

Ten weeks late! Was this an omen? Didn't she want to go into the water? Was I tempting Providence building the boat half in one country and half in another? Childish forebodings, but forebodings nonetheless, and not to be dispersed by logic.

On Good Friday I saw her in the water for the first time. She looked bigger than in the yard, an odd, unfinished thing, with no mast and high in the bows as a result. Below, she was a black, empty shell, the steel of the hull coated with bitumastic, the toilet in solitary splendour for'ard on the port side, and in the stern the engine, a monstrous and unfamiliar piece of machinery on which our lives were going to depend—a devilish contraption it seemed to me, for it was a diesel engine and I'd never had anything to do with a diesel engine before.

For three months now, all through the winter—all during the time the Dutch yard had been prevaricating and delaying—there had been nothing but calm weather; an almost unnatural stillness had lain over the North Sea. True, it had been foggy. But I had radio-direction finding equipment and I was confident that I could home on that. Fog was a small hazard compared with rough weather, for without her mast to act as a pendulum, we knew her motion would be swift and violent in anything but a flat calm sea.

On Friday night it began to blow from the south-west, almost the first strong wind since Christmas, and I went to bed in my comfortable Amsterdam hotel wondering how I should feel the next night; for the next night we were due to take her across.

On Saturday morning, in the peace of Amsterdam's yacht haven, I took the stores aboard, enough for four men for three days. If all went well, the crossing would take us twenty hours, but I was taking no chances, for if anything went wrong with the engine, there was no knowing how long we would be at sea.

It was bright that morning, bright with a brittle chill to the sunlight. Hans, a journalist from Holland's largest newspaper, joined ship; he was coming with us for the story and I wondered whether he had any real idea what it would be like if the weather were bad, for he wasn't a sailor. Between us we began to check the compass the yard had loaned us for the voyage. And as we did this I began to realise how very tricky the navigation was going to be.

A ship's compass, when properly installed, is adjusted by small magnets to counteract the magnetic effect of all adjacent steel fittings. In a wooden hull adjustment is mainly on account of the engine, and usually not very large. But this was a steel hull. I placed the compass box on top of the main hatch for'ard of the cockpit, I was horrified to find a deviation of anything up to 5°. Worse still, the hand-bearing compass itself showed considerable deviation, according to whether I stood in the cockpit or on the deck. The most satisfactory reading was obtained by standing right in the stern, but even here the bearing showed a deviation from the reading obtained by standing on the quay.

There was nothing I could do about this, and shortly afterwards the engineering partner of the shipyard arrived and we motored out of the yacht haven and down the

Noordzee Canal, the three miles to the yard. Shipwrights came aboard, the other partners, too. A flurry of last-minute preparations, a few final alterations, warps and fenders aboard, a boat hook, a 30-gallon drum for reserve fuel, a Primus stove fastened to the floorboards on the port side, an inspection lamp fitted to the batteries to give us light at night. By 1400 hours we were off, motoring down the Noordzee Canal in bright sunshine.

Robert and his engineer, Harry, were due to arrive by plane from England at 1450. They would be driven down to meet us at Ijmuiden where the locks take boats out of the Canal into the North Sea. The engine ran smoothly, giving us over 6 knots at 1,800 r.p.m. in the smooth water, engine temperature low, oil pressure good. For the first time I began to feel confidence in the engine.

We covered the 10 miles to Ijmuiden in an hour and a half, arriving at the same moment as the car bringing the other two members of the crew. A quick refuel and then we were lying alongside the wall close by one of the locks. "Have you got a BEME Loop on board?" Robert asked.

A BEME Loop is a direction-finding radio and I brought it up on deck, thinking it a very natural and seaman-like inquiry. He sat in the cockpit, put the earphones on and tuned in. "It's all right," I said. "I've checked that it's working." I wanted to get ashore for some food before we sailed. I had had a cup of coffee for breakfast and nothing since, except a brew-up of tea on the Primus as we came down the Canal.

He held up his hand for silence. "Ten minutes, that's all." And after a moment he added. "Oxford leading by two and a half lengths. They're at Hammersmith Bridge."

I had forgotten it was Boat Race Day at home!

We found a restaurant in the town and drank Bokma to the accompaniment of the most gloomy pre-sailing conversation I have ever heard. This from the two partners. They had obtained a weather forecast and it was not good;

by the time the soup arrived we were practically sending up distress signals. Over the fish they reduced us to the stage of inquiring about rooms for the night. " If we don't get out of here right away," I said, " we'll be too scared to move at all."

Back to the boat for the English weather forecast. Winds south-westerly, Force 4-6. Not good. We squared things up and made ready for sea, put on cold-weather clothing and oilskins and motored round to the lock gates. At least we'd get outside and see what it was like.

A final good-bye to the two partners and then we were in the lock. We had it all to ourselves and motored out of Ijmuiden at 2000 hours Dutch time. We were off.

The night was clear and there were stars. We set a course a little south of west, checking our compass bearings by the stars. There was not much sea close under the land, but down below in the black, empty shell of the hull the movement was violent enough to keep all four of us up on deck in the cold night air.

What I did not know was that Harry, our engineer, was a violently sick man. Within an hour of our leaving Ijmuiden he was violently ill. White-faced, he took to his sleeping-bag on the lurching cabin floor. We reached deep water and the rolling and pitching became more violent, the movement very fast. About ten I tried to get a little rest, lying out on the bare boards in my oilskins. The cold was intense, the engine sucking every vestige of warm air out of the hull. Harry was blue about the cheeks and shivering.

The lights of Ijmuiden gradually dipped below the horizon. But away to port the lights of Scheveningen still showed clear, for the coast of Holland trends almost south-west at this point. Every now and then the bows lifted on a broken wave and water poured along the deck, spray drove in our faces for we were bucking a head sea. Just before midnight we brought the BEME Loop on deck and tuned

in for the English shipping forecast . . . wind south-west
5-6, increasing to gale force 8. Robert looked at me. " It's
just not on, is it?"

My spirits sank. We were a quarter of the way across to
England. If we turned back now, it would be another five
hours before we reached the coast. Ten hours' steaming;
if we held to our course we should then be half-way across.
I thought of *The Times* weather map Robert had brought
with him. It had shown a high-pressure system covering
the continent of Europe with depressions to the north.
Clearly the low-pressure system was gaining the upper
hand, but by how much? " Forecasts aren't always accu-
rate." All the months of waiting, all the days of prepara-
tion. . . . Damn the weather gods! To turn back now, to
admit defeat—and if we turned back, should we ever start
again?

I was at the helm and every instinct urged me to drive
on for the coast of England. " There's a front passing over
early to-morrow," Robert said. " We've no means of accu-
rate navigation and to close the coast with all those banks
in bad visibility. . . ." And he repeated, " It's just not on."
And then he said, " I'm worried about Harry." He then
explained that he wasn't just suffering from sea sickness, as
I had supposed.

There was nothing for it then. I put the helm up and
turned the boat's head for the lights of Scheveningen, still
just visible on the horizon to the south. The end of all my
hopes of a quick crossing. And after this we'd have no
engineer. " It just isn't on." That phrase kept running in
my head as we motored along the line of the waves, the
movement more violent than ever, a quick, muscle-
exhausting, jerking roll. An unlucky break . . . or even the
boat herself unlucky?

At five in the morning we closed Scheveningen and
began paralleling the coast, heading for the entrance to
The Hook of Holland where the packet had landed me two
days before. Robert was resting below. Hans and I were

in the cockpit. Very tired now. But the moon was bright, the shore lights close and very clear. Difficult to know how far off we were. The sea was lumpy and it looked shallow. Why couldn't I see the lights of The Hook? A quick check on the chart below. . . . The Hook was less than ten miles from Scheveningen and the main light had a range of fifteen miles. Something wrong.

And then a wrack of cloud went racing across the moon, low scud, thick as smoke. I called Robert as the lights of Scheveningen vanished astern. Fog or cloud, it didn't matter—we were suddenly isolated. "That front has caught up with us sooner than we expected." He went below and managed to work out some sort of a course, and then he steered whilst I balanced in the stern with the hand-bearing compass, hoping that the magnetic effect of the steel hull— greatly increased by the fact that the boat had been built east and west—would be too small from this position to seriously affect the course I was giving him.

Viewed from the stern like that, at night and in an unpleasant, churned-up little sea, *Mary Deare* looked as though she had been dismasted, the decks flat and awash with water. She rolled like a bitch, quick as lightning in the short seas, and it was difficult to keep one's balance, let alone read out a compass course.

The situation was distinctly unpleasant. If we had gone on, instead of turning back, we should have been in deep water in the middle of the North Sea, where no harm could have befallen us. But now the front was upon us. We were on a lee-shore and a gale imminent. If the engine packed up now . . .

Dawn came reluctanly, cold and grey. Was that the shore away to port? But tired eyes produce strange hallucinations. The air was thick and moist; visibility could be anything from a hundred to a thousand yards. I got the BEME Loop up and we stopped the engine and got a fix on The Hook radio beam; it confirmed our course.

An hour later, the air suddenly thinned, and then we

saw the coast. It was very close, much too close; and straight ahead of us was the long breakwater guarding the entrance to The Hook. The first and only break we'd had, for if visibility hadn't improved at just that moment we might have run slap on to the breakwater or on to the sandbanks of the shallows.

By nine o'clock we were tied up alongside a floating crane in the little haven that lies just seaward of the railway station and the quay where the packet boat docks. We stumbled ashore to lick our wounds and discuss the situation over a huge Dutch breakfast in the station restaurant. It was only then that I realised that Hans, who had never been at sea in a yacht before, let alone an empty, mastless hull with the motion of a maddened seahorse, had not been sick, had not once complained and had stuck it out in the cockpit throughout the night. Quite a boy, Hans.

We slept the morning through. But I managed to wake for the weather forecast. Not at all good. And the evening forecast gave gale warnings for the Thames Estuary and right away down the Channel as far as Finisterre. And all these weeks and weeks of still weather. Dazed with exhaustion, convinced now that the boat was jinxed, I sat over coffee and listened to Robert making arrangements to get Harry home on the night boat. No engineer—and I'd always said that I wouldn't dream of doing the crossing under engine alone without a qualified engineer on board. And then Robert saying that he thought the only thing to do was to take the boat up to the Royal Maas Yacht Club haven at Rotterdam and leave her. " I'll make a pact with you . . . we'll come over and try again the instant we get a firm forecast of fine weather conditions." And he added something about knowing the movement would be bad, but never expecting it to be quite as bad as it had turned out.

I didn't say anything. What was there for me to say? The boat was ten weeks late already, the English yard desperate to set to work on her completion. And Robert, I knew, would be completely absorbed for some time after this in the launching of his big schooner. I phoned my wife and asked her to telephone the Customs at Harwich, for we had cabled them to expect us that night and with a gale blowing I was afraid a search for us would be started as soon as we were overdue. Though exhausted and ill, Harry gallantly checked the engine for us. We refuelled, just in case, and then booked rooms for the night at a local hotel.

A late meal, and Harry on his way to England. There were only three of us now. An atmosphere of gloom hung over us. "Well, you've got your story anyway," I said to Hans.

"Yes." He nodded, and with a charming smile added, "But it has not any ending, not yet." No, no ending. Would it ever have an ending? Suppose we tried again, a week, two weeks hence . . . there would just be Robert and myself then. Now we had Hans. If only the bad weather would let up, just for one day. A comment of Robert's showed the first glimmer of a return to optimism : "Why do you say you would never attempt the crossing without an engineer? It's like saying you'd never go to sea under sail without a carpenter on board for fear the mast broke."

At two in the morning I came struggling out of an exhausted sleep to hear the wind battering at the window and the rain lashing against the glass. A hell of a night, and I knew Robert had been right to insist that we turned back. And I lay awake for a long time, thinking about the boat, thinking that the rain would damp down the sea if only there was a pause in the succession of depressions coming at us out of the Atlantic.

Morning and Dutch coffee. I found Hans waiting for us down below, his dark hair slicked back, good looking and abominably cheerful. "I have listened to the radio. This afternoon it will clear from the west." A ray of hope, but it was only the local land forecast designed for Easter holiday-makers. Down to the boat to get the shipping forecast, but in the daze of the previous day's weariness, we had

muddled the Dutch and English times and missed the forecast by an hour. Breakfast at the hotel then and a new
mood permeating the three of us. Hans went off to ring
the signal station for a proper forecast. Then minutes later
he returned smiling. The signal station had no forecast,
but very intelligently he had rung the Dutch international
weather bureau at Bilt. Winds south-west, decreasing, and
the nearest depression a thousand kilometres west of
Ireland.

We paid our bill and left quickly, before anyone had
time to change their mind about the weather. It was cold,
but the wind was not so strong. Half an hour's work gave
us at least the illusion of comfort below—sleeping-bags laid
out ready, a chart table rigged, everything shipshape and
ready to hand. We let go the mooring lines and motored
out into the Maas, the world's busiest inland water highway.

In a mood of consummate optimism we set our watches
to English time as we passed out through the arms of the
breakwaters. Nine-forty, and Robert, seated at the impro-
vised chart table, ruled off courses and distances across the
chart. We were taking the long way round so that we
would be motoring from light vessel to light vessel, the
longest hop the 26 miles from the Noord Hinder to the
Galloper.

It was an incredible day. The wind died away completely. Visibility gradually improved. By afternoon the
sun was out and we lay sunbathing on the coach roofing,
took pictures with the boat rolling only slightly. Even
when we reached deep water there was only a slight swell
to show the passing of the gale, the rain had damped the
sea right down. By nightfall the water was so calm we
felt as though we could have walked it if necessary. And
looking along the length of the beautiful teak-laid deck,
watching the water curving back from the bows to the
thrust of the engine and lying behind us in a broad wake, I
knew at last that the boat was all right.

I had known this, I think, from the moment it had

cleared on the Sunday morning and we had sighted the entrance to The Hook just where it should have been. It is, of course, less the boat than the people who sail her, but it is impossible not to have one's confidence affected by the chance of circumstances, and all that night, as we bumbled across a flat calm sea with the moon bright overhead, I kept saying to myself : " She's all right. She's going to be a lucky ship."

And at four o'clock in the morning we sighted the Sunk light vessel, fifteen miles from the English coast, sighted it and lost it again. Fog closed in. The moon vanished. Nothing to steer by now except the hand-bearing compass. And then, right over the bows and high and eerie in the fog, the sudden yellow flash of the light, the shape of the light vessel itself, shadowy in outline and only a hundred yards away. No diaphone blaring, and as we passed the weird shape, everything suddenly became clear again and the quick flasher of the buoy marking the Roughs anti-aircraft tower coming up ahead.

We lost it in another fog bank, closed it and motored round it, wondering whether we had identified it correctly, for there was no sign of the tower or of the other buoy, a quick flashing red. And then, in the dawn, the double-footed shape of the tower, wreathed in fog and very close. We passed within a few yards of it, stirring up a whole gang of cormorants; and as it vanished astern, the red flasher came up on us very quick with the tide.

A compass course again; shallow water and no lead line. The tide had carried us right across the Cork Sands. We must have almost touched the bottom, but we were across, and in the deeper water we picked up the witch cry of the Cork light vessel's reed whistle, and ten minutes later were tied to her stern and brewing coffee and bacon and eggs over the Primus stove.

Strange to look back on that voyage now, so bad a start and in the end such a perfect crossing. If we had waited all summer we could not have found better conditions.

Luck? But then in sailing there is always an element of luck. And for that reason it is essential to have at least the illusion that the boat herself is lucky. This I now have. Two great seafaring peoples have had a hand in her construction. *Mary Deare* is going to be all right, and in the years to come she will take me to some of the places that I still long to write about.

Hammond Innes

The Conquistadors £1·95
Hammond Innes's brilliantly told, lavishly illustrated history
of the Spanish conquest of the New World. 'Mr. Innes's
lucid and fast-moving prose is enhanced by the traveller's
feel for the land and the sailor's experience of the vagaries
of the sea. With its high quality and superb photographs
The Conquistadors deserves a wide audience.'
Times Literary Supplement

Hammond Innes has also written two travel books, tracing
his own journeys to remote parts of the globe to collect the
raw material for his novels.

Sea and Islands 45p
In his ocean-going yacht, the *Mary Deare*, Hammond Innes
and his wife Dorothy explored the coasts of Europe from
Scandinavia to Turkey, as well as the Indian Ocean and the
Western Isles. 'Here is a book which makes you feel that a
lifetime passed without cruising in your own boat from one
to another of the Greek islands is a lifetime wasted.'
Maurice Wiggin, The Bookman

Harvest of Journeys 45p
The story of Hammond Innes's many journeys overland—
with a survey team in the Rockies, with the Hudson's Bay
eskimos, with Arabs in the Hadhramaut on the explosive
Yemen border—to the very outposts of civilization. 'It has
all the punch of a Hammond Innes novel plus the qualities
of the great travel books.' *Books and Bookmen*

 Fontana Books

Fontana Books

Fontana is best known as one of the leading paperback publishers of popular fiction and non-fiction. It also includes an outstanding, and expanding section of books on history, natural history, religion and social sciences.

Most of the fiction authors need no introduction. They include Agatha Christie, Hammond Innes, Alistair MacLean, Catherine Gaskin, Victoria Holt and Lucy Walker. Desmond Bagley and Maureen Peters are among the relative newcomers.

The non-fiction list features a superb collection of animal books by such favourites as Gerald Durrell and Joy Adamson.

All Fontana books are available at your bookshop or newsagent; or can be ordered direct. Just fill in the form below and list the titles you want.

———————————————————————————————

FONTANA BOOKS, Cash Sales Department, P.O. Box 4, Godalming, Surrey. Please send purchase price plus 5p postage per book by cheque, postal or money order. No currency.

NAME (Block letters)

ADDRESS